"Bob Edlin personified the image uncommon valor and modesty, his the campaign to capture Brest and the ordeal of the Hurtgen Forest, reveal the terror, the horror, the bravery and camaraderie of World War II combat."

Gerald Astor
Acclaimed WWII Author

"First Lieutenant Robert Edlin made local history as the first GI to board a landing craft at Weymouth Quay, and his face became one of the enduring images of World War II. From the moment he set foot on Omaha Beach, his war record was nothing short of heroic, yet no one was more surprised than he, when he received a hero's welcome from the people of Weymouth on his return to the town 55 years later. Having grown up with the picture of the laughing GI as part of our local folklore, I was honoured to at last meet the man himself—a hero still!"

Denise Harrison
Weymouth, England

"He was some kind of a guy, this guy Edlin. I'll admire him till my last breath."

Staff Sergeant William Klaus
A Company, 2nd Ranger Battalion

"Bob Edlin was one of the top platoon leaders in the 2nd Ranger Battalion."

Captain Sidney Salomon
B Company, 2nd Ranger Battalion

"I wish I had had a platoon of him. He wasn't afraid of anything and he was a very good soldier. He was a born combat soldier."

Captain Ralph Goranson
C Company, 2nd Ranger Battalion

"I just can't say enough in praise of Bob Edlin. He was a great soldier. He wasn't trying to make a name for himself; he's just one of those people that did things unconsciously. It just worked out that way. He had something that a lot of us didn't have, although we were in the fight together— he liked to live on the edge."

Captain Preston Lamar Jackson
Headquarters, 28th Infantry

"I guess we all know that pound-for-pound Edlin was about the best front line combat officer in Europe."

Captain James Tate
Headquarters, 28th Infantry

THE FOOL LIEUTENANT

"To the front"

THE

FOOL

LIEUTENANT

a personal account of D-Day and World War II

by Marcia Moen and Margo Heinen

MEADOWLARK PUBLISHING, INC.
Elk River, Minnesota

Library of Congress Control Number: 00-092036

ISBN 0-9705257-3-7

Second Printing 2002, revised

Cover Design: Ben Harris at VA Graphics
Front Cover Photo: Weymouth Museum
Back Cover Photo: Erin Warfield

Manufactured by Malloy Lithographing
Ann Arbor, Michigan, United States of America

I dedicate this book to my wife,
who was truly the center of my life for all our married years.
She left this world in 1994 but she has never left my heart.
I continue to talk to her daily and share with her my thoughts.

I'd also like to dedicate my story to my family—
my children and grandchildren, brothers and sisters,
nieces and nephews.

Lastly, I'd like to dedicate these stories to my big family of the
Rangers. Those times with you all were some of the best moments
of my life. I will always be honored to have known each and
every one of you. You're the GREATEST.

Bob Edlin
"The Fool Lieutenant"

Graf Spee guns at largest fort on Brest Peninsula

CONTENTS

THE RANGER IN WORLD WAR II

Rangers are an elite group of the Army Infantry—they are all volunteers! They have been used throughout America's history for special assignments in times of war. The Army Ranger exemplifies the highest standards of courage, initiative, determination and ruggedness, fighting ability and achievement. Rangers were the first American ground soldiers to see action against the Germans in occupied Europe during the Dieppe Raid conducted on the northern coast of France along with the British and Canadian Commandos. Fifty Rangers participated and became the first Americans to die in the European theater.

Ranger involvement in World War II began with the decision to form a specialized fighting unit as a part of the American Army Infantry, much like the Commandos of Canada and Britain. This would create a unit much like the Rangers in early American history. They picked a commander, one of their staff leaders whom they greatly admired, named Darby. Major William O. Darby organized and activated the 1st Ranger Battalion on 19 June 1942 in North Ireland. The members were all handpicked volunteers.

When they called for volunteers they got an absolutely enormous response. The 1st, 3rd, and 4th Ranger Battalions were formed. These fought in Italy and North Africa. Next to form was the 2nd Ranger Battalion, first started at Camp Forest, Tennessee in the year 1943. The 5th Rangers were formed in 1944 in England. There were many volunteers for these elite group of fighters "so one had to stay up or you got dropped." The 6th Ranger Battalion served in the Pacific Theater of World War II.

The history of the Rangers, as a specialized fighting unit, goes back to early America. In 1756 Major Robert Rogers recruited nine companies of American colonists to fight for the British during the French and Indian War. The group used techniques characteristic of the American frontiersman. This was the first time that such a fighting doctrine was used by a permanently organized fighting force. It was Rogers that first came up with the idea to fight the Indians as the Indians fought. "Conduct yourself in the woods as if you were hunting a deer." Those are Rogers' Rangers Rules.

The Ranger's Standing Orders are carved in a large stone plaque that stands in front of the 75th Regiment Ranger Headquarters at Ft. Benning, Georgia. These orders were issued by Major Rogers in the 1700's during the Revolutionary War.

RANGER'S STANDING ORDERS

1. Don't forget nothing.

2. Have your musket clean as a whistle, hatchet scoured, sixty rounds powder and ball, and be ready to march at a minute's warning.

3. When you're on the march, act the way you would if you was sneaking up on a deer. See the enemy first.

4. Tell the truth about what you see and what you do. There is an army depending on us for correct information. You can lie all you please when you tell other folks about the Rangers, but don't never lie to a Ranger or officer.

5. Don't never take a chance you don't have to.

6. When we're on the march we march single file, far enough apart so one shot can't go through two men.

7. If we strike swamps, or soft ground, we march single file, far enough apart so one shot can't go through two men.

8. If we strike swamps, or soft ground, we spread out abreast, so it's hard to track us.

9. When we camp, half the party stays awake while the other half sleeps.

10. If we take prisoners, we keep 'em separate till we have had time to examine them, so they can't cook up a story between 'em.

11. Don't ever march home the same way. Take a different route so you won't be ambushed.

12. No matter whether we travel in big parties or little ones, each party has to keep a scout 20 yards ahead, 20 yards on each flank, and 20 yards in the rear so the main body can't be surprised and wiped out.

13. Every night you'll be told where to meet if surrounded by a superior force.

14. Don't sit down to eat without posting sentries.

15. Don't sleep beyond dawn. Dawn's when the French and Indians attack.

16. Don't cross a river by a regular ford.

17. If somebody's trailing you, make a circle, come back onto your own tracks, and ambush the folks that aim to ambush you.

18. Don't stand up when the enemy's coming against you. Kneel down, lie down, hide behind a tree.

19. Let the enemy come till he's almost close enough to touch, then let him have it and jump out and finish him up with your hatchet.

Major Robert Rogers

RANGER CREED

Recognizing that I volunteered as a Ranger, fully knowing the hazards of my chosen profession, I will always endeavor to uphold the prestige, honor and high "Esprit de Corps" of my Ranger Regiment.

Acknowledging the fact that a Ranger is a more elite soldier, who arrives at the cutting edge of battle by land, sea, or air, I accept the fact that as a Ranger my country expects me to move further, faster, and fight harder than any other soldier.

Never shall I fail my comrades. I will always keep myself mentally alert, physically strong, and morally straight and I will shoulder more than my share of the task, whatever it may be. One hundred percent and then some.

Gallantly will I show the world that I am a specially-selected and well-trained soldier. My courtesy to superior officers, my neatness of dress and care of equipment shall set the example for others to follow.

Energetically, I will meet the enemies of my country. I shall defeat them on the field of battle for I am better trained and will fight with all my might. Surrender is not a Ranger word. I will never leave a fallen comrade to fall into the hands of the enemy and under no circumstances will I ever embarrass my country.

Readily will I display the intestinal fortitude required to fight on to the Ranger objective and complete the mission, though I be the lone survivor.

Courage Immortal

'Twas the night before invasion,
And all the boys were there
Cleaning their rifles and pistols,
Each with the tenderest care.
They thought not of their daily lives,
They thought not of their past,
They even failed to realize
That this might be their last.

They only knew the time had come,
When each would play his part
Without reward of a Silver Star
Or maybe a Purple Heart.
Their laughing voices filled the air
With a spirit that has made
The American Ranger what they are
With a victory on every raid.

—Joseph J. Cleaves
Company E, 2nd Ranger Battalion
World War II

FOREWARD

Growing up in the 60s, as the son of a Ranger, I always knew that my dad was part of something special during the war. Back in those days he was rather tight-lipped about his wartime experience. I could only imagine what he went through, and really, all I had to gauge it by, were the Hollywood war movies I saw, and the TV show "Combat." (By the way, Vic Morrow would have made a great Ranger.) Back then, my dad had an old cigar box in his top drawer that was full of ribbons, medals, and souvenir German belt buckles, and badges. I wasn't supposed to touch it, but of course I couldn't resist. I would also wear his "Ike" jacket, of course carefully returning it to the closet before he came home.

As a kid playing Army with the guys in my neighborhood, I was always a "Ranger," and of course that meant that I always won the battle of our neighborhood war. Many an argument arose about "Hey, I shot you" and my response was "No you didn't, I'm a Ranger."

Through the years, my dad began to open up a little more, and was willing to talk more about the war. I found that asking the right questions after a couple of beers, helped to loosen his tongue, and jog his memory. Through much research, and from speaking to the Rangers themselves, I've learned much about their combat history. And with each bit more that I learned, my admiration and respect for these Rangers has reached a level of absolute hero worship. The immense pride and respect I have for my dad, is equal only to the immeasurable love a son can have for his father.

Since the release of the award winning Steven Spielberg film, "Saving Private Ryan," the Rangers are finally receiving the respect and notoriety which they so justly deserve. This book, I'm sure, will enlighten readers to the exploits and individual heroics of the men of "A" Co. 2nd Rangers.

During the war the Rangers always seemed to draw the short end of the stick. With their highest headquarters at only the battalion level, there was really no voice for the Rangers at the Divisional, Army, or Corps levels. Subsequently, the Rangers were often misused as a regular infantry, wasting their talents as quick strike assault troops. In the course of the war, the 2nd Rangers were attached to nearly a dozen different divisions, and to whatever task force that needed their extra firepower. But no matter what duty they pulled, they always performed to the highest level of their expectations.

To my father, and to all the men of the 2nd Rangers, I extend to you, my deepest respect and admiration. For you are, positively, the finest example of the "Greatest Generation," and truly do "Lead the Way."

Jon Jacobus
Son of Dave Jacobus
Secretary, Militaria Collectors Society of Florida

Dave "Jake" Jacobus
A Company
2nd Ranger Battalion

PREFACE

Bob Edlin, a one-of-a-kind individual, has many attributes that shine by themselves. Getting to know him has been an honor and a remarkable stroke of luck for the two of us. In the writing of this book, we also had the privilege of having conversations with many other 2nd Ranger men and are struck by their similarly impressive qualities. They are intelligent, humble, warm and just down right awesome. We hope that this book is worthy of their story, that it lends the reader some insight as to their accomplishments and character, and gives an inkling of what it meant to be a United States Army Ranger in World War II. Thank you, men of the 2nd Rangers, for sharing your memories so generously.

We ourselves were steered in the direction of writing about World War II and the Rangers when we first started interviewing our uncle, Captain Charles H. Parker, of the 5th Ranger Battalion, in 1998. He has since passed away, but we are forever grateful to him for sharing so benevolently with us his "war stories" and his personage. Ace, as his war buddies called him, ignited in us an interest and respect for World War II and the men who fought in it, that we otherwise, would never have had. He was truly a great man.

The very first time we met Bob Edlin, we knew he was special. We had just published our first book, *Reflections of Courage on D-Day*, which told of our uncle's war memories. We were attending the 1999 Ranger Reunion at Fort Benning, Georgia with "Ace" and our cousins.

As a result of conducting research for the book, we had a chance to talk with a lot of World War II Rangers. From phone conversations, we had grown to know several of them. They graciously welcomed us into their Ranger family. So it was wonderful to finally meet these heroes in person.

One of the stories we included in our first book was the famous capture of the Brest Peninsula Fort by Bob Edlin's patrol from the 2nd Rangers. We had read about it but we wanted to capture more of the personal side of it. So through a phone interview with Bob, we had already been exposed to his gracious spirit and quick sense of humor.

When we were introduced to *the* Bob Edlin, we were very excited! From the get-go, it felt like we had known him for a very long time. We caught a glimpse of the young man that fought his way across France, confident and feisty. We saw him not as an older gentleman but a quick-minded, devilish son-of-a-gun that would just naturally be at the center of any gathering. The 1999 Ranger reunion was no exception. The idea for our next book was born.

A comfort level between the three of us was established giving Bob the confidence to accept our offer of putting together his World War II stories. To Bob's credit, he had been writing his story for some years and had gotten a good start on the manuscript you now hold in your hands. For the next 11 months, through hours of phone conversations and visits down to Corpus Christi, we tried to capture on paper the essence of this soldier and family man that we have grown to know and love.

Our two visits down to Corpus Christi, where he lives, were highlighted for us by attending the Edlin Auctions in the evening. Watching how the whole family systematically kept the items coming, sold items moving, and the popcorn popping, mesmerized us and made us feel like we were in another time, another world. It's something we'll never forget.

Many people contributed to this book. We wish to thank our friends and families, who put up with our long stints at the computer and gave us an abundance of support.

Thank you to Peter Laughlin for creating the thorough glossary for which he most graciously volunteered. Well done!

Thank you to Randy Moen, Marcia's husband, for placing the document and pictures into a format ready for print. Yes, it was way over our heads!

We sincerely thank Jon Jacobus, the son of Dave Jacobus (A Company, 2nd Ranger Battalion), who devoted a great amount of time to send us his father's pictures from World War II so that they may be included in this book. He also graciously accepted our invitation to write the "Foreward" for our book. He was the perfect person for the job. Thanks a million, Jon.

We wish to extend a very special thank you to Erin Warfield, a young woman that inspired us along the way, typed thousands of words listening over and over to taped conversations with Bob, and for her editing skills. She also traveled with us to Corpus Christi in July to continue our interviewing and took pictures of Bob Edlin and his auction house. The back cover is one of those pictures. Her most special talent, however, was her spirit and incredible enthusiasm for this project which never waned.

We also wish to express our appreciation to Bob's family who so graciously welcomed our endeavor to capture their dad's, their uncle's, and their grandpa's memories/life story down on paper in order to share it with everyone everywhere.

And last but not least, thank you Bob Edlin. Thank you for all our evening conversations on the phone this past year. You were charming, endearing and witty and usually ten steps ahead of us in our conversations. Your sense of humor kept us on our toes but usually left us in the dust with your quick mind. You honored us in many ways—by giving us your time, your thoughts, your words and your respect. You truly believed in us and that kept us going! You were a gracious host when we visited you in Corpus Christi at your home. Over this past year we have gained insights into the real you, your integrity and even your vulnerabilities.

You have become a true friend, a confidante and our hero. We hope our friendship never ends.

Marcia Moen and
Margo Heinen

Lt. Robert Edlin and Lt. Stanley White on LCA in Weymouth Harbor

1

D-DAY—THE WAY I REMEMBER IT

Absolutely nothing that had been planned for on that part of the beach worked.
–Robert Edlin

I f every Ranger in the 2nd and 5th Ranger Battalions put down their recollections of D-Day, there would be more than one thousand versions. Even men who were side by side saw the events differently. The following account of D-Day is the way I remember it. You must understand that there was much confusion, excitement, exhilaration, fear and apprehension on that day. I believe most of the Rangers felt as I did—the mission was necessary. Even though very heavy casualties were predicted, there was never any doubt in our minds it would be successful. I believed then that I would not be killed or injured or hurt in any way. The thought of one's own death does not come easily into the mind of a young man in his early twenties.

It was June 1, 1944, that it began for A Company, 2nd Ranger Battalion. It was a beautiful day in Weymouth, England. We moved down the dock to load into small boats to be taken out to the *H.M.S. Prince Charles*, a British ship that would take us across the Channel. Morale was very high. I remember joking with Lieutenant Stanley White, who was commander of the 2nd Platoon of A Company. I had a lot of respect for this big, blonde-headed fellow. Newsreel photographers, correspondents, and high brass were everywhere. The British dockworkers were yelling, "Give 'em hell, Yank!" My platoon, along with the rest of A and B Companies and part of Battalion Headquarters, had made several practice assaults with this British crew. We felt prepared!

After we were on the *H.M.S. Prince Charles*, our company commander, Lieutenant Joe Rafferty, was promoted to captain. This took place before we moved out across the Channel. There was a little celebration and the officers were issued a liquor ration. We had a pretty good time. I took my ration back to the platoon and gave it to Sergeant Bill White to share with the other members of the platoon. I went back to "officer's country" and helped Rafferty and the other officers get rid of their jugs. There was a little grumbling from a couple officers about the mission. Looking back on it, it's understandable I guess, but I didn't want to hear that bullshit.

So I went back to my platoon and my salvation. These were the guys that wanted to win the war. If Eisenhower, Bradley, Hodges, Gerow, and Rudder had problems, let them handle it themselves. The 1st Platoon of A Company, 2nd Ranger Battalion was fixin' to kick some Kraut ass! That's just the way we felt.

The invasion was planned for June 5th but as we were getting ready to leave Weymouth, it was delayed due to the weather. Then they called it for June 6th. Of course, that's been shown in the movies and the books. Everyone knows about that.

I remember the night before the invasion, about sundown on June 5th. It was cloudy and the seas were getting a little rough, but the sun came through; it was a beautiful sight. I was standing with Pfc. Roy Latham on the bow of the ship. Roy was just a fine look-ing young southern boy from North Carolina. Roy and I talked about home and about our chances of making it. One of us said, "There'll be a lot of sad people tomorrow."

I walked away to be alone. I thought of my mother and father—the trouble and worries they had of raising four boys and three girls through the Depression years. My older brother, Sam, although married and with a family of three small children, had enlisted in the Navy and was destined for submarine duty in the South Pacific. My brother, Marion, was only eleven months younger than me. We'd gone into the service together and had stayed together all through 1941 and 1942 until I went to Officer's

Candidate School. I knew he was a platoon sergeant with an infantry division on the way to the Pacific. I thought, of course, of Doris, who became my wife in 1946. She was the sister of Sam's wife and we were all very close. My sisters Betty, Alta, and Aileen were all in their teens and I had seen none of them for more than a year. My youngest brother, Morty, was only about five or six years old and was destined for Viet Nam.

For the first time I was scared. Doubt came into my mind. Could any of the Rangers possibly make it? The sun dropped behind the horizon. I went below, miserable and homesick. My platoon sergeant, Bill White, came over and asked how I was doing. I told him I was a little down. He grinned at me and quoted that well-known Ranger phrase, "Well, what the hell, you volunteered, didn't you?" Fears and worries left me again. I realized I had family here too. We got the platoon together to go over the mission again. I heard one of the sergeants say, "That damn fool lieutenant ain't afraid of nothin'." It was a good thing he hadn't been inside my head a few minutes earlier.

On June 6th, I'll let the historians set the time, we watched the Paratroopers and gliders go over. It was a dark, cloudy night. The seas were very rough. Every once in a while we would get a glimpse of the moon or the stars. When the Paratroopers and glider planes went over, they almost completely blackened the sky. As far as you could see in every direction were troop planes, gliders, bombers, and fighters. Ten years before, in the rural southern Indiana county that I came from, one plane was a big event. People would gather to watch small planes fly over. Now, here, there were more planes in one place than the world had seen in all of time. Maybe this is an exaggeration, but it seemed so to me. We were about ten miles from the beaches of France when the bombers went to work. Flashes of fire from exploding bombs against the low hanging clouds lit up the sky. It seemed the whole world was ending. The beaches were being saturated with bombs to explode the German mines and create shell holes in the beach for our cover.

We had breakfast before we loaded into the small crafts. This was a meal that not too many people were hungry for. Pancakes and coffee. Dr. Block, our battalion doctor, thought pancakes would not be so hard on the stomach. I can recall, when I went through the line, one of the mess cooks said to the man in front of me, "Don't get sick now and puke in the pancakes. The 2nd Platoon hasn't eaten yet."

After we had breakfast, we went back to our bunks. The call came, "Rangers! Man your battle craft!" We loaded into the small assault boats. There was some joking and laughing going on. Then it began to get a little serious. Bombers were still blasting away.

The boats were about the size of one of our motor homes today, without the top of course, about 25 or 30 feet long with a high ramp in front and a motor in back. They were manned by a British crew of two. It was pretty crowded with 35 men or so plus two British sailors.

As we were lowered into the English Channel in our LCAs, we realized we'd be lucky to stay afloat. The water was very rough. The waves were much higher than the boat and we bobbed around like fishing corks. Every time that a wave came in, 12 or 14 feet high, the boat would drop. Actually, we felt as if we were going to slowly sink. Many of the boats did sink. The boats went around in continuous circles, one boat with A Company 1st Platoon, one boat with the 2nd Platoon A Company, and several boats with the 5th Rangers. We continued around in what we called the marshalling area about seven or eight miles out from shore until it was time to make the run into the beach. It seemed like it took about an hour from where we were and all during that time the sea was very rough.

The Navy opened fire. It seemed like the whole world was exploding. There was gunfire from battleships, destroyers, and cruisers. The bombers were still hitting the beaches. We thought no one would be able to survive the amount of firepower that was being laid down by the American forces.

The lead craft suddenly straightened out and started in towards shore. We knew that we should hear from D, E, and F Companies. They should have landed on the cliffs about this time. We had to move in toward the landing area an hour before they were to make their landing. As we went in we could see small craft from the 116th Infantry, which had gone in ahead, that had sunk. There were a few bodies bobbing in the water, even out three or four miles.

We waited until 0700 (7 a.m.) for the code word "Praise the Lord" from D, E, and F Companies that they had reached the top of the cliff. It never came! Colonel Schneider, the head of A and B Companies of the 2nd Rangers and the whole 5th Ranger Battalion waited 30 minutes after the code word should have reached us. There was a lot of gloom amongst us. The few people that were able to talk, or were willing to talk, were very upset. We thought we had lost the three Ranger companies at the Pointe. We knew now that we had to land at Vierville sur Mer and that the complete mission to knock out the guns on the Pointe was up to us. There was nothing that could be done for D, E, and F Companies.

We were out about two miles when the lead boat made an abrupt turn to the left and paralleled the coast from Pointe du Hoc past Pointe el Raz de Percee on down to the Vierville sur Mer exit. As we turned to make the landing, I took stock of the condition of the men in my boat. This included the 1st Platoon of A Company and a couple of men from headquarters. Many of the men were sick from the action of the waves. They were vomiting on each other's feet and on their clothing. It was just a terrible sight.

When we came in, there was a deep silence. The only thing that I could hear was the motor of the boat that we were on. It was dawn; the sun was just coming up over the French coast. I saw a seagull fly across the front of the boat, just like life was going on as normal. All the gunfire had lifted for a very short time. The Navy was giving way to let the troops get on the beaches. I didn't hear anybody pray. I didn't hear anybody say anything. We knew that the time was here.

Up till now, we had not been fired on by the enemy. Then there came a peppering of heavy hail on the front of the ramp. I realized it was enemy machine-gun fire. Then all hell broke loose from the other side with German artillery, rockets, and mortars. It was unbelievable that anybody could have lived through that barrage. Enemy fire came into our boats directly. We crouched in the bottom of the boat in the vomit, urine, and seawater.

Our assault boat hit a sandbar. I looked over the top of the ramp and we were at least 75 yards from the shore. We had hoped to make a dry landing. The way I remember it, I told the coxswain, the operator of the boat, "Try to get it in further." He was screaming that he couldn't get in any further. That British seaman had all the guts in the world, but he couldn't get the assault craft off the sandbar. The ramp dropped and we started off the small landing craft. We had been trained for years not to go off the front of the ramp for fear the boat would get rocked by a wave and run over us, so we went off the sides of the ramp. I looked to my right and I saw that a B Company boat next to us had taken a direct hit by a mortar or mine. Lieutenant Bob Fitzsimmons, a good friend of mine, was in that LCA. I thought, "There goes half of B Company."

I realized as I went into the water, even though it was June 6th, it was miserably cold. We were carrying heavy packs with ammunition. I was carrying an M-1 rifle with a helmet and gas mask, fighting knife, 40 rounds of ammunition, two hand grenades, and three D-ration bars, which was all we had to eat until we got more food. But we weren't worried at all about eating at the time.

The water was up to my shoulders when I went off and I saw men sinking all around me. I tried to grab a couple but my job was to get in and get to the guns. I looked in front of me and started through that endless 75 yards of water. The waves were heavy coming in behind us and we kind of bounced along. There were bodies floating everywhere from the 116th Infantry, face down in the water with their packs still on their backs. Their life jackets were inflated. Fortunately, most of the Rangers did not inflate their life jackets or they probably would have turned over and drowned.

When I hit the sand at the edge of the beach, I saw soldiers clinging to the German cross-iron obstacles. I kept screaming at them, "You have to get up and go! You gotta get up and go!" but they couldn't move. They were worn out and defeated completely. There was no time to help any of them, so I continued across the beach, trying to get to the seawall. I got about 20 feet from the seawall. There were mines and obstacles all up and down the beach. The Air Force had missed the beach entirely. There were no shell holes on the beach to take cover in. The mines had not been detonated. Absolutely nothing that had been planned for on that part of the beach worked. I knew Vierville sur Mer was going to be a hell-hole, and it was.

About twenty yards from the seawall I was hit in the left leg by what I assume was a burst of machine-gun fire. It tore the muscles out. My thought was, well, I've got the Purple Heart. I fell, and as I fell, it was like a searing, hot poker ramming through my leg. My rifle fell 10 or 15 feet in front of me. I began to crawl forward to get the rifle. I managed to pick it up. As I got up on my right leg, a sniper bullet hit my right leg, went directly through, shattered and broke the bone and knocked me down again. I lay there for just seconds. I looked ahead of me and saw several Rangers lying just ahead of me on the beach.

One of them I recall was Butch Bladorn from Wisconsin. I screamed at Butch, "Get up and run!"

Butch, a big man, a powerful and handsome man, just looked back at me and said, "I can't!"

I got up and hobbled toward him. I was going to kick him in the ass and get him off the beach. He was lying on his stomach with his face down in the sand. And then I saw the blood coming out of his spine. I realized he had been hit in the stomach and the bullet had gone through his spine, completely immobilizing him. Even then, I was sorry for screaming at him, but I didn't have time to stop and help him. I thought, well, that's the end of Butch. Fortunately it wasn't. He lived and became a very successful dairy farmer in Wisconsin. As I hobbled forward, my legs were slowly stiffening up, not all at once, but slowly. The pain was indescribable.

I fell to my hands and knees and tried to crawl forward. I managed just a few yards, then blacked out for a few minutes. When I came to, I saw Sergeant Bill Klaus. He was up at the seawall. When he saw my predicament, he crawled back to me under heavy rifle and mortar fire and dragged me up to the cover of the seawall. He had been wounded in one leg and had been given a shot of morphine. Then a medic came and gave me a shot. My mental state by that time was such that I told him to shoot the morphine directly into the wound on my left leg as that was the one that was hurting the most. The medic reminded me that if I took it in the ass or the arm it was going to get to the leg. He consented to give me the shot in my left leg just to make me feel better. So then, I told him to give me a second shot because I got hit in the other leg too. He laughed at me but gave me no more shots.

I looked back and there were still men struggling across the beach. I saw Sergeant Courtney, Private First Class Dreher, T/5 Garfield Ray, Private First Class Gabby Hart, and Sergeant Berg from company headquarters and some other Rangers gathered at the seawall. I yelled at them, "You have to get off of here! You still have to get up and get the guns!" They were immediately gone. Sergeant Bill White, my platoon sergeant, we called him Whitie, took charge of my platoon. He was a very courageous man. He went across the beach leading what few men were left of the 1st Platoon, 2nd Ranger Infantry Battalion and started up the cliffs.

Omaha Beach 1999

The Edlin boys. . . Bob, Sam and Marion

Bob . . . just a boy

Figuring they might make the Golden Gloves tournament a family affair, the Edlin brothers playfully poke each other on the "button." However, it won't be playful punches they're swinging if Marion (left), and Bob (center), meet in the lightweight division. Sam (right), the eldest, is a featherweight.

The fighting Edlin brothers

2

BATTLING BOB

The first nickname that I had was "Battling Bob." That's when I was six years old because I was fighting all the time.

–Robert Edlin

On D-Day, my first real battle experience, I was only 22 years old. It was a frightening ordeal, but I think my background prepared me for that day and the days that were to follow. My beginnings were humble and not so different from the rest of the country at that time. It's pretty hard to dig back into my past. It's kind of like scrubbing out a dirty old iron skillet with a brillo pad. It hurts. But when you get it cleaned up, why fried chicken tastes real good.

I'm going to start out by saying most people call me Bob. My name is Robert Thomas Edlin. I was born on May 6, 1922, in Evansville, Indiana. World War I had ended in 1919 and there were war veterans everywhere. Jobs were very scarce and it wasn't easy for my mom and dad. They had seven children. There were three boys, Sam, Marion and myself and three girls, Betty, Alta, and Aileen. Morty was born quite a few years later.

My mother's name was Alice Elizabeth Stewart and my father's name was Lewis Lee Edlin. My mom told me that they met on a streetcar between Louisville, Kentucky and New Albany, Indiana. She told her friends with her that she was going to marry that man (my dad) and of course she did.

My mother went to school through the third grade. She could read and write, but that's about it. However, my mother definitely had leadership ability; she ran our house with an iron fist. She wasn't mean. She wasn't nasty. When we did something wrong, she would tell us to go out and cut a switch off the peach tree in the back yard and she would whip us. But we had to cut our own switches. That's the way she raised us and she raised us all equally. One day she told me to go out and cut her a switch. I went out and I couldn't reach them. Marion, my little brother, had taken a pair of scissors and had cut all the switches off the tree. I told my mom, "You can't whip me because there's no limbs left." She told me to get a ladder and reach higher. I went and got the ladder. You get a little discipline that way.

I remember my first day at Harwood School in Evansville, Indiana. I went home and found my mom sitting at the kitchen table peeling three potatoes and crying. I asked her what was wrong and she said, "This is all we have for supper." I didn't really understand what was happening. I walked outside and walked down the sidewalk. It was raining. There was a little puddle of water there and lying in the middle of it was a coin. I reached down and picked it up. It was a fifty-cent piece. It's not much money today but it was a lot of money back then. I guess the good Lord had put it there for me. I put it in my pocket. I was rich. I walked back and my mom was cooking the potatoes. My brothers and sisters and I began to eat. My mom was still crying.

I remembered that whenever we sat down to eat my dad wouldn't eat anything. He would say, "I'm just not hungry." And I wondered about that. But then I realized it was because there wasn't enough food for all of us. I took the fifty-cent piece out of my pocket. I laid it on the table and I said, "I found this."

My mom said, "Did you steal that from somewhere?"

I said, "No, Ma'am. I didn't steal it. I found it in a puddle of water."

And when I gave that to her, boy she just changed. You could buy a lot of stuff with fifty cents back then. So anyway, that fifty cents was a bright spot.

In spite of the Depression, my father was able to find work in a veneer factory. We had a nice home. However, my father was a rabble-rouser. At that time he got blackballed from working for the veneer factories in Indianapolis and Evansville because he was one of the founders of the first labor union in Indiana. He got so mad that he joined the KKK. My mother was pretty upset about that. I sat there and listened. I remember her remarking, "What did any colored do to you?"

One day I can recall my father came to me and said, "Do you know why they have black people?"

I said, "I guess 'cause God made them." And he looked at me like I was some kind of a nut or something.

"Who told you that?"

I said, "I don't know, I just know it." Pa dropped out of the KKK immediately.

We moved to Memphis and were there probably six months when the Depression banged out in full force. The last two weeks down there he was night watchman, the only job that was left. Later, out of a job, we headed back to Indiana looking like the Okies in an old truck.

I was about seven when we moved to Inglefield, Indiana, a couple miles out of town into a little three-room shack. The kitchen had a stove, an old four-burner iron cook stove. We could burn coal or wood in it. We also used it for heat in the wintertime. We had to carry the water into the house from the outdoor well. And of course we had an outdoor toilet.

My dad worked for the WPA (Works Progress Administration) when the Depression started. He didn't make very much money, but it was a good life in that three-room shack, food-wise and fuel-wise. We had a big garden and we could cut tree limbs to burn for fuel.

When mom was doing the washing, we'd carry the water from the well using two tin pails for one trip. When you're eight or nine years old, that is a pretty big job. My mom had two tubs in the kitchen. A washtub and a rinsing tub. Some people had electric washing machines. But the washing machine that she dreamed about getting was a hand turned machine; you turned the handle to agitate the blades on the inside. She had the hand ringer that bolted to the back of a chair. She was working from the time she got up in the morning till she went to bed at night. Plus she had all us kids.

Us kids were always busy doing physical activities. My first experience with going hand over hand climbing ropes was when we had to clean the well out. We washed the rocks at the bottom of the well with soap after Dad lowered us down with a rope. I also used to climb ropes when climbing up on the billboard across the street. We used to climb up on that big old sign board and wait for Dad to come home from digging ditches for the WPA in Evansville.

We also climbed up onto the roof of our house. We made a big lasso, when Mom wasn't looking, and threw it up to lasso the chimney. Then we'd climb up the rope, get up on the house and slide down the rope again. It was big fun! When I got into the Rangers, I'd already had a bunch of that experience. That helped me a lot!

I went to a little school there from the second grade to the eighth grade. There were only 15 or 16 kids in the whole school. We walked a mile and a half to school. Miss Martha Bower was our teacher. I will always remember that lady. She did a lot for me.

Across from our home was a farm. The farmer, Mr. Rexing, sold milk to my dad. We didn't buy bottled milk; it was in pails. We'd walk (we didn't have bikes then) down to the farmer's house every morning and if he had time he'd pour us a quart of milk; if not, we could milk the cow and get our own. Then he'd put us down for a nickel.

A few years back, after I got out of the army, and got married, I was up in Indiana. I was traveling for an insurance company selling stocks for them. I didn't know much about it but they hired me and paid me three hundred a week. (Previous to that I was making three hundred a month on the police department.) I came to a road that looked familiar. I turned to where our old house was and it was gone. I turned into the Rexing's driveway. A guy came out about my age. I said, "You probably don't remember me."

He said, "Yeah, you're Bob. And I'm Walter."

"How's your dad?"

Walter said, " Oh he's doing fine. He's still working." We walked up to the house. Mr. Rexing looked at me and said, "Well, you're one of the Edlin boys. How's the rest of them?"

I said, "They're all doing great. I wanted to stop by to see you. I also wanted to see how much money we owed you for that milk."

He busted out laughing. "Surely you don't think I kept track of all that milk."

I said, "My mom and dad said a nickel a quart. They said one time we must have owed one hundred dollars. I've come to pay you. I'm doing real well and I'm going to pay you. I can't give you a whole lot of interest but I'm going to pay you one hundred dollars." Big tears ran down his cheeks. He replied, "You just paid me back without the money." That's the way folks were back then.

My aunt, the greatest person in the world, would send us a check for six dollars every week. She just gave it to us. We used that to buy our staples like flour, sugar, coffee, and tea. Once a week, like on a Saturday, we'd walk over to Inglefield to the grocery store. We'd go a half-mile and then we'd cut across country under the barbed wire fences to town. Mom would give us a list of stuff to get. Marion would go with me. Sam would usually be working.

Mom told us, "Now, if you have any money left, you can buy a nickel's worth of candy. But don't eat one piece. Not one piece. Bring it all home because the girls have to share in it."

So I would say to the storekeeper, "How much money do we have left? How much do we have left?"

"You'll have a nickel left. Don't worry." He would fill a big "ole" bag full of candy.

I'd respond, "I don't have that much money left."

And he would say, "Yes you do. It came out just exactly even." He probably gave us a quarter's worth of candy for a nickel. But that's the way they were back then. Then we'd haul it back. We had a couple of wagons and we'd carry some on our backs. That was a big event!

Up on the hill behind us was a big three-story mansion, like a ghost house or something you'd see in a horror movie.

One day the sheriff came and talked to my dad. We were all

awestruck. We couldn't believe it; here was a real live big-time sheriff of Vandenburg County, Indiana. He and my dad went into the back room and were discussing things. Then the sheriff left. Pretty soon Mom and Dad gathered us all around the table and said, "We're moving into the big house on the hill."

"Aw, c'mon. Nobody could live in that old mansion."

We didn't know what was happening, but we moved up to the house. Not only did we each have individual bedrooms and heat— fireplaces, but we had electricity in the house. They even had a well that you could pump water into the sink in the house. I mean it was as modern as you could get back in those days. They had radio hooked up and everything.

First thing after we moved in, my mom and dad sat us down at the table and told us there were going to be two people living with us all the time. "They are married and they're going to have a room here. They will eat with us and everything." The second thing they told us was, "Never ever go down into the basement." We responded, "Yes, ma'am and yes, sir," but man, we had to know why.

So Sam and I had a little meeting. We cut Marion, the youngest, out. Sam reasoned, "We've got to find out what's in the cellar. There might be some vicious animals down there."

I agreed, "That's right. We've got to go."

He said, "There's a way in there from the outside so we don't have to go down the steps like Dad told us not to."

So the next night about dusk, Sam went down and came back up with big eyes. He said, real low, "Come on down here." I went down the steps and saw what looked like a torture chamber. There were great big old brass tubs with brass piping that twisted around and ran over into a vat. It was a "still." The "still" belonged to the Sheriff. The two people living with us ran the "still." About every two weeks a truck would pull up to the cellar and load up some cases. This went on for a good long time. Then we moved back up to New Albany. But we lived above that "still" for about a year and a half.

I worked at the age of 10 or 11 along with Marion, who was 11 months younger than I, and Sam. We worked for 50 cents a week picking peaches. Then I got a big paying job of shocking wheat, which is not an easy job if you know what it is. I think it paid me 50 cents a day. We were able to work six days a week.

I also remember the big threshing dinners. I was just a kid. The way they did it then all the farmers in the area formed an informal organization. The farmers would go to each farm during the threshing season with their teams. This was standard then throughout the midwest. Everybody showed up. My parents weren't farmers but I was hired to shock the wheat and get the grain off. I worked at every farm eventually during the threshing period. I worked from daylight to when the sun went down for 50 cents a day and felt like I was getting overpaid.

When, the farmers would show up with their teams, their mules and horses and wagons, all of their wives and children came, too. Anybody that was of working age worked for free because they turned around and did their farm next. So it was a community thing. But young girls, 12, 13 years old would help their mothers prepare the dinner.

The threshing dinner, a big old country meal, would take place at the stroke of noon. The dinners were just one of the greatest things I'd ever seen. There'd be about 25 to 30 men and boys, big boys, sitting at the table. The ladies would serve the food to them. They talked politics, about Franklin Roosevelt. They would talk about the government and the people in the schools. And every once in a while some old guy, grandpa type, would look down and say, "Well, what do you think, Bob?" Here I was, a little kid being included in the conversation. What a wonderful feeling it was for me to be included. I was only 10 or 11 years old and made to feel important. They have psychiatrists now to take care of that type of thing. But it was great! So that's what the threshing dinners were.

I remember wearing over-alls. We each had two pairs. We'd wear them for a week and then Mom would wash them and then we wore the other pair. I can remember that my mom used to go over to the township trustee, about 10 or 12 miles away. Some farmer's wives would come by and pick her up in a horse and buggy. She'd come back with a couple pairs of pants, a pair of shoes and socks and underwear for each one of us. I would ask her, "How did you get these?"

She answered, "Well, you go to the township trustee. You talk to him and he gives you a little coupon and you go to the store and exchange that for the clothes."

So it was welfare, I guess or a form of it. We didn't do that for very long because my dad didn't like that at all.

Dad was working in Evansville digging ditches on the WPA. It was 12 miles out to where we lived in the country. Sometimes he would hitch a ride but sometimes he had to walk all the way.

Then we moved back to Evansville. My dad had a job still with the WPA. Then I got a job at the golf course, right across the street from where we lived. The first day I went onto the golf course the caddy master asked me, "Do you want to be a caddy?" I didn't even know what a caddy was. I didn't know anything. I think I was 12 then.

I said, "Yeah. What is it?"

"You just carry the golf clubs."

So I carried them for a man that same day. It turns out he was a writer for the Evansville Press. He was drunk like a lot of golfers were back then. We got up to the 18th hole and he said, "What kind of club do you think I should use here, Caddy?"

I didn't know one club from another. I just picked one out of the bag and handed it to him. And he hit the ball and knocked it right up by the hole. Normally they give you a quarter for caddying but he handed me three dollars. I went back and said to the caddy master, "I thought he was just supposed to give me a quarter?"

"Well he can give you whatever he wants to. But he has to give you at least a quarter."

I said, "Well, he gave me three one dollar bills. What do I do with them? Give them to you or what?"

"No. That's the tip!" He said, "That's yours. You're going to do good here."

After six hours of caddying I went home. I had five dollars. At that time, my dad was making six dollars a week! I started making six or eight dollars a week on that doggone golf course. Then I got both of my brothers over there and they were toting bags, too. I think my dad was proud of us and happy for the family. It was just a matter of survival.

My brothers and sisters and schoolmates would call me names. The first nickname that I had was "Battling Bob." That's when I was six years old because I was fighting all the time. It started with a guy named Chief Ritter. We were in the first grade. He had come from a tribe of Indians that were well known as great athletes. He and I used to fight every day. He whipped me every day for nearly a year. I probably learned one of the greatest lessons that I ever learned in my life right there when I was six years old. One day after the fiftieth fight or so, he knocked me down and beat me up pretty bad. Then, low and behold, one day I knocked him down. He got up and said, "You're too good for me." And it finally dawned on me—if you don't quit, if you just keep on going, one day sooner or later, you'll win."

When we went to fight for the Golden Gloves, I told my brothers we shouldn't. They called me a coward and a chicken and then they called me the "Preacher Man." Our parents didn't have any money and if we got hurt they wouldn't have any way to pay our medical bills. There wasn't such a thing as medical insurance back then. They said, "We won't get hurt. If you get hurt it's you're own fault." It was the same old Ranger thing—I went because they went. So from peer pressure, I went to the Golden Gloves. I was scared though.

I used the philosophy *don't quit* in the first sanctioned boxing match that I ever had. I was about sixteen then. Back in my corner, my manager said to me, "You can't win this fight. This guy is too good for you." The second round I came back and he said, "You look like you're completely exhausted. Why don't you just give up?"

I said, "No, I'll try it again." It occurred to me, I wasn't in my opponent's shoes. I didn't know how he was feeling. I went out and in the third round put my head against his chest and just kept swinging and swinging and swinging. All of a sudden he was gone. I opened my eyes and he was lying on the floor. I had knocked him out. Then I learned again—if you don't quit, you eventually turn up a winner.

Bob, Grandmother Edlin, and Marion

Sam

Bob

Marion

Lt. Bob Edlin in 1942

3

ARMY LIFE

Little did we know that it would be more than five years before some of us would return. Others would never return, but would lie forever in countries and places we didn't even know existed.

–Robert Edlin

Just before my senior year I quit school. I was working for a veneer factory trying to work to get enough money to help my mom and dad. We knew that Marion and I, with the war seeming to be close, would probably be gone for a year. We wouldn't be able to help them any then. So I went to work, took only a dollar or two for spending money and gave the rest of my pay, all of ten dollars, to my mom.

"W. W. 2," as Archie Bunker called it, began for me in 1939, June 6, to be exact, with the dogs of war barking in Europe. I knew I was going to be called to active duty anyway, so I enlisted in the Indiana National Guard at the tender age of 17. I went one night a week to drill and got paid one dollar a night. They paid us quarterly $12. We thought we were rich. This was still in the days of wrap leggings and piss-pot helmets, 1903 rifles and stovepipe mortars. A few old time sergeants trained us in the WW I tradition. But what could you teach a bunch of green-ass rookies who were interested only in baseball, boxing, basketball, and girls, and not necessarily in that order.

We went to Fort Knox, Kentucky for our two weeks summer training. That '03 rifle kicked like a mule and the wrap leggings were a mystery I never solved.

In August of 1940 we went to Wisconsin for training. Even to a country boy like me, it was obvious things were gearing up. That was the year I won the Inter-Falls Cities Golden Gloves championship. In November, we were told to get our affairs in order. Everyone was listening to the radio breathlessly while they were passing the draft law. It passed by only one vote. A senator from Iowa who was a pacifist changed his vote at the last minute and the draft went into effect. If the draft hadn't gone in, we probably would be talking German or Japanese now.

December 1, 1940, we were called to active duty. Many of the younger people enlisted to be with friends. All the married men and the guys over 28 were let go. My older brother, Sam, married with three children, got out.

Ten days after we were activated, we were ready for the train ride to Camp Shelby, Mississippi. Damn, I could hardly wait to get on that train! Look out, Hitler, here we come! We were going to war! My brother, Marion, also active duty, went with me to Camp Shelby. Drastic changes were about to take place.

When we left New Albany, hundreds of people lined the streets to see these "elite" units following the high school band to the train depot. Wrap leggings were proudly flapping in the breeze while full field packs were falling apart, dropping blankets and mess gear in the streets. Little did we know that it would be more than five years before some of us would return. Others would never return, but would lie forever in countries and places we didn't even know existed.

My company, Company B of the 152nd Infantry, had about 60 guys and basically consisted of my old National Guard unit. I was promoted to the heady rank of corporal and was given command of a 60mm mortar squad. Even General MacArthur had never received such an honor. I had two stripes and command of four men, even though I had never seen a mortar and didn't even have a weapon of any kind. But I was a soldier!

Many events took place during the next few years. I trained in Mississippi, Louisiana, Virginia, and Texas. I remember furloughs home, parades down Canal Street, trips to the big cities of Laurel and Hattiesburg, Mobile and New Orleans. I experienced drinking my first beer in Mobile and my first fancy house in Gulfport. I earned $21 a month for the first three months and then was promoted to buck sergeant in April of 1941 when the first draftees came in. I became platoon sergeant with three stripes and then a staff sergeant. I began to take things a little more seriously.

I remember the first time Marion and I went into Hattiesburg. I was a buck sergeant (the lowest ranking sergeant) and he was a corporal. A sign on someone's lawn read, "No soldiers or dogs allowed." We went downtown and the restaurants had postings in the windows, "No soldiers allowed on the premises." We were not at all welcome.

After three months, one guy in my platoon got a 10-day pass to go home. He came back driving one of those big convertibles. Evidently his family had a lot of money. Then he approached me, since I was the sergeant, the boss man, and said, "How would you like to go into town with some of us?"

I said, "Fine. Just because I'm a sergeant, don't let that bother you when we go to town and do whatever we're going to do. But when we get back, I'm the sergeant and you're the private. You don't want to ever forget that. I'm not going to do you any favors and if it can't be on that basis then I don't want to play." So that's the basis it was on.

December 7, 1941, put an end to the boys' games and turned most of us into men. Where in the hell was Pearl Harbor? Who ever thought the Japanese would dare to attack the United States of America! When Pearl Harbor happened there was a great turmoil for two or three weeks. We were scattered all over the coast. They brought us down to New Orleans. Hell, we didn't even have weapons. The few weapons that we had we didn't have any ammunition for. I wound up over near Orange, Texas with a platoon of 45 men. We were there to stop a possible Japanese invasion by submarine. I thought, "How stupid can this be?" But when things settled down, a couple of weeks later we went back into town. In the restaurants, the waitresses fell all over us and the bartenders came over with free drinks. There was a great turn around in the country then. We became great heroes without hearing one shot fired.

Bob Edlin at Camp Shelby, Mississippi, 1941

Bob Edlin, 2nd from right, Camp Shelby, Mississippi, 1941

We have so many good memories that we love to talk about, even today. We were close then. We still are a very close family. We didn't have anything but we didn't know it because nobody had anything. The farmers at that time were considered to be the rich people. But we never knew it. We'd still go down to their house and they'd come to our house and play. There was no social difference at all.

I was mad at Roosevelt. He said the boys would only be gone for a year. They were gone much longer. I wanted my brothers back home.

—Alta Turner (Bob's sister)

Then came the Phillipines-Bataan-Corregidor. Legends were being made while we sat on our ass in the swamps of Mississippi and Louisiana. We heard stories of Colin Kelly and Sergeant Louis Diamond. Sadly I learned that my cousin was murdered in the Bataan death march. And who would have ever thought that the boys with the flapping leggings from New Albany—my brother Marion, Buck Corley, Pottsy Maraman, "Sunshine" Slaughter, Kenny Brewer, Cliff and Earl Basham, and the Harrell Brothers would fight so bravely and earn the name "Avengers of Bataan" just a few years later? God bless them all.

Back in Camp Shelby, Mississippi in 1942, I was a platoon leader at the rank of staff sergeant. They had posters up asking for volunteers for the Rangers. I thought about going. A friend of mine advised me to go to OCS, Officers Candidate School first. So on June 14, 1942, I began OCS at Fort Benning, Georgia. The top sergeant had to change the date on my records so I could qualify. You had to be 21. So with the stroke of a pen he aged me one year.

I have vivid memories of my OCS days. When we arrived at Fort Benning we were assigned to barracks. The 1st sergeant set us straight right from the start. In a general assembly he informed us, "The first thing I want you to do is tear your stripes off." I had three up and two down, a tech sergeant. I took off my shirt and tore them off along with everybody else. "Now, take off any ribbons. Put them away. You are a nondescript nothing. You don't even exist right now."

They were tough. We marched 30 to 40 miles a day, and studied all night long. I wasn't that good so I'd stay awake till 0400 or 0500 studying and then get up at 0530 and go again. We were there for six weeks before we even got a one-day leave. Day and night. Night and day. Night problems and day problems. It was terrible.

Then we went to the rifle range. That's where I was good. The guy who was tops in the class in marksmanship also graduated tops overall. I was told early to try to be in the middle of the class. Not in the top ten. Not in the bottom ten. If you're in the top ten they're going to watch you close and give you a tough assignment. If you're in the bottom ten they'll cut you out quick. I was just trying to do the best that I could.

I remember one incident there in particular. I was carrying the base of a light machine-gun. Another guy was carrying the machine-gun itself. On a machine-gun, a pintle hangs down from it, a kind of prong, that drops through a slot in the base helping them to stay together. When the base man puts down the base, then we were supposed to count, "one, two, three." Then the other guy puts the machine-gun down. Well, I got to two and he dropped the machine-gun. That pintle went into my hand. I still have the scar. It went all the way through and I was bleeding out the other side.

A lieutenant came over and said, "Does that hurt?"

I said, "Yes sir, it hurts like hell."

He said, "Well, I'd better send you back to the medics."

I said, "No sir. If you send me back to the medics you'll wash me out. I know that. I know you're looking to get rid of people and you ain't getting rid of me."

He said, "I don't own a first aid kit and I don't like the sight of blood." A guy close by me had some band-aids and we put one on both sides. That was the only treatment that I had.

The instructors threatened us every day. The first thing we wondered each morning when we got up at 0530 was, "How many guys are going to get kicked out today?" They didn't have a ceremony about it. A guy would just be gone. At the end of the day we'd get back and if we weren't too tired to get to chow, we'd notice that Pete, for instance, was gone. He wasn't there anymore. We didn't know what happened. But the guys I knew, we were hanging in there together.

One guy stood out, Preston Lamar Jackson of Laurel, Mississippi. "Jack" was a fine gentleman and we lifted many a glass together. I was in close proximity to Jackson. "E" and "J" are close together in the alphabet, so we were in the same platoon. He was a very levelheaded young man, about 23 years old while I was only 20. He took me under his wing. He would say to me, "Now, Bob, don't get mad. Don't get mad at that 1st sergeant. Your time will come. Stay cool. Stay cool. They're trying to get you mad and throw you out of here."

I said, "Well, they're damn near ready to succeed because I don't know if I want to be an officer in an outfit like this."

He said, "The outfit you're going to won't be like this."

We got through and that was a bright day. We didn't know if we were going to make it until a week before when the tailor came down and measured us for our uniforms. Back then we got straight leg pants, a blouse, a belt that went across our chest called a Sam Browne belt, and a fancy hat. I'd never been dressed like that before in my entire life.

The day of the ceremony arrived. We had to be discharged first. We put our stripes back on to get discharged. They called us by name and rank and we marched up. We were then officially discharged from the United States Army. I think there were 212 of us that graduated out of a class of 260. That was the most that had graduated in a long time because there was a shortage of junior officers all over the country. They needed lieutenants bad. We were experienced lieutenants. Some of us, like me, had already been in the Army for two years and in the military for four or five.

As soon as they discharged us, we lined up on the stage. A band played and they called our names. The mothers and fathers were there. Some of them had their girlfriends. When it came my turn, Jackson pinned my bars on and I pinned his on. That's how close we were. I named my son after him. We were together during all our training time. (Jackson stayed in the military and retired as a general.)

Then we went down to the 1st sergeant to get our traveling orders and our assignments. This is the guy that had given me pure hell for the last 90 days. He'd called me everything in the book. There he sat. It's an old custom that you hand the 1st sergeant a silver dollar. It's just a tradition that probably goes back to the Revolutionary War but is still in effect today. I handed him the silver dollar. He said, "Here's your commission. Take care of this and be careful with it. And here's your orders for your leave."

I looked at him and said, "Do you know who you're talking to?"

He said, "Yeah. Edlin."

I said, "Get on your two feet and bring your hand to a salute and stand at attention until I tell you otherwise. You're talking to a 2nd Lieutenant in the Army of the United States."

Boy, he hove to and said, "You're the first son-of-a-bitch that's done that today."

"I hope that I'm not the last one."

He said, "That was the final test and you passed. I wouldn't want to serve under you but you're going to be a good one." That's the way it went.

As soon as I graduated, I immediately went over and applied for the Paratroopers. I took the physical and was accepted into their organization. At that time, very little was heard about the Rangers. Jackson said to me, "Don't join the Paratroopers now. Stay here and we'll go on together."

After three months of pure hell at Fort Benning, I became a 90-day wonder, an officer and a gentleman. I wore a Sam Browne belt, all gold bars gleaming in the sun and an officer's hat about three sizes too small for the biggest head in the U.S. Army. In all my splendor I headed back to New Albany for a 10-day leave. We each got a 10-day leave. For me, it would be the last time I would be home for more than three years. To my mom and dad and sisters I was a big hero.

The first night of my leave I stayed home with my mom and dad and spent some time with them. The second night I went on an excursion boat that went down the river about 10 miles or so. They had a bar on there. I was drinking some. Boy, I felt I was something else. As I recall I was the only officer in the town. I had the dark brown uniform on and that beautiful hat, like an air force cap, and that black hair I owned back then. The boat docked. As I was going down the ramp, I heard a girl say, "My God, he looks like MacArthur." I thought, "Oh man, look at me now!"

At that time I was also dating Dodie, the gal I married. I called her my Sunday girl. We'd go out on a Friday night or a Sunday and I'd have her home by 10:30, her father's rules. Then I'd head downtown to Gib's Grill, a sports bar. About that time if you were wearing a uniform you could do just about anything you wanted to do and you didn't have to spend that much money for drinks. All of the civilians were buying them for you. I also noticed the shortage of young men and the abundance of young women. Life was great and I felt the good times would last forever.

Then we reported to Camp Livingstone, Louisiana, just outside of Alexandria and the 28th Infantry Division. Camp Livingstone was my first experience being in officer's quarters. Jackson took me in hand and taught me some manners about using napkins and wearing pajamas and all of that stuff. We lived in little one-man Quonset huts. We got to town occasionally, to Alexandria. Here there was a Mirror Room at the Bentley Hotel that was a kind of hang out for some of the guys. I can remember one time I got appointed to MP duty. I had to stand outside the hotel in a lieutenant's uniform. If an enlisted man walked by and didn't salute me, why, I was supposed to write him up. I think I was there two nights and never wrote one ticket. I was too busy inside drinking the beer.

Then I was back in the swamps again to Camp Carrabella, Florida, for assault training on the beaches. We were in tents right across from the beach. We would go out to an island, Dog Island, and come in and make amphibious landings on the coast. I remember a big storm came up. Of course, being from southern Indiana I didn't really know what a hurricane was. There were eight or ten men killed there on the ground. Then to West Virginia for a stint of mountain climbing and to Camp Pickett for more training. I was the most trained man in the damn army and I still hadn't seen any Japanese or Germans. We didn't know whether we were going to the South Pacific or Europe, but we figured we were close to going somewhere. Our outfit was getting pretty good.

Late September of 1943 we went to a little camp, Camp Miles Standish, hacked out of the woods near Taunton, Massachusetts. It was a cold and miserable place. It became very obvious to us then we were going to Europe!

SEEN IN THE COMPANY STREET shortly before their departure for Officers' Candidate Training School at Fort Benning, Ga., are, left to right, Staff Sergts. Robert Edlin, Charles Saylor, George Olson, and Joseph Condra from New Albany, formerly members of Company "B," 152d "Indiana" Infantry, 38th "Cyclone" Division.

4 New Albany Sergeants At Shelby To Enter Officers' School Today

All In Training Since Jan. 11

Special to The Courier-Journal.

Camp Shelby, Miss., June 13.—Four staff sergeants from New Albany, Ind., will leave Camp Shelby Monday for Infantry Officers' Candidate Training School. They are Staff Sergts. Joseph E. Condra, son of Mrs. J. E. Condra; George A. Olson, son of Mr. and Mrs. George F. Olson; Robert T. Edlin, son of Mr. and Mrs. Lee Edlin, and Charles R. Saylor, son of Mrs. Nelly Saylor, formerly of New Albany, now residing in San Diego, Calif.

All four boys have been training at Camp Shelby since January 17, 1941, when their National Guard unit, Company B, 152d Infantry, 38th "Cyclone" Division, was inducted into federal service. Their military records have been exceptionally good. Sergeant Condra, a graduate of the 38th Division Rifle Marksmanship School, was in charge of rifle instruction for Company B and 99.8 per cent of the men he instructed qualified as rifle marksmen. Prior to his departure for Benning, he was acting first sergeant.

Sergeant Olson graduated from the 38th Division Chemical Warfare School, and at the time of his departure was commanding the Weapons Platoon of Company B and gas non-commissioned officer for the First Battalion, 152d Infantry.

Sergeant Edlin graduated from the 38th Division Bayonet School and served as bayonet instructor for his company. Before entering the army he won the 1940 Intercity Falls Golden Gloves championship. At Camp Shelby he continued his champion's stride, participating in numerous regimental boxing matches without a loss.

Sergeant Saylor for two seasons was a star on the 152d Infantry regimental baseball team, for which he played center field.

These boys have much in common. Before induction they worked with the same concern under the same boss, who after induction was their "boss" as captain of Company B. They all qualified as expert rifle marksmen on the same day, went before the examining board for Officers' Candidate Training School on the same day, were promoted to the rank of staff sergeant on the same day—and even used to take their furloughs at the same time. And in about three months they may add don second lieutenant's bars—on the same day.

3 New Albany Men Commissioned Captains

Three New Albany men—James Perry, son of Mrs. Dolph Harmon; Kenneth Brewer, son of Mr. and Mrs. Calvin J. Brewer, and Clifford Bassham, son of Mr. and M' Earl Bassham—have been missioned captains in th All are stationed at Ca'

New Albany newspaper article

Cliffs at Swanage, England

4

OVERSEAS

I knew that to live through this war, someone had to go. So I began looking for a way out.

–Robert Edlin

October, 8, 1943, we climbed the plank to an old banana boat called the *USS Santa Paula* and sailed out of the Boston Harbor. We, however, called it the "Santa Roller." This old ship rocked and squeaked like a roller coaster. We became part of a convoy and were escorted by several destroyers while crossing the very frigid north Atlantic. The accommodations were terrible and the food was worse. We all got seasick. It took 10 days, and they were bad days, to reach Scotland. We had a "U" boat scare every day, but I don't think we ever saw one. I had time to read the popular book, *The Robe*, and part of the *Bible*. I did a lot of praying too. I wasn't praying for myself. I was praying that I would be able to do the job and wouldn't let the guys down.

We landed at Greenwich, Scotland. I was transferred to Company I, 112th Infantry and stationed at Carmarthenshire, South Wales. Our barracks were way up in the hills. Five miles the other way was a woman's army camp. On a night off, a couple of the guys and I would run down to the pub and meet some of the girls there. Our time was limited so we only had time for a pint or two together. Then we had to jog back to camp to make curfew by 2200. There wasn't much action there, you know. I remember it was here at these barracks that Jim Tate decided to teach me how to dance. He taught me the jitterbug. The only problem was that I was always on the wrong side.

Jackson and I were separated and life was not good. I had a run in with a major that suggested I seek other employment. He had planned a training problem in which we were supposed to be attacked from our right flank by a much larger force. I chose to pull my platoon off this flank to move around to the left and attacked the attackers from the rear. The major had a screaming fit, critiquing me in front of all the brass. He accused me of being everything but brilliant. I asked permission to point out something to him on the map. Our right flank was on the water. The attacker would have had to wade through water 40 feet deep for two miles to attack from that direction. There was an embarrassed silence until some colonel said, "That's true lieutenant, but you should follow orders." I knew that to live through this war, someone had to go. So I began looking for a way out.

No one heard my request for a transfer, but if you want something done, go to the first sergeant. He was on my side and pointed out that if I volunteered for training at the Commando school, the request couldn't be turned down. So on December 28, I was assigned to the British Commando unit at Dover, England, on a temporary basis. I was promoted to first lieutenant in January.

I spent three or four months at the 61st British Battle and Commando School. During that period of time I had what they called a "striker." That term means a batman. He was my own private soldier. I told him, "You're older than I am. I'm only 21 years old. (He must have been 30 or something.) You don't have to wait on me."

He said, "That's the way the British Army is. I'm you're batman and I take care of you. I fill your plate, dig your foxhole and do everything for you."

"Not me you ain't. If I'm going to dig a hole then I'm digging my own hole and I'm going to get my own food."

He replied, "All the guys are going to laugh at me."

"Well, I'll go along a little bit then, but not very much. I don't like that stuff." Everybody there was British. I was the only American. I'm not sure why. There were Rangers that went through that school, however. They had all kinds of schools all over the country.

Boy, the food was terrible. I got down to about 115 pounds and probably first developed stomach ulcers there. I think I was eating too much dirt or something. It was very intense training and those Commandos gave me a whole new education on cliff climbing and all the rest.

It was about here that a division athletic director and a master sergeant, contacted me and asked me if I would do a fight with a division light-weight champion. There would be no winners. We would just fight and put on a show.

I met this young fellow in the ring. We both weighed around 135. We fought the first 30 seconds and I knew that I could handle him all right. I told him, "Let's just go ahead and put on a show." Well we put on a pretty good show and the colonel congratulated us. He said, "I believe you could have beat him." I didn't say anything but I knew he was right.

Then I returned to Carmarthenshire and my outfit.

Here I was, sitting in the mountains of South Wales, five miles from the nearest pub, and miserably cold rainy days. I decided to call Jackson on the telephone. He was stationed at another village that I've since forgotten the name of. I got the operator on the phone and I told her that I was looking for a Lieutenant Jackson. She said, "You mean Lieutenant Jackson?" But I couldn't understand her because of the accent. I said, "Whatever you say. We call him lieutenant." She said, with that accent, "You're the first American that I've ever talked to. Where are you at?" I said, "I don't know, somewhere up here in the mountains at a place called Wales, wherever that is." She said, "Well, I'll get your friend on the phone but I want to talk to him because he's here in town." Evidently Jackson later met that lady.

Everyday I put in a transfer to anywhere. I thought, how in hell do I get out of here? I was training with a battalion commander who disliked ex-sergeants with OCS commissions and an infantry unit that was destined for hard times. This wasn't a fit place for a 21-year-old 1st lieutenant. I wanted to get out of that outfit as I knew it was a loser. I knew they were going to get the hell shot out of them. And that's the way it turned out as later in the war they would earn the name, the "Bloody Buckets." The guys were good but the commander was a louse. He was another George Patton without the guts. The commander wouldn't transfer me and I couldn't go over his head. He told me that I was going to stay there until the war was over.

I went up to the 1st sgt. and told him, "I've had my transfer in here a dozen times and the commander won't transfer me out."

He said, "The colonel said you were going to stay in this company and you were never going to get a promotion and that's it."

I said, "There's got to be another way."

Then one day the 1st sergeant slipped me aside. He said, "Well, Bob, I'm going to tell you something, but don't you tell the colonel that I told you this. Here's some orders that he told me not to put on the bulletin board because he didn't want you to see them."

The document stated they were looking for recruits to be in the Ranger battalions. I didn't even know what a Ranger battalion was. At that time very little was heard about the Rangers. I said, "Well, I'll get the papers and fill them out and send them in."

He told me, "I've already done it."

Bob Edlin and Ed O'Connor

5

JOIN THE RANGERS

I found the Rangers to be a very exclusive outfit; most of them were very intelligent, athletic, and high spirited. They were the best and they knew it. They would fight anyone, anytime, anywhere!

–Robert Edlin

I reported to the Rangers for an interview. They had 3000 enlisted men and 200 officers volunteer. I was told four officers would be selected. I thought there wasn't any way I could make it.

I got by the first interview with a 1st sergeant who passed me on to a captain. Captain Lyttle was, boy, spit and polish and sharp. He was the company commander of A Company. He took 20 minutes with me and finally said, "Well, I don't know if you can make it or not but you can go in and talk to the colonel."

I next met with the finest officer and man I've ever come into contact with, Lieutenant Colonel James Earl Rudder from Texas, commander of the 2nd Ranger Battalion. He told me to sit down. He had just two questions for me.

"Why do you want to be in the Rangers?"

I replied, "I had better tell the truth. The outfit I'm with now has a battalion commander that is going to get a lot of people hurt and I need to be with an outfit that believes in itself."

"I've looked at your records. You've been in for a good while. You've had a lot of training, however you have some bad reports here. They say you're a rebel and a renegade."

"Yes, sir, I guess so."

He said, "Well, I liked the part about wading out into the water. By the way, were you ever in the boy scouts?"

I said, "Yes, sir, I was. For a short time."

He said, "What was their motto?"

"Be prepared."

"All right. Now, I'd like to ask you another question. If you were leading a company of Rangers and you were on a hillside, completely surrounded by 500 German soldiers and they were attacking you and you were plumb out of ammunition, what would you do?"

I said, "Well, I'd surrender."

I thought to myself, "Well, I got to see the top man anyway."

He said, "You're the first soldier that's been in here today that would surrender. Everyone else would fix bayonets and charge. Now, why would you surrender?"

I said, "Well, there might be a chance that maybe some of us could get away and tie up some of the Germans guarding us. We could do that much to help anyway."

I couldn't believe what happened next. Rudder shook my hand and said, "Go back out and tell the 1st sergeant to put you on the Ranger roster. Report back to your battalion, get your gear, and report to the Assault Training Center."

I got out of there before he could change his mind. I had been through the assault school before and it was no picnic, but if I could cut it with the Rangers I would at least have a chance to get back home someday. I went back and thanked everyone in the 28th Division that I could find. I was on my way to becoming a Ranger.

Lt. Sidney Salomon was with the 2nd Rangers almost from the beginning. He remembers those early days:

The first day that I came into the 2nd Ranger Battalion in Camp Forest Tennessee, I thought I was going from the frying pan into the fire. I thought, "What did I get into?" When we had retreat at night, each company would give their report, which included a lot of AWOLs. We had the dregs of the army actually. Division commanders sent their *eight balls* to the 2nd Rangers in order to get rid of these men. The Rangers were so new then, that the Army really didn't know what to do with us.

We had a succession of two or three battalion commanders before Colonel Rudder took over. The battalion was in very poor shape. One of the commanders we had prior to Rudder was a West Pointer. He didn't want any part of us but he was ordered to take over the battalion. Bear in mind that in the Army in World War II, the highest rank a battalion commander could be was a lieutenant colonel. This West Pointer didn't want to be sidetracked as every West Pointer thinks they're going to be a general someday. But in a battalion, all you can reach is a lieutenant colonel.

Colonel Rudder was the one that really shaped us up. Rudder had the expertise of coaching and administration. He was the one that really put it together and made something of it. It was Rudder that had the managerial experience to weld us all together as a battalion. After he took over, we had almost 100% turnover of men and officers. I have a photo on the wall in my office of all the officers at Fort Dix prior to going over seas. We got rid of a lot of those officers because they didn't measure up to Rudder's standards. Edlin came in when we were over in England. That's where we got a lot of new ones.

I reported to Major Max Schneider. He told me that I didn't need to go through the assault school again and to report to the battalion. I didn't see him again until much later because about that time the 5th Rangers arrived from the States and he was assigned to be their battalion commander.

In February 1944, I went to Bude, on the northern side of Cornwall. I got off the train about dark. I was cold, miserable and lonesome - no one was there. I thought, "These Rangers don't care either." I was homesick. All the guys that I knew in the 28th Division were gone and I didn't have any friends. Then a jeep came around the corner. Captain Ed Arnold stuck out his hand and said, "You look like a Ranger that needs a drink and a hot meal." I was home! He said, "I'll take you over to your house. A guy by the name of Lt. Fitzsimmons lives there but he's gone off to another school. You'll stay with his people."

He took me over to their house in the jeep. We knocked on the door. Everything was blacked out. No street lights or anything. They had to turn the lights out in the house before we could enter. Then we went in. The people greeted me like I was their son. It was the best time. The family consisted of a fella about 30 or 40 and his wife about the same age with a daughter around 16. They asked me if I had had dinner yet. I told them a little bit, but the truth was I hadn't had anything to eat for 12 hours. The man said, "We'll make up a good American dinner for you Yanks." We had pork and beans and hot dogs. They were so proud. They were standing there, waiting for me to sit down because I was their guest. I tried to remember how a gentleman acted. I pulled out the chair for the lady and the girl. Everybody was beaming. I said, "Boy, just like my mamma's meals." I ate it and I thanked them. She said, "We saved these special for you." They had saved that can of pork and beans for three or four weeks to give me an American treat. No wonder we won the war with people like that.

The next day, I told a couple of the guys about it. They said, "They do that all the time. You've got to tell them, Bob, you don't like that stuff. You don't like chocolates, you don't like cookies, because they'll give you all of theirs and they won't have any for themselves. They probably gave you half their food rations for the month right there." I tried to pay them back. I smuggled a couple of K-rations. The mess sergeants understood all about it. They'd give me a couple of boxes and a couple of cans of stuff. I'd drop it off on the table. These people were getting paid something, but I don't know how much. Some of them took the money and some didn't. They had been bombed. They had been through it. These people were truly war veterans.

After the war, Pfc. Morris Prince, A Company, wrote the history of A Company, 2nd Rangers. He had it published in Czechoslovakia while we were still stationed there in 1945. He entitled it *Co. A, 2nd Ranger Battalion, Overseas And Then—Over The Top*. We all treasure that book. I'd like to share with you some of his words about the British:

> It seems like there weren't any barracks or Army camps about and being it was too cold for outdoor life, it had been decided to put us into private civilian homes where we were to become similar to boarders in these private homes. . . .The people had been requested to give up a room or two or as much space as they could spare and they had complied. . . .we found ourselves billeted in civilian homes, living the life of Riley. This was a fine gesture on the part of the British

people and it showed the spirit and enthusiasm these people have in their pursuit of the war. They had made sacrifices previously but now they were giving up parts of their own homes, so that we could be billeted. A friendlier gesture than this could never be made by anyone, anywhere.

Bude is a peaceful, small town on the southwestern coast of England. Its normal population in peacetime couldn't have run over 5,000, but then being on the west coast and removed from the danger vicinity of air raids, its population had naturally increased a great deal. It was a lovely resort town, fairly modern and up-to-date. . . .At first it was a bit awkward to get friendly with the people we were living with, as we didn't want to over-do taking advantage of them; but as time wore on, these people got to know us and we to know them. We felt as though we were back in our own homes, working on a civilian job. For when our working day was ended and retreat formation over, we could do whatever we pleased. We could either go home and pass away the evening with our people we lived with, or we could go to town without a pass and spend the evening there. All that was required of us was that we remember that we were gentlemen and that we were Rangers. There were many things that we could do in town. There was a local movie house that was fairly up-to-date and which featured American film. The café and pubs always welcomed our entry into their establishments, and the fish and chips places were a good place to go to always satisfy our appetites. The bonds of friendship that grew up out of this relationship has never been severed, and even today our correspondence with the people of Bude continues to go on, on a most amiable level. It was here at Bude that not only did we become acquainted with, but we became a part of the British. Such food combinations as fish and chips, cheese and jelly, tea and crumpets, etc. etc. became ritual with us. . . .

We sang all the time, we were here. *Roll Me Over in the Clover*, that famed English ballad, became synonymous as our battle cry. We Rangers must have presented a strange picture in this quaint and peaceful town. We were just about the opposite, lively, noisy, and playful, never once serious. . . .

We saw for ourselves from very close range the effects of the war upon these people and on their country. We began to learn the extreme hardships these people were enduring. We learned what rationing really was, the darkness of a total black-out, the shortage of petrol, and the absence of motor vehicles. Our battalion underwent a reorganization while at Bude. A few men and some officers were released and transferred to other outfits. It appears that although these men had put out to the best of their ability, it didn't quite meet the rigid standards and moral requirements of the Rangers. . . .But, in return we got Lt. Edlin and several other swell soldiers. . . .

Due to the facilities and different kinds of cliffs, we had nearby, we could experiment with many different ways of surmounting this kind of obstacle. We would climb certain cliffs without the use of rope, some with and then for others we used little steel ladders which were four feet in length and which had ends which could be connected to one another. We built up ladders which extended in length to 80 to 100 feet. With these all we had to do was place the ladder against the cliff and walk up. Very simple, all you had to do was hope and pray that the ladder wouldn't break or that the construction rods weren't loose and would give away while you were going up and down.

Our life settled into a routine. We got up, had breakfast with our family (pork and beans with mutton), reported to the training area, did a days work in the field there and back to our family for supper. The evenings were usually free. My number one girlfriend (now my wife since 1946) sent boxes of canned goods and chocolates. These English people hadn't had some of these items for years. It was a pleasure to see them enjoy it. They had given us so much.

After about the first or second week there, I really felt like I was home for the first time in my military career. I felt that this was the place I belonged. Morale was very high. Rank did not mean much to the Rangers. Junior officers were usually called by their first names, even by the lowest private. Most of the lieutenants did not wear bars. The men knew us.

I found the Rangers to be a very exclusive outfit; most of them were very intelligent, athletic, and high spirited. They were the best and they knew it. They would fight anyone, anytime, anywhere! We were convinced we were better than the British Commandos or the American Paratroopers. I'm sure that we didn't win all the battles, but we sure as hell tried. These guys were the greatest!

Pfc. Ray Tollefson remembers when I joined the Rangers in England:

> Bob Edlin started with our battalion just prior to the invasion. My recollection is that immediately he had a great impact with those of us that were doing the legwork, the GI that was taking the orders. There was a change in officers and that's where Bob Edlin came in. Myself, I was always interested in athletics, like football. Well, Edlin was a great athlete. He was fantastic as a softball pitcher. In Dorset, waiting to go in for the invasion, we played a lot of softball. The only officer that participated in any of that stuff at all was Edlin. He didn't do it just to butter up to us fellows as much as he enjoyed it. And he was also a great boxer. I think from day one we were just glad to have him.

> One thing is that look that you see in that famous picture of him —that was there all the time. He was a nice looking person and he always had a smile.

> As for Colonel Rudder, we weren't running up to him asking him the time of day, but again he had that look and smile. As a private first class, I wasn't running up to him and talking to him, but again I knew he was one of us. We had so many officers that were that way.

I was given command of the 1st Platoon of A Company. By this time Captain Arnold had been promoted to battalion executive officer and Lieutenant Rafferty was now our company commander. He took me over to the group and had the platoon line up. He introduced me to the platoon. He told them I was their new platoon leader. And that was it. Then I met with the first platoon sergeant, Bill White. Bill White was a little short fellow, about 5'6", 120 pounds. I heard he used to be a jockey. As time went on I discovered he was a great leader and a great young man and probably one of the bravest men I've ever met.

He said, "Lieutenant, can we talk frank with you?"

I said, "Yes, let's do. Let's get it out in the open. What's the problem?"

"Well," he said, "you're a 90-day wonder."

I said, "You're right. Do I talk like I'm a college graduate or something?"

He said, "No. I wondered about that." So I told him about my

National Guard days and going into the military at Camp Shelby.

He said, "Hell, you've been in longer than anybody in the platoon." So he spread the word amongst the men. Back in those days in the Rangers, rank didn't mean anything. That's the way I saw it anyway. You had to prove yourself. So, the second day we were out in the field somewhere, I had somebody bring along a set of boxing gloves. I was a pretty fair boxer at about 5'9" and 145 pounds. At noontime I asked if there were any boxers around. There were 35 men in the platoon and of course all 35 of them were boxers.

I said, "Well, I'm going to box with you any way you want to do it. So let's just start." I worked through about four of them and the rest of them said, "Naw, that's not necessary. We've seen enough." One big old boy by the name of Roy Evan stood up. He was about 6'3" and about 180 pounds.

He said, "Well you're too little for me but I used to box." I got another lesson that day. He did everything but wallop me good. When we got through he said, "That's the last time I'll box you because you're going to get better."

A couple of days later we met up with a couple of B Company non-coms and I boxed with them. Then C Company. We were working our way through the battalion. Whitie was my agent. It was all in good fun. But really, what I was just trying to do was prove to these guys that I belonged there. I ran into the 1st sergeant of C Company, Steve Golla. He was a great soldier and a good first sergeant, but he was one hell-of-a boxer. He gave me boxing lesson number two in the Ranger battalion. He was killed on D-Day.

I ran through the rest of them. Somewhere along about then we had a USO show that had some boxers, heavyweight champions. Joe Louis was there and Bach and some others. Anyway, they asked me if I would fight in an exhibition with some fellow. I can't remember the fellow's name but his brother had been a contender for the world's championship. We met in the middle of the ring and he asked me how many fights I'd had.

I told him, "Serious, other than just amateur, maybe about 15."

He said, "Well, I've had 200. We'll put on a show if you behave yourself. Now don't get too brisk here." So we went along there for about a minute or so.

Then I told him, "I think I'm going to give you a try."

He said, "Go ahead." And I hit him. He flinched and moved back and for the next minute and a half I had education number three. That guy must have been wearing eight or nine boxing gloves. He hit me with everything all at the same time; three or four hands hit me up the side of the head. Then he eased off.

He said, "You want to put on a show for the guys?"

I said, "I think we had better put on a little slower one." So we went ahead and did about five rounds taking it easier.

In the Rangers we had a platoon of 35 men. In the regular infantry there were 45. We had three or four squads with 12 men in each squad with the machine-gun squad being a little smaller. In my past military experience I'd usually discipline my privates and corporals by going through their platoon sergeants. If the platoon sergeant couldn't work it out, he was to go ahead and take appropriate action. Some would say, "Well, like what?" I would say, "I don't care if you take him on a five-mile hike or put him outside all night marching with a rifle. Whatever you do, I'll back it up. You can tell them if I have to come in to it, it's going to be a court martial or an ass kicking, whichever way we have to go with it."

Now with the Rangers, discipline was a whole different matter. We didn't have to discipline for the most part. There were situations when we took hikes or climbed cliffs or whatever it might be. With thirty guys behind me going up a cliff, I might hear, "Go to hell, you yellow-bellied lieutenant" or something like that. I didn't know which one it was, so I ignored it. Maybe a couple or three hours later after we'd stop for a break, I'd notice a guy with a little black eye or some lump on the side of his cheek, or maybe his face was red. Then I'd know which one it was. Somebody had thumped him. In the Rangers the non-coms took care of the discipline. They were for the most part just top-notch.

Somewhere in this time period, Colonel Rudder told me to take five days leave. I went to Manchester to see a nurse I had known in the States. About all I can remember was that everywhere I went, the Ranger patch brought a lot of attention. The 1st, 3rd, and

4th Rangers had received a lot of deserved publicity on their exploits in the Africa, Anzio, and Cisterna campaigns. I'm sure they didn't mind that I basked in their glory for a while.

In February we moved to the Assault Training Center outside the small village of Braunton. This was my third time, but the first time with my platoon, the 1st Platoon of A Company. I remember one training exercise in particular. My platoon was to be the first to perform. The rifle sections were to advance under our own machine-gun sections. Our own mortar section was to lay fire in front of us. I wondered, "Do we have enough confidence in each other to do it?" I had only known them for about a month or so but I thought they were the greatest. I was giving them instructions. I said, "Are you ready to go?" Nothing happened. The whole platoon froze, scared shitless as we lay there.

A full colonel came over and said, "Lieutenant, you can't seem to handle these men. You step back and I'll take them through here."

I said, "Colonel, let me tell you something. You aren't going to be there when D-Day comes. I'm going to be there. If these guys aren't going to follow me, they aren't going to follow anybody. You son-of-a-bitch just get out of the way and I'll do this." I turned around and hollered, "Whitie, come on!" I went and I didn't look back. They had snipers firing at us as close as they could get without hitting us. Bombs were going off all around us. When I got through the obstacles, I was surrounded by 35 guys. Not one of them flinched; not one of them backed off. All of them were up firing and assaulting the position. It was picture perfect, right out of the field manual. The high brass were ecstatic, best they'd ever seen. We could have whipped the whole German army at that moment!

The rest of the platoons in the battalion were just as good or better. We were a confident combat unit. I went back and the colonel slapped me on the back and congratulated me. He said, "You did a wonderful job but don't ever call me a son-of-a-bitch again." And that was my introduction to the real Rangers right there.

When I joined the Rangers in England I was in good shape,

about as good as shape as you could be. I went around boxing any-body that would box and played baseball, softball and basketball. We had speed marches. Five miles before breakfast! Then we'd take 20-mile hikes and 40-mile hikes. A 40-mile hike in 12 hours! These were speed marches. I mean we moved.

One day, about two months before D-Day, we were on another speed march when I developed shin splints. I had been at the head of the column because I was the platoon leader. I told Bill White that I was going to have to drop back because my legs were hurting me. I dropped back and the next thing I knew I was at the back of the column. I finished up that day and some guys were looking at me kind of curious. Rafferty looked at me kind of funny, too.

A couple of days later we did the same thing and then my legs locked up completely. It was the second run that day. I thought, "I can't make it. Guys are dropping out, but I can't. I've got to stay with my platoon." Sergeant White was carrying my rifle and Sergeant Courtney my pack, but I still couldn't make it.

I went to the back of the column again. Along came big Bill Dreher. He came running along and picked me up and was going to carry me on his back, if you can believe it. I told him, "You can't do that Bill. They're going to kick me out, that's for sure." Then the 2nd Platoon went past me. I was over at the side of the road. I was-n't stopped, but I was hobbling. Then I was crawling. I actually crawled 200 yards. When I crossed the street coming into the town of Swanage, I looked up and I was crying. Tears were running down my filthy face. When I got there the whole 1st Platoon was standing along the side of the road. The 2nd Platoon was standing on the other. Behind them most of the rest of the battalion was gath-ered. When I got across that line they just went wild. They stood up and cheered and hollered and yelled. Whitie said, "Now they'll have to kick us all out." Lieutenant Rafferty, our company com-mander, just slapped me on the back and said, "You're the biggest gold brick I've ever seen." Rafferty would die a hero's death on D-Day; he was one of the finest.

Now I had to face Rudder. He just grinned that big grin and said, "What's the matter with you *gold brick*?"

I said, "I guess I'm gone, huh?"

"Nah. D-Day ain't tomorrow. You go over and see Doc Block and see what the hell is the matter with you."

I went over to see Doc Block. He examined me and said, "There isn't anything wrong with you. You're just stressed and your muscles are swelling up on you because you've been doing too much and you're pinching your nerves. That's what's causing your shin splints. What you need to do is rest your legs about five or six days."

I said, "You know I'm not going to do that. If I do that they're going to have to turn me loose because time is getting tight, Doc."

"I know that. I know that you aren't going to do that. So I'm going to give you the next best thing. I'm going to give you some painkiller. For heaven's sake, be careful. Don't take anymore than I tell you to take. But try not to twist your leg or anything because you could break it and you wouldn't even know that you broke it."

I don't know what he gave me, but it helped. Rudder told me to ease up. The guys told me to ease up. I guess I eased up for a few days. Then pretty soon I was well again. That's where I first got to know Doc Block. He was just a great guy. Come to think of it, they all were. I never really knew any bad ones in the whole bunch. Especially Rudder. Colonel Rudder was the best leader there ever was in any Ranger battalion we ever had. When I would voice an idea, he would listen to it. He didn't always do it or let me do what I wanted to do. He didn't always take my suggestions. He would say, "Well that sounds like a good idea but I think that we'll do it this way. But if you have anymore ideas let me know." I suspect he did that to a lot of people.

Every morning at dawn, we did a five-mile speed march to Baggy Pointe. Five miles up to the Pointe, climb the Pointe and then five miles back.

The training at Bude was centered on cliff climbing. I'd had mountain climbing training but nothing like this. The first time I stood on the beach and looked up at those 90-foot high cliffs it just scared the crap out of me. Sheer cliffs. I saw rope ladders and ropes hanging on them and some guys were climbing up them. I thought, "What kind of a nut would climb up something like this?" Some of those monkeys were free climbing. Free climbing was without rope or ladder, just natural handholds plus some chopping with a fighting knife. We started out with a six-foot section of light ladder, then we added on a section until we reached the top. Then we went to ropes, climbing 90 feet on a wet muddy rope will tucker you a little. There was no rank here either. Bars or stripes didn't matter a thing. If we couldn't make it, we were gone. Some people quit, they were gone the next day. This seemed like senseless stupid bullshit. When would we ever need to climb 90-foot cliffs under fire?

When I realized I had to climb them also, I decided to take the toughest one first. I went up the rope and did pretty well. Fortunately, I never looked down. I got to the top and wondered what the hell was I doing there. Then we went back down. We did so well; we got to do it again, four or five times. Then we ran back to camp and ate breakfast, did some maneuvers and then we ran that five miles back to Baggy Pointe again. Then we went up and down 100-foot high cliffs all day long.

A couple of guys went off to London and were taught how to operate 100-foot fire ladders by a London fire brigade. We wondered again, "What the hell kind of a job are we going to get?"

Old Whitie contemplated this with me. I said, "What kind of place was this going to be where we're going to have to climb up and attack something?" We started looking at maps of France. We wondered, "Where is a beach area five miles from high cliffs?"

So we laughed and joked about it. We didn't know what we were going to get into. We did our training. Every day it was Baggy Pointe again. We did that through March, April and May.

In early May, we moved to Swanage in the county of Dorset. Here we stayed in a big old high school building. The whole 2nd Ranger Battalion stayed there. Just down the street about a block was the British Women's Army barracks. We went to the clubs and dances. Our stay here was enjoyable.

Morris Prince offers more memories of Swanage from his book:
    We detrained and proceeded to make our way to our new home, which was to be a school house that sat on the crest of a hill over-

looking the bay at Swanage. I'll never forget our first run in with the people of this town. It seems as though the American troops who had been billeted in this town before us and had just departed . . . had warned the local residents that the Rangers were a bunch of hood-lums, gangsters, and prisoners who were out on parole. They had said that they had assembled us out of volunteers from state and federal institutions and were letting us do the dirty and dangerous work of the Army. So that when we first started to walk around town during our leisure time we began to receive funny and inquisitive looks. The weaker sex particularly didn't have anything to do with us, shunning us as though we all had B.O. Well finally the truth and reason for this snobbing leaked out and it didn't take long until we straightened things out and proved to these people the kind of soldiers we Rangers were.

At Swanage, it was a five-mile run and climb the cliffs again. Whitie and I sat down with a map of the coast of France. We were determined to figure out where this invasion was going to take place. We went from the end of one coast to the other—a lot of places. We decided it had to be sort of an isolated place so we nar-rowed that down and came to the Normandy area. Cherbourg. Nobody could get in there. So we went on down the coast from there and came to the little town of Vierville sur Mer. And exactly, almost exactly 5 miles to the right of Vierville sur Mer coming in from the sea was a place called Pointe du Hoc. Whitie and I agreed that we had figured out where we were going. And damn if we weren't right. Good thing the Germans weren't watching us!

Ed O'Connor, Adolf Sorestad, and Ray Tollefson with football
Bude, England, March 1944

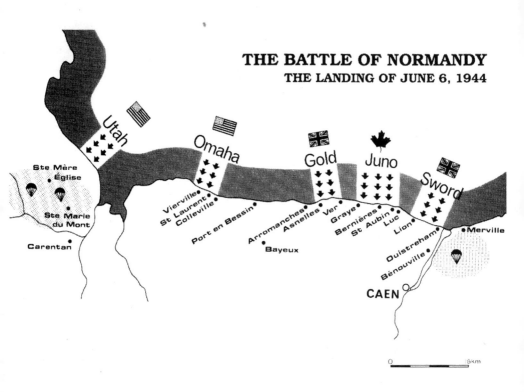

THE BATTLE OF NORMANDY
THE LANDING OF JUNE 6, 1944

Utah

Omaha

Gold

Juno

Sword

Ste Mère
Église

Ste Marie
du Mont

Carentan

Vierville
St Laurent
Colleville

Port en Bessin

Arromanches
Asnelles
Ver
Graye
Bernières
St Aubin
Luc
Lion
Merville

Bayeux

Ouistreham

Bénouville

CAEN

0   5km

6

PREPARING FOR D-DAY

We knew where France was, but where in the hell was Normandy?
–Robert Edlin

On May 20, 1944 the 2nd and 5th Ranger Battalions moved into an area at Weymouth, England, a small town on the English Channel. The officers of the 2nd and 5th Battalions were billeted in large Quonset huts. As I remember it, the weather was beautiful; there was sunshine and no rain. We knew that the time was getting close for the invasion of France, however, we still had no information about when or where the invasion was going to take place.

During those four or five days, we were visited several times by German bombers. They incurred very little damage, but it was a very scary situation. I thought that they were closer than they really were. Many times in London, when I was on leave, I had come under air raids. I would look outside and see two or three searchlights pick up a German bomber, as if they had pinned a moth. When the anti-aircraft would fire at them, I almost felt sorry for them. The last raid that I can recall at Weymouth, I was lying on my bunk laughing at the guys that took cover in an air raid shelter. Then a bomb hit the motor pool about 100 yards away. I think I set a new speed record for lieutenants in the army at that time.

The first four days we were there, were carefree, almost like a picnic. We could go into any nearby town and do just about anything we wanted to do: drink, gamble or whatever and nobody

would bother us. It was pretty much a period of relaxation. Bob
Fitzsimmons, a good friend of mine, Bill Sharp, a super lieutenant
in B Company, and myself would go to town. We'd sometimes stay
overnight.

We took a train down to Portsmouth or Southampton. It wasn't
too far. We would drink some beer and stuff and mess around, you
know, and then we would start on back. We'd get back around
2200 hour. The old train was always full of Paratroopers from the
101st or the 82nd.

We got into some fights with the Paratroopers over who was the
greatest. We usually didn't have fistfights with them because we
were all three lieutenants and they were mostly enlisted men. They
wouldn't fight us unless we were all drunker than what we should
be. We'd kid each other and be joking and laughing. Then we'd get
full of beer and on the way back we'd argue, talk, yakkety-yak—
who was with who and all that. We'd make motions at each other.

About the third or fourth night, coming back on the train, we
noticed the train was almost empty. There wasn't one Paratrooper
on the train. We kept pretty quiet. We realized what was going on.
I told Bob, "Well, that was our last shot." He said, "Yup." So we
went on and checked into camp.

The next morning, May 25th, 1944, the party was over. From
then on we were padlocked in the marshalling area for briefing. As
I recall, the area was surrounded by barbed wire. Armed guards,
Military Police and British were stationed outside the fence. We
were ordered not to communicate with them in any way. Nobody
came in. Nobody went out, not even to empty the garbage. We were
not to talk to any of the guards nor to let them talk to us. We could-
n't have conversations with anybody that wasn't more or less
imprisoned in the compound. In fact, we felt more like prisoners
than we did invading troops. From May 25th to June 1st we were
literally prisoners of the U.S. Army.

Then began the briefing for D-Day. We were told the date, time,
and location of the invasion. We were briefed on the complete
invasion, including what the British, the Canadians, the Americans,
the Paratroopers, the 20th Infantry Division, the 4th Infantry

Division, the 1st Infantry Division, and the Ranger battalions were to do. Then each company was briefed on its mission. Each platoon and each section was briefed on the job they were to do. I can remember someone saying, "Hitler would give ten million dollars to know what I know."

H-Hour was to be 0630 June 5, 1944. The overall picture was that the Allies were to land on several beaches in Normandy, France. We knew where France was, but where in the hell was Normandy? Until the briefing team put up a map of France very few Rangers, or for that matter, very few of the invasion troops had ever heard of it. Brittany and Normandy were not places we had studied in school. But, in just a few days the whole world would know all about Normandy.

We were initially shown the beaches. All the beaches were code-named. Utah Beach and Omaha Beach were to be the American beaches. One American infantry division was to land and establish a beachhead on Utah. The 1st and 29th were to land on Omaha and establish a beachhead. Every book that I've ever read assumes that everyone knows what a beachhead is. For those that don't, this is my version: a place where assault troops land with all the support they can get, knock out the enemy defenses, and try to make operating space for larger forces to come in. These forces get organized and push on inward to make room for other forces to come in and move forward to make room for larger forces. This goes on and on until you have a damn war going. After the beachheads are set up, the house-cleaning group comes in. They remove all the bodies and burned out vehicles, and so on. By the time the big brass get there, it looks like nothing happened. So they tell reporters that everything went as planned, when really the assault force just had more men than the defense had ammunition. I'm sure they have a better description in higher headquarters and at West Point, but none of them ever made a beachhead.

I know that 22-year-old lieutenants are not supposed to be military geniuses, but I saw a gap of 15 or 20 miles between the beaches. But the briefing wasn't over yet. The 82nd and 101st Airborne Divisions were to land behind the beachheads a few miles, capture and hold the high ground and stop any enemy counter-attacks.

They let us think on that a little while. It looked to me as if one of two things were going to happen to those guys: one, they were going to get shot down on their way in; or two, they were going to be dropped in the English Channel. I'd never been in Normandy, France, but I'd sure as hell spent a lot of time on the beaches in Mississippi and Louisiana. In those areas, behind the beaches, there wasn't anything but swampland. But, as I said, you don't have to know much to be a lieutenant.

Back to the briefing. We had large-scale maps of the Omaha Beach area. The 29th Division was to land at Omaha, Dog White, which was the beach nearest the 1st Division area. There are high bluffs behind this area but no exit roads. Some lieutenant must have planned this part. Dog Green is in front of an exit road going to Vierville sur Mer. A regiment of the 116th Infantry was to land here, go up the draw and take out the defenses so tanks and artillery could get off the beach. We could see this was going to be a mean son-of-a-bitch. We were taught better than that at Officer Candidate School. Why not go around the strong point and take it from the backside? Whitie and I discussed this a little, while we were setting up the aerial photos. Sergeants and lieutenants didn't decide these things. Anyway, that was 116th's problem. We wondered what would the Ranger problem be. We were just about to find out. Incidentally, I never did hear how they lit on the names for the beaches. Why not Indiana and Kentucky Beach or Pennsylvania and New York Beach? Well, it had to be something I guess.

A close-up look at this area would show why there was a 15 or 20-mile gap between the landing beaches. There were no exit roads and no way off the small beachhead areas except up the cliffs. No way the Krauts could attack the beaches from that area either, but on defense you don't have to attack with troops. You can attack with automatic weapons, mortars, rockets, or artillery. The offense, of course, can use these same weapons, but eventually someone must physically force the defense out of the pillboxes, unless one kills them all. But we still had to occupy this ground.

These two points had real names, not code names. The one nearest Vierville su Mer, about two miles to the right, was Pointe el

Raz de Percee. The largest one, about five miles to our right, was Pointe du Hoc. The Allied command had received information from the French Underground. They knew there was a strong point located at Pointe el Raz de Percee that could sweep the beach in front of Vierville with machine-gun, rifle-fire, mortar-fire and artillery. This position had to be destroyed at any cost. It was located on cliffs approximately 90 feet high. Some say 40 feet, some say 60, some say 90. All I know is that they were damn high. And they were strongly defended from the backside. The Germans were not worried about the channel side. They felt no one could possibly get up those cliffs and, if they did, Grandma Moses could push them off with one hand. Not much has been written about this part of the invasion.

We were still at this time getting an overall briefing but it was becoming obvious that the Ranger mission had something to do with the 15 or 20-mile gap between Omaha and Utah beaches. Whitie and I were doing some speculating. Now, we had maps and aerial photos of Pointe du Hoc. Intelligence had information that there were five or six large artillery pieces on this cliff. These guns could cover not only the beaches of Omaha and Utah, but were also a threat to the transport area and support fire from destroyers and battleships. It was obvious, even to me, that something had to be done about these guns. This was believed to be the strongest point in the whole German defense.

I don't intend to tell the story of the Pointe again; it's been told many times. It is important, however, to realize that the Rangers, from top to bottom, recognized the importance of this position. Concern about these guns influenced the two Ranger battalion activities over five miles of beaches on D-Day. They were our sole reason for being there. Since the war, of course, some have wondered if it was necessary. I can only speak for the 1st Platoon of A Company, the 2nd Ranger Battalion. The whole invasion depended on these guns being taken out. You must risk one thousand men for the liberation of France and freedom for the world. To say a month, a year, or forty years later it was unnecessary is just not reasonable thinking. Suppose those guns could have been brought into action and had stopped the invasion. The Germans could have developed the atomic bomb. Maybe Hiroshima wouldn't have happened. Maybe we would be speaking German or Japanese today. But I believe every Ranger always felt that this mission was necessary.

Colonel Rudder took over the briefing. Big Jim was very intense. "This job can and must be done." He told us about the meetings he had had with General Bradley and his staff. Some thought it wouldn't work. Some thought it was possible. It boiled down to, "Here's the mission. Tell us what you need and do it the Ranger way."

Without getting into the statistics, logistics, and ballistics, here was the plan: C Company of the 2nd Ranger Battalion was to land at Point el Raz de Percee and take out that strong point. It's unbelievable to me now that they would send a 65-man Ranger company in to do a job that looked like the work of an infantry battalion, but that's what they did. C Company was commanded by Captain Ralph Goranson. Lieutenant Sid Salomon and Lieutenant Bill Moody, the platoon leaders, along with their key non-commissioned officers, went into a separate briefing with part of the battalion staff. They reviewed aerial photos and a rubber mockup of the area. It was left to Captain Goranson and his officers to work out the plan they would use later. All other officers and non-commissioned officers of the 2nd and 5th Rangers were still being briefed on everybody's mission so, if necessary, anyone in the battalions could work with them or take over the job.

Then we came down to Pointe du Hoc. I began to understand. It was pretty complicated, but the staff broke us down into two teams. Each team had an assignment and a mission. Colonel Rudder decided that D, E, and F Companies would assault and take the cliffs. The key thing was to take the cliff tops within thirty minutes before the Germans could recover from the naval bombardment and air force bombing and strafing. When the beachhead had been established, A and B Companies of the 2nd Rangers and the entire 5th Ranger Battalion were to follow up the cliffs and take out the guns. He said, "Now, if they don't make it up the bluffs, and we expect 80% casualties getting there—if they don't get up there within 30 minutes, you'll get the code word *Tilt*." If this were to happen, then A and B companies along with the 5th Rangers would land at Vierville sur Mer, bypass all enemy opposition in ones and twos or whatever, get up the road, get up to the Pointe and get the guns out. That was the mission—to get the guns. He preached on that and preached on that.

I felt a little let down at first because I felt that A Company was the top company in the Rangers and should be given the toughest part of the job. Each Ranger company, of course, felt the same way. So he told us to go back and think about it and we would get together in a couple or three hours.

I went back and thought about it. "Why are D, E and F Companies going up the cliffs when A Company is the best company in the battalion." I felt like he had mistreated us. Of course, I wasn't the company commander. "Hell," I thought, "I'm going to ask him anyway. He can't kick me out now. It's too close." So, I went over to where he was and I said, "Colonel, why D, E and F Companies? Why not A and B Companies?"

He looked at me and said, "Well, Bob, I was wondering when you were going to ask that. I knew you would. You think A Company is the best in the battalion, don't you?"

I said, "Well, yes, sir."

"That's the reason we gave you, A and B, the mission we did. Because you've got two missions. You can either come up the cliffs behind D, E and F or you can go down to the left, then come up the highway and take the guns out from that way. We took that into consideration." I knew he was just pulling my rope, but it made me feel pretty good.

A couple of hours later we came together again. Everybody had it down pretty well. They laid out the display areas of foam rubber and sand to show us what it looked like. We went through that briefing for about three or four days. We went over and over the plan. We had information on all of it, what every unit was going to do. I've read in books since then that some of the other outfits weren't briefed on what they were going to do. But I guarantee you, we knew everything that there was to know and all the odds. Everything to the tee.

June 1944. American Rangers march along Weymouth seafront to embark for Omaha Beach. First Lt. Robert Edlin (outside top right) gets his platoon to march in step with Lt. Col. James Rudder (front right). This picture was reproduced in ceramic and placed on the town's American War Memorial in June 1999.

7

D-DAY—ON THE BEACH

We knew we were going to hell. We didn't know how bad it was going to be, but we knew we were going.

–Robert Edlin

Thousands of British people had gathered, cheering and yelling as we marched along the quay. We had arrived in covered trucks to the docking area. They had let the school children out and they were singing the national anthem and waving American flags. As I turned to wave at the cheering crowd, I thought of the years of hardship these people had endured. I remember that moment well. Our mission was top secret but I believe the people of Weymouth knew more about it than we did. We were pretty solemn as we marched toward the waterfront where we would board our assault crafts. We knew we were going to hell. We didn't know how bad it was going to be but we knew we were going.

I didn't want to look rowdy dowdy in front of all those thousands of people so I thought it might help to keep in step. "Hut, two, three, four." I had my whole platoon in step, swinging arms. The 2nd Platoon immediately picked up on it and I think that behind them B Company did also. I expect it followed all the way back to the 5th Rangers.

I was in the lead with Rudder and the battalion staff. I dropped back to the middle of the column. Rudder was up front where he should be, but out of step. There's an old saying in the Army that you don't tell a colonel the time of day. You don't tell him anything, you ask him. When you've got a guy out of step that just can't keep step you holler, "Everybody but Corporal Jones change step, *harch*." That word is actually march. But in the Army we'd say *harch*. It's a harsher sound. We'd say *order harms* and *present harms*. I don't know where that came from but it's been around since the Revolutionary War. No need to change it now.

Well, I thought, this might work here. So I said, "Everybody but Colonel Rudder change step *harch*." So the whole platoon changed step. There were snickers and laughter up and down.

Rudder asked me a little later, "Bob, who told you to do that?"

"Nobody."

"My God," he said, "you loosened things up for a minute. I even heard them laughing and joking and making fun of me." He wasn't upset. That's the kind of guy he was.

I said, "Well, better you than me."

I realized Rudder was uptight. He knew where we were going and what we were going to do. He knew we were going to lose eight out of every ten men. That means only two guys out of ten weren't going to get hurt. I looked at it this way—I wasn't going to get hurt; who would the other one be? That's the way I think most everybody looked at it.

The LCAs transported us out to the mother ships waiting in the Channel. My unit boarded the *Prince Charles*. We were on the ships for five days, delayed one day due to bad weather. While on ship they promoted Lieutenant Joe Rafferty to captain since he was given command of A Company. On the night before D-Day they had a little party. The British always had a little whiskey aboard ship where as the Americans had to slip it in. At the party, I was talking to Lt. Stanley White and Bob Fitzsimmons. An argument started between Major Lyttle and some other officers. They got loud and violent. Lyttle said, "This is a suicide mission. We're all going to be killed. There's not going to be one man left and it's all going to be absolutely for nothing." That was the wrong thing to say!

Weymouth Museum Collection

I was the first American soldier to board a Landing Craft Assault boat at Weymouth Harbor. People get confused when they hear the story about me being the first one aboard the landing craft. They immediately think that I was the first one to land in France, which is absolutely not true. The rotation was that the 2nd Rangers were to load first, and behind us were the 5th Rangers and behind them was the whole 1st Infantry Division. The reason they went in that form is that's the military, not because they were going to land first but because somebody had to go first. So they went in numerical order: two before five and five before the regiment. A Company was first of the 2nd Rangers and the 1st Platoon of A Company went first. The 1st Platoon leader was naturally the number one man, and that was me. It took three or four days for all the troops to get loaded on to the ships. They loaded a total of 500,000 men from that harbor. About 200,000 landed on D-Day.

That night, when people's nerves were short, Lyttle was kicked out of the Rangers. I saw Lyttle at a Replacement Center weeks later. He told me that he didn't think that he'd ever go back to combat—he was actually crying about how upset he was and what a terrible thing he had done. I've since read the stories about what happened to him after that. He went into another infantry outfit and got promoted to a lieutenant colonel and was awarded the Distinguished Service Cross. He was known as the best officer in that particular infantry division. He overcame what happened to him on the boat and he overcame getting kicked out of the Rangers and was promoted to full colonel before the war was over. That story needs to be told.

The original plan was for Rudder to be back on a ship with General Bradley, the Army commander and General Gerow, the corps commander. When the landing took place, Lyttle was to take the 2nd Rangers in and Schneider was supposed to take the 5th Rangers in. We were to keep in contact with Rudder and Rudder would get reinforcements to us as needed. When Lyttle was relieved and Rudder took his place going in with the 2nd Rangers, we lost our key man. When we asked for fire support, they didn't even know who the Rangers were. That's what happened.

What it cost us to have Lyttle relieved, people can only guess. What would have happened if Lyttle had gone in instead of Rudder? What if? Nobody will ever know. The way I figure it, the Lord made it happen the way it did.

There were many sound military reasons to pick Normandy for the invasion, but for a while on D-Day, June 6, it looked as if they had made a tragic mistake. Dog Green Beach loomed before us. The 5th Rangers had come in further down under cover of smoke but we landed right where the guys from the 29th, A Company of the 116th Infantry, sustained the real slaughter. Two hundred and forty of them landed just 15 minutes ahead of us. It was a terrible sight. There were bodies everywhere. I had to step on some of them to get over them.

The first man that I saw get hit on the beach was Roy Latham, my runner at the time. Rea Carroll, my original runner, had gotten the measles and spent D-Day in the hospital in England. His replacement, Roy Latham, a 19-year-old from North Carolina, had stood with me on the deck of the ship talking the night before the invasion. On the beach, I heard him grunt just to my right and a step or two to my rear. I turned to look and I saw him falling, the blast just took away his face.

As in the movie, *Saving Private Ryan,* I saw rivulets of blood going out with the tide. I saw some guys huddling up behind the beach barricades. I screamed at them to get off the beach. Even a stray round would have blown up one of those barricades because they were all mined.

I got up to within ten feet of the seawall. I looked back and saw only two or three guys coming. I have no recollection but I've been told that I turned around and went back almost to the water's edge. Our job was to get up the cliffs and get the guns but I must have been thinking that I couldn't do that myself. So I must have gone back to stir up some help. There were some guys that got up and started moving when I was yelling. The story went that I was moving around the beach trying to help. I don't remember that at all. I know that Captain Rafferty was killed, but I don't remember how I knew that. Captain Carter swears that I saved his life on the beach but I don't remember. Once in a while someone will prod my memory and something else comes out.

When I became wounded, the thought came to my mind, "Hell, I haven't been here 15 minutes and I have a Purple Heart." Bill Klaus had been wounded pretty badly in one leg. He crawled over and dragged me by my backpack up to the seawall when I couldn't move anymore. I was just completely done. He covered my body when a couple of artillery rounds came in. Then a medic gave me a shot of morphine. After that, some events are clear to me and some others are not. We were still under machine-gun fire, mortar-fire and sniper-fire. It was right in the middle of the worst part of the thing. And here's this sergeant kind of covering me with his body and a medic crouching over me to give me a shot. They were the heroes.

I've read a lot of books that stated Bob Edlin led A Company ashore. Well, I did not lead the Rangers ashore. Captain Rafferty did, the company commander. When Rafferty got killed on the beach, I became company commander, because the company commander was dead and then the next ranking officer automatically takes over. I had seniority. Stanley White had the 2nd Platoon and I outranked him by a number of months. My time as company commander was probably a half hour at the most.

I got hit the first time in the left leg, regardless of what the books say, by machine-gun fire. It brought me down but I still had command of the company. I was still hollering at both platoons, "Get up and go." Then when I got hit the second time and went down, I got up about ten yards and Klaus crawled out and saved my life, dragging me up to the seawall. I was still company commander then. But when I hollered at Bill White, my platoon sergeant, "Bill, get out of here. You've got to get to the top of the cliff," then I relinquished command of the company. The senior officer had turned the command over to the senior non-commissioned officer. That made Bill the ranking officer and the company commander getting off the beach.

Bill White was, at that time, a tech sergeant, three stripes up and two stripes down. When I told Bill that he was in charge of the company and hollered for them to get off the beach, Courtney, Dreher, Gabby Hart and everybody that could move, went with him. There were only four or five of them that got up and went. That was all that we had left. They went. No questions asked. Bill commanded A Company all through the rest of D-Day and D-Day+1. On D-Day+2, when they were going up to relieve D, E, and F Company on Pointe du Hoc, he was still the company commander. When my small group of 4 or 5 men went up the bluffs, to the left of them the 5th Rangers were moving up to climb the cliffs at the same time, about 150 - 200 yards away.

After the morphine set in, I thought, hell, I feel pretty good now. I managed to get up and hobble a little bit. I looked back at the sea, nothing, no reinforcements. I thought, "We are going to be dead or prisoners pretty soon. Everyone has withdrawn and left us. Well, we tried." After I got up to the seawall and got the shot of morphine, I crawled up to a small villa. The bluffs were about 90 to 100 feet high behind the beaches. I crawled forward as far as I could. I got up and hobbled to some cover over there, some bushes at this villa. It was a sort of vacation house. Around at the back of it there was a well and a garden. It was a round stone well and I can remember, even now, how it was mortared together. It had a wooden bucket and a handle that turned the rope. It was so inviting. I was there alone and I wanted some of that water so bad, but years of training told me, that's booby- trapped. I looked up to the top of the cliffs and I thought, "I can't make it on this leg. Where is everyone? Have they all quit?" Then I heard Dreher yelling, "Come on up. These trenches are empty!" Then a Kraut burp gun cut loose. I thought, "Oh God, I can't get there!" I heard an American Tommy gun and Courtney yelling, "Damn it, Dreher. They're empty now!" There was more German small arms fire, and the German's grenades popping. I could hear Whitie yelling, "Cover me!" I heard Garfield Ray's BAR talking American. Then there was silence. They had broken through the thin German lines. There were no generals here, no colonels. Just three sergeants and a couple of PFCs.

Now I thought, "Where are the 5th Rangers?" I crawled back to the beach. I saw the 5th Rangers coming through the smoke of a burning LST that had been hit by artillery fire. Colonel Schneider evidently had seen the slaughter on the beaches and used his well learned experience from the 1st, 3rd, and 4th Ranger Battalions in Africa, Sicily, Italy, and Anzio. Using the smoke as a screen, he moved in behind it. He saved the 5th Ranger Battalion many casualties. There were no field manuals here and Colonel Schneider had just written a new one.

I got back to the beach to check on the wounded members of my platoon. My years of training told me there would be a counter-attack. I gathered the wounded by the seawall and told them to arm themselves as best as possible. I said, "You guys pick up your guns or whatever weapons you can find and turn and face up the draw. You've all been taught like I have that the enemy is going to counterattack. And when they counterattack, I don't know if they are going to kill us or take us prisoners, but we're going to take our shot at them." Now, if you can imagine 15 wounded Rangers sitting there and we're going to fight the German army. I know it sounds ridiculous, but 12 or 15 wounded Rangers lay there in the sand facing up to the cliffs just praying that Sergeant White, Courtney, Dreher, and the 5th Ranger Battalion could get to the guns. Our fight was over unless the Germans counter-attacked. Then we were going to take some of them with us. The 5th Ranger Battalion had now moved inland. Someone had to get the Pointe. Those guns would start firing any time. I looked back to the sea; there was nothing. There were no reinforcements. I thought the invasion had been abandoned. I thought we would be dead or prisoners soon. Everyone had withdrawn and left us. Well, we had tried. Some guy crawled over and told me he was a colonel from the 29th Infantry Division. He told me to relax and let up; that we were going to be okay. He said that D, E, and F Companies were on the Pointe. The guns had been destroyed! A and B companies and the 5th Ranger Battalion were inland. The 29th and 1st Divisions were getting off the beaches. This colonel looked at me and said, "You've done your job." I remember very bitterly telling him, "Yeah, I did a hell of a job. I used up two rounds of enemy ammunition. That's a hell of a part to play in the war."

We were lying there. There were people sheltered all along the seawall. By this time there were hundreds of people on the beach that still couldn't get across to the top. They were auxiliary troops like engineers and mine experts. The artillery-fire was heavy and there were people taking cover under the seawall. They wouldn't come and help us. Finally, two black soldiers, part of an engineer battalion, came out under heavy fire and dragged us to cover. They would have made good Rangers.

Despite the awful pain, I hoped to catch up with the platoon the next day. I got another shot of morphine. It was warm. The sun was warm. I was lying there. It made me feel good. I slept. I must have slept two or three hours from exhaustion and from the morphine. I asked somebody what time it was when I woke up and they told me 1300 (one o'clock). There was a lot of artillery. The tide was going out taking bodies and debris with it. It kept reaching back to pick up another body, but they didn't want to go. They had earned this part of the beach with their lives. All that day we were under constant fire.

The artillery was coming almost as bad as it was early in the morning. We were bringing tanks ashore and their artillery was firing and blowing them up. From somewhere I had heard that there was an aid station down the beach away from the Vierville exit.

A tank came along. It stopped. I asked the crew where they were going. They said they were going to try to get up the Vierville draw. I knew that that's where the 2nd and 5th Rangers were at, somewhere up there. I thought, well, maybe we will take a ride that way. Otherwise it was hard to move around. I asked a couple of guys if they would help me up on the tank. They helped me up. I couldn't walk by then at all. Sgt. Klaus got up there with me. He also had been wounded pretty badly.

I said to him, "What are you going to do?"

He said, "I'm going with you."

I said, "Well, I'm going to get back up with the company and make sure they're all right. I'm going to see if there is anything that I can do to help them." That's how nutty I was, full of morphine. I don't know what I could've done once I got there. That was silly, gun-ho stuff.

We got up right in front of that draw and I'm telling you, there sat a big gun that had been knocked out. That thing was a dinosaur. There was another one next to it coming out of a pillbox looking right in our faces. The driver stopped the tank. I don't know why. Maybe he was trying to make up his mind if he should go ahead and attack past the pillbox or go back and get out of its range. I thought, "This is no place for me. We're stopped right in front of that gun." I bailed off. Klaus fell off. We rolled away a little bit. About that time their artillery hit that tank and blew it all to hell. We took cover again at the wall.

I've often thought about that tank since. It was a stupid thing to do. I say stupid, because a tank is a big target for somebody. It was a mistake to get on the thing in the first place. We were just thinking about getting transportation.

I was on the beach for 16 hours under heavy fire. There were people that went in even the next day and were under fire. There were people that went in on D+3 and they were still under fire.

I knew Rafferty was dead. Rafferty was the company commander. I didn't know where Lt. White was. I learned later, following D-Day in just four days time they had three company commanders. They brought Salomon down first to command A Company. And then someone else whom I've forgotten. Then they brought in Arman. There's a lot that I can't remember.

Things were beginning to loosen up a little bit then. It was getting along toward about 1600 in the evening. There were still some artillery and mortar-fire and rockets coming in but it was obvious we had established the beachhead.

As it got along toward dark, a boat came in to evacuate the wounded. I was immobilized by that time. A full colonel came in and said they would only take walking wounded out to the ship. I'm not sure who the colonel was. By that time there was a lot of brass on the beach. The men that couldn't walk would have to wait until the litter bearers could come and pick them up.

Two or three of the Rangers put me on a stretcher. One of the sergeants stood up and said, "This is one lieutenant that's going with us on the boat. That's it."

The colonel replied, "Well, this is a direct order. Nobody but the walking wounded are going on that boat."

The sergeant and about 15 other guys told him, "Lt. Edlin is going with us or we're not going and you're not going." That is the truth. The colonel responded it wasn't going to be that way. One guy pulled out a .45 and slipped the slide back and threw a shell into the chamber and said, "Yeah, he's going." The colonel said, "Put him on the boat." That was the Rangers.

It was almost dark as we got on the small landing craft. The American Air Force had finished their job now. They had moved back. There were no landing strips for them in France. The Germans took over. The Messerschmidt (German planes) started to come in; their fighter planes and light bombers began to attack the beachhead. We went out in the landing craft and came up beside the ship we were to get on. We were to climb a rope ladder to board. Sergeant Ted James of B Company had lost all of the fingers off one of his hands right to the knuckles. It was impossible for him to climb the ladder. I was lying in the bottom of the boat still on the stretcher. Most of the people had gone up the ladder except Ted James and myself. A German fighter plane came in strafing; it looked like he was coming right at our boat. I'm telling you James went up that ladder, about 40 feet up, one handed like a monkey. He was safe up at the top. I was still down at the bottom. Then they kind of cut my boat loose. I thought, "They've got to take me back to shore. They've got no choice. They can't get me up there." The strafing and bombing around the ship was so heavy that I thought they were going to leave me. I looked up, it seemed quite a distance, and there was a redheaded, heavyset American sailor. He was probably 20 years old and weighed about 230 pounds.

"I'll get that son-of-a-bitch!" He dropped a big net over the side and down into the boat and then climbed down the ladder. He told me, "This is probably going to hurt."

I said, "I don't give a damn. I've got to get off this thing." He put me, stretcher and all, into the net. He got in there with me and they hoisted us up to the top with a winch. I'll never know who that redheaded sailor was, but he was a good one.

We began to feel more secure, me, Sergeant Klaus, Sergeant James and whoever was there from A Company. We felt like we were going to make it. All night long the German strafing and bombing continued. It seemed so unfair that we were out of it and still not out of it.

I remember they took me down into the hospital section of the ship. I was given some more morphine. As I lay there on the operating table, I heard a conversation between an Army doctor and a Navy doctor. One of them said, "We're going to have to take his leg off." The other one said, "It's not going to get any worse. Why don't we just leave it alone? We don't have time to fool with him anyway. Let's get to the seriously wounded people first and work on them. We'll get this man back to England and then they can decide there what's going to have to be done." Thank God they were busy, because that leg is still working.

We sailed back across the Channel. We were out there on that ship the night of June 6th and most of June 7th. When we came in sometime in the afternoon of June 7th, that same red-headed American sailor came down to the bunk where I was laying and picked me up and carried me up to the top deck.

MORE D-DAY STORIES

WILLIAM KLAUS
Private First Class
1st Platoon, A Company

I also was there on D-Day. Bob Edlin and I went in on the same landing craft. I knew the boat had touched down on the beach but the ramp didn't drop. I thought, "What's going on?" We were being shot at all the while. It was a British seaman that was responsible for lowering the ramp, but the poor man had been killed. I saw his body; his body was there but he didn't have any head. I looked at him and said, "He doesn't look right." I probably was in a little shock. Then I noticed that his head was gone. Edlin was in the front and I was in the back. Edlin was familiar with this boat. We were all familiar with the boat. We had been operating with the British sailors ever since arriving in England. So, Edlin got the ramp down.

Then when we got ashore, we happened to wind up together in the same area. Edlin had both his legs wounded. I had one leg wounded but I didn't have any broken bones. After I got a shot of morphine, I could hobble a little bit, but I couldn't continue with the mission because I couldn't keep up with the other guys. Edlin was in pretty bad shape but he was conscious. We were lying there and there were wounded all over the place. Somewhere near, within a few feet, one of our men was lying, badly wounded. Really badly wounded. I recall a medic coming up the beach. He had a blanket on his arm. I don't know who he was or where he was from. Lt. Edlin said to this medic, "Put that blanket on our wounded man." The wounded man was lying there out of it, in shock, freezing to death. This medic said, "I can't. I've got to go up the beach. I'm taking this blanket to somebody else." So Edlin pulled his .45 out and pointed it at the medic. He said, "Put the blanket on that man." The medic had no choice. He put the blanket on the man. I'm sure that probably saved the man's life because he did survive. Edlin gave that medic an offer he couldn't refuse. That's the way he was. He took care of his people. We were close before that, but it just bore out my opinion of him. I just can't say enough about him.

INNES R. ROBERTSON
Technician Five
2nd Platoon, A Company

I remember it just as well as if it had happened yesterday. The LCAs with the 1st and 2nd Platoons came in side by side. I was in the weapon's section and in the back of the LCA. Everything was happening up in the front. Everybody was getting shot. So we bailed over the back end. I struggled in the water up to the beach. It was about four feet deep where I went in. Everything was just flying around. I saw one of B Company's landing craft running loose, just spinning around in a circle. The throttle was stuck wide open. It was just a roaring going round and round in circles. I could see that there wasn't anybody aboard. The British coxswains were probably all dead.

Smith, the section sergeant, was shot by a sniper. He was lying right in the middle of the trail that led up the cliff to where Courtney had wiped out the German machine-gun. I remember Edlin was lying up off the beach, far enough away so he wasn't getting fired upon. As I was going up the cliff I ran into him. He was lying on his back. I stopped and leaned down and asked him, "Can I help you?" He said, "No, keep on going! Keep on going!" I can remember that very clearly. His injuries didn't seem to be bothering him much; he just couldn't walk any further.

RAY TOLLEFSON
Private First Class
2nd Platoon, A company

I was one of the youngest Rangers there on D-Day. I was born on December 4, 1924 and was 19 ½ years old on the invasion day. The fire was directed at our LCA. Edlin was on the other LCA. We were in different platoons. The three British men on our boat got wiped out while we were out there, a long way out yet. So we had nobody to pilot the boat.

There we were. Somebody dropped the ramp down and I saw Ed Sowa, the first sergeant go forward. He was hit right away. I know myself and O'Connor jumped over the side. I think the majority of our men after seeing what happened, went over the sides. I was over my head in the water, but I was comfortable. I had been around water all my life. That didn't bother me. The waves and everything were heading in towards shore anyway, you know, so I wasn't concerned. I had my rifle with me. I don't think that it was over a couple of minutes before I could feel bottom. Then I fired the only two shots that I did in the war. As I got in there a little bit, my rifle had been in the water and I just wanted to see if it was okay. I knew where that one machine-gun was coming from. So I aimed up there and I fired two shots. It was seconds after that that I got hit. It spun me around and that took care of me. I was hit by a machine-gun in the arm holding my gun out of the water. I made noise about it. One of the fellows came over to me and wrapped up my arm. He gave me a shot of morphine and off he went. I was still out in the water when I got hit.

I want to relate a little story about that. When we were at the San Diego Ranger reunion, in 1989, I registered. Someone said, "Ray, someone is looking for you." Well here, Doynoff was his last name. He was a radio operator in Headquarters Company. He remembered that he had been the one that put the bandage on my arm. He never knew what happened to me. When we finally met up with one another he said, "I didn't know if you lived or died." We were pleased to see one another. I couldn't believe that he remembered me because we never talked after I was hit.

After I was given the shot, the morphine put me in la-la land. From there I just struggled my way into the beach which took a considerable amount of time. I would walk a few steps and then the waves would pull me in some more. Then also when the machine gun fire was firing, ptr-rrrrrrrr, and getting worse and worse, well, there was no sense in me standing up. I wasn't going to do anybody any good, so I stayed low and swam as much as I could in to shore. I was basically washed into shore those last yards. And who's along side of me but Jim Slagle. We were in the same machine-gun squad. We'd been friends and I ended up right next to him. He had been hit in the back and had floated in. He couldn't move. He was paralyzed. I thought he was done with. But later on he recovered so that today you would never know the difference.

There was one other fellow by the name of Joe Daniels that was lying there on the beach with us. He was in our company too, and he was just full of holes. Joe knew he was going to die and he was whimpering. I think he was lying between Slagle and myself. He was bringing up his mother, you know, when he was crying away there. So the three of us were just laying there. But Joe, oh jeezz, blood was just coming out of every place. I don't know how he had gotten that far. Finally he expired. Then I fell asleep with the morphine.

MORRIS PRINCE
Private First Class
2nd Platoon, A Company

Our CO, Captain Rafferty, was the first man off the assault boat. He had just waded through the water and had reached the beach, when a spray of machine-gun fire had wounded him in the leg. It hadn't taken him long to size up the fighting situation. He realized to stay on the open sandy beach was suicide. He repeatedly shouted, hollered, cajoled and urged his men to keep going ahead, refusing to budge from his own uncovered place, so that he could be in a better position to control his men. He was masterful and inspiring as he yelled and directed his men forward. When the last man passed him, he made a move in an attempt to seek personal safety, but a direct hit of an enemy 88 put a climax to his career as an officer and a Ranger. A quick ending to a most courageous leader.

ED O'CONNOR
Private First Class
2nd Platoon, A Company

On D-Day my LCA got snagged on an under-water emplacement that was supposed to block a tank. When that happened, the coxswain let the ramp down. Then we all started piling out and started getting hit by small arms fire and machine-gun fire. It was pretty dreadful. I went off the side and found myself in water up to my chest. I had a life preserver on called a Mae West. I had it inflated. I was able to get my feet to the ground and started in. I was over by myself. I could see to my side a sniper shooting at me. The bullets were landing right next to me, hitting the water like kisses.

We were to go in with a position called high port. I was holding my

M-1 with both hands with the barrel to the left and higher. I thought, "Well, hell, while I'm walking in, I'll start shooting up at the bank." They called it harassing fire. "Maybe I can keep somebody's head down or maybe kill them." I went to pull my trigger and it didn't work. I thought, "My God! My gun doesn't work. All the training and keeping the gun clean!" I looked at it sideways and there, where the little operating handle was, it was splintered. A German bullet had hit my gun. A German had been aiming for my chest as I walked in and had hit my gun with my gun across my chest instead.

I went a little bit further. I dropped down behind one of the German obstacles and looked at the trouble. I saw that it wouldn't work so I left it lay there. I looked to my right. I looked to my left. I saw guys that were running, trying to make it ashore. Every once in a while a guy would fall. In the meantime I was lying down and I thought, "I've got to make a run for it." So I ran halfway to the beach, which maybe was 40 yards. Then I took a great big belly flop, making believe that I was hit, so they couldn't zero in on me. I did that all automatically. Never did I believe that when I got up to run that I was going to take a flop. From our training it just came naturally. We were also trained not to run too far because then we're less likely to get picked off.

So I took that flop. Finally after a few seconds, I lifted my head and looked to my left. I saw guys still struggling trying to get to the beach. Every once in a while, just as in *Saving Private Ryan*, I saw guys falling. A guy would get hit and drop to the ground.

I started running. I got to the shelter of the shoreline and some cover. I met some guys from Company A and we started up the hill. That was an unbelievable experience, getting across that beach! God sure was with me when I had that gun across my chest, then looking down and seeing those two shells kiss the water. Maybe more than one guy was shooting at me.

We started down a nice black-top road with little ditches about 12 inches wide on each side and about that deep. Finally the Germans zeroed in on us with 88's. Whoom! They would hit the road or the trees along the side of it. We could hear them coming in and when they did we all stopped running and hit the ditches. The shrapnel flew over our heads for what seemed an eternity. Then when the shrapnel stopped, we ran further. This happened for about 20 rounds. Two of our guys were killed outright with that attack. The Germans knew right where we were. They knew we were coming down the road. But it was all we had to travel on to go that way.

Somebody back further hollered, "retreat," so we started to go back.

Then there was a guy by the name of Robertson in my platoon. A bullet went through the meat of his leg muscle so he was limping like hell. He couldn't go very fast. I said, "Robertson, you try and catch up with the company. They're retreating. I'm going to stay back here and be a rear guard." We always trained to have a rear guard in a situation like this to watch and prevent the enemy from setting up a machine-gun in the middle of the road and mowing us down.

I stayed back there for a while. The company was about 100 yards off, retreating. Robertson was catching up to them. Finally they made a little bend in the road. I thought, "OK. I'll get out on the road. Nobody's coming." I started to go back on the road and I looked to my right. Then I looked to my left. I looked to my right again and then to my left. Pretty soon I looked to my left once more. There were some Germans, about six, waving some white hankies. I motioned my hand for them to come out to me.

I was scared, but I got my gun lowered on them. I was just about six feet tall then and they could see I meant business. I didn't show any fear. I took control. I got those guys out on the road. I motioned my hand for them to put their hands above their heads and clamp them tight. OK. Then I made them get up in front of me. "OK , all right, let's start going down the road."

Pretty soon I caught up with Company A and I felt pretty big. I felt pretty happy. Here comes Ed with six prisoners.

There were a lot of troops below us on the slope. Somebody suggested that we send the prisoners back through the American lines to the beach. So we told our prisoners, "Go ahead and keep that way." Down they went. That was quite a moment for me. I've wondered a few times if those were the first Germans captured on D-Day. It was a break for me that they gave up when they did. They sure could've wiped me out pretty easy.

That was another example of good training—staying back and playing rear guard. Instead of jogging back along the road, my head was going back and forth, checking automatically to see if anything was there. And sure enough, there these jokers were with their hankies up in the air. Who knows, maybe they were running out of ammunition.

I need to add a little introduction for this next story. Everyone knows about how D, E, and F Companies climbed the cliffs and took out the guns on Pointe du Hoc. However, little has been written about C Company's accomplishments on Pointe el Raz de

Percee. They completed their mission and were the only Rangers to do so in the prescribed amount of time, actually for that matter, of anyone on the entire beach. They've never been given recognition for that and they did a great job. Who better to tell their story than their company commander, Captain Ralph Goranson.

RALPH GORANSON
Captain
C Company, 2nd Rangers

I was 24 years old when we made the invasion. I had been made a captain just a month before. When I volunteered to be in the Rangers, I was shipped to Camp Forest. We went through a couple of commanders. Then we got Rudder. I would have followed Rudder to hell and back! He was always there, right up at the front.

We were in the marshalling area in England, when we were sequestered, the last couple of days before D-Day. I and my two lieutenants, Bill Moody and Sid Salomon, went to a briefing of the 29th Division because we were going to come in on their flank. They had very good pictures and mockups of Normandy and the beaches. Our planes had done some flying over the area and had it all mapped out.

Bill, Sid and myself went back and sat down with our first three graders, three stripe sergeants and higher. That was about 20 of our guys. The Ranger companies had a lot of stripes in them. "What are we going to do?" We decided that we would have two plans. If the 29th had good fortune in crossing the beach, we would follow right behind them and come up the highway and do a right flank and take out Pointe el Raz de Percee from the back side. That's always easier. That was plan one. Plan two was to have the 1st Platoon with Bill Moody leading the way, free climb the 90-foot cliffs, drop some toggle ropes, get top side and do what was there to do. Everybody knew what we were going to do. Either execute plan one or plan two. Plan two is the plan we actually did.

We didn't think about how many men we were going to lose. I do remember that shortly before we left the ship my company said the *Lord's Prayer* together. Then I said, "Give 'em hell."

Vierville had the only paved road from the coastal highway down to the beach. Where the road met the beach was the biggest pillbox you ever saw. It was like a motel! I believe it was the 1st Battalion of the 29th that was to hit that at H-hour. They were to pave the way.

A few minutes behind them, I was supposed to land on their right flank. We decided that Sid would land on the left of the three boats that we were in. The cliffs were 90 feet there. About half a mile west of there was another point called Pointe el Raz de Percee. The Germans here had mortars, cannons, and in other words, it was the gun position to protect the western flank of what was to become Omaha Beach. We were to neutralize that Pointe. From there over to the road there were some other guns.

We landed in the British landing craft, which is smaller than the American ones. The front went down. When I left the boat, the front was gone, shot off, and six or eight were dead in the boat.

I recently found out that the beach master, the man in charge of the beach there, had shut the beach down shortly after we came in. He made the boats land further to the east because that first group just ahead of us had received 85% casualties. The poor guys were laying at the edge of the water line and shooting up at the cliffs, but they didn't know what they were shooting at.

The minute I got across that beach and realized I was all in one piece, I took a fast look. I looked over at Bill Moody. He was looking at me. I put up two fingers, meaning plan two. He gave me a high sign and off we went. I got across the beach. You never saw so many dead bodies in all your life. We lost 23 men there. We had 65 men in the company with 3 officers and 2 attached. Out of 70 men we lost 23 people. Twenty-three were dead. My boat was destroyed when they blew off the ramp the minute we dropped it, but the 3 coxswains survived. The huge pillbox was giving us hell and we were also getting fire from Pointe el Raz de Percee behind us.

We climbed up the cliff then. We carried some 10-foot lengths of rope. It had a loop at one end and a cross bar at the other. Imagine taking a broom handle and cutting them about 10 to 15 inches and having one end of the rope tied around that. The other end of the rope had a loop. They dropped about three or four of those when they got to the crest. There were "mine" signs all over, but I think that was just camouflage.

When we got topside we couldn't believe it. It was just like a maze. The topside of the cliff was just honey-combed with trenches and dugouts everywhere, reaching from the guns to the road. There were also pillboxes cut right into the cliffs. Our landing site was to be an old farmhouse, chosen from pictures that we had seen. What we found when we got up there, in the farmhouse, was the master control center with the whole fire plan for that western edge of the beach. It was all painted out on the cement floor.

We took out the control center in that old farmhouse. Then we got some Germans that were guarding the pillboxes hanging out from the cliff. The pillboxes were fed from the back by these trenches, which were cut all over the place. It was made to order for hand-to-hand fighting. I'd rather have that than charging across the beach any day. We'd blow out the back door and then throw in white phosphorous. White phosphorous will burn the hell out of you. We used that to flush them out and when they did come out we shot them. Some would hole up. We'd tell them to come out.

We accomplished our mission. We had killed 63 Germans and captured 1. Then we turned it over to the 29th Division.

I had only one casualty on the topside of the cliff and that was my lieutenant for the 1st Platoon, Bill Moody. Bill Moody got it right between the eyes by a sniper. I was very sorry about that.

Sid Salomon, the lieutenant for the 2nd Platoon, had been hit, but we patched him up. We might have had some other minor wounds but if we could put some tape on them, then they could still fight.

A section of the 29th had somehow got lost coming in on their boat so I used them top side. When we got an area cleaned out, I had one of those guys guard it so the Germans wouldn't be able to infiltrate back in. I later ran into Lt. Heaney on the beach. By that time the road was open.

We made our way to Pointe el Raz de Percee and found that had been pretty well flattened by the navy. Our small arms fire had also contributed to neutralizing the area. We joined up with the 5th Rangers in going into Vierville. Our company was made "point" company the next day when we headed down the road toward Pointe du Hoc—what was left of it! We suffered no more casualties in that action.

I never got wounded on D-Day. My hands were a little scratched up from barbed wire, but that happens. I found out later that I got nine bullets in my gear from just going across the beach. My rations were shot off my back. My canteen had two bullets in it. I had an extra pouch strapped to my middle for the aid man with extra plasma in case we needed it. That had stopped three or four bullets. We carried stuff for the aid man because he couldn't carry it all. I had a flare projector in my pocket and a bullet had come in and was lying just on top of the flare. The flare projector could be fired to let the navy know where we were. The Navy, however, got too close to us several times. We had extra pockets going down the side of our fatigue pants. The Paratroopers had them. We copied them.

They had a big pocket that went from their knee to just above their hip, divided into two sections. We had gotten extra material and had sewed pockets down the side, or we hired people to do it. Some guys did it for a fee. It enabled us to carry more things.

I'm proud of my company and their spirit. I just happened to be a captain. Somebody had to run it. It's as simple as that. There were guys there that did a lot more than me.

WESTERN UNION

1201

·(25)·

A. N. WILLIAMS
PRESIDENT

The filing time shown in the date line on telegrams and day letters is STANDARD TIME at point of origin. Time of receipt is STANDARD TIME at point of death.

VEAA41 26 GOVT=WUX WASHINGTON DC 25 253P

LOUIS L EDLIN=

1944 JUN 25 PM 3 37

605 MACARTHUR DR NEWALBANY IND=

REGRET TO INFORM YOU YOUR SON FIRST LIEUTENANT ROBERT
T EDLIN WAS SERIOUSLY WOUNDED IN ACTION SIX JUNE
IN FRANCE LETTER CONTAINING PRESENT MAIL ADDRESS FOLLOWS=
ULIO THE ADJUTANT GENERAL.

THE COMPANY WILL APPRECIATE SUGGESTIONS FROM ITS PATRONS CONCERNING ITS SERVICE

Telegram received by Bob's parents on June 25, 1944, informing them
that their son was wounded on D-Day, June 6, 1944.

8

THE BEAUTIFUL NURSES

Am being awarded the Purple Heart and some other decorations for bravery in action, etc. If they knew how scared I was when I hit that beach they'd change their minds.

–Robert Edlin

The sun was shining brightly in the early evening. The English countryside was a beautiful green with flowers beginning to bloom. It was like we were coming back into civilization, and the hell we had just been through was behind us. There were bands on the dock playing, crowds of British civilians lined up cheering, yelling and praying. We could tell by their reaction that the invasion was a success. They were applauding and yelling for the wounded. There were about 15 of us 2nd Rangers there and also men from the 29th Division and Paratroopers and whatever happened to be on the boat. We were in a temporary hospital right there on the docks. They got us off the boats so they could go back into the English Channel to bring back more wounded. It must have been a pitiful sight when they carried me in there on a canvas cot.

I have never been treated any kinder, gentler, or with better care in my life. The Navy corpsmen were very careful with us. A young nurse came up to me; all the nurses looked young and beautiful to me back then and especially at that time. But I was so filthy dirty from the beach and blood. She said, "Don't you worry about anything. We're going to give you some morphine to ease the pain until you can get back to where they can fix your legs and do it right. You just lay here in this nice bed and your hot meal will be coming. I'll feed you and everything's going to be just great." I never did get that hot meal because I guess I fell asleep.

I woke up about 0300. Nightmares. I'm telling you it was just terrible. I was crazy. A nurse was sitting by my bed, holding my hand, wiping my forehead with a wet cloth, and assuring me that I was going to be all right. Evidently I had had a violent nightmare. She gave me more medication to put me to sleep, but before I went to sleep I heard the awful sounds around me. Men were screaming and groaning and I knew they were having nightmares too. I heard guys yelling, "Oh, my God! Oh, my God! John, John, help me!" and that kind of stuff. In the half hour or so that I was awake it was like being back on the beach again. These men, about 150 of them, were going through a terrible torment in their minds after the invasion.

When I woke up in the morning, that would be June 8th, we had breakfast. This was the first time we had real eggs—not the dehydrated kind—but real eggs, in many months. They loaded me into an ambulance and took me to Oxford, England to the 97th General Hospital. It was a civilian hospital that the Army had more or less taken over. There was a large circular driveway with a flagpole in the middle of the lawn. I believe we were the first casualties brought in. Ambulance after ambulance were coming in from field hospitals along the dockside.

Two aides put me down on my stretcher under the flagpole. I saw a chaplain coming through, kneeling, talking to people, consoling people, and giving last rites to some of them that had made it that far and couldn't make it any further. I looked up and the sun was shining, little clouds were in the sky and the American flag was flying directly over my head. I was very proud and honored to have been given the privilege to take part in the "great crusade," as Eisenhower had called it. Then a couple of aide men picked me up and took my stretcher into a ward. I was the first man in the ward. I still had on my original combat clothes I wore since June 1st. I still had the original blood-encrusted bandage around my left leg. I was filthy with sweat, vomit, and blood.

As I lay in my filthy uniform on the bed with those clean, white sheets and my head on a pillow, I felt as if I had all the comforts of home. About that time a young nurse came in, Marjorie was her name, screaming and yelling, livid with rage. She said, "You dirty so and so! Why are you laying on that bunk? You've been out drinking and wrecked a jeep! Got yourself in a mess of trouble and vomited all over yourself and here these wounded combat veterans are coming in from Normandy. You ought to be ashamed of yourself. You should be court martialed!"

She went on like a raving maniac. But, I was feeling so good lying there, pumped full of pain pills, that I didn't give a damn what she did. I was going to stay there until somebody moved me. She went storming out and brought in some more wounded men and started putting them around on the bunks. They were as filthy, dirty, and ornery-looking as I was. We all looked like something out of Bill Mauldin's cartoons and it didn't take very long for us to stink up the place. In a few minutes a doctor, who was a major; a nurse, who was a captain; and the young 2nd lieutenant nurse, came back. Marjorie had big tears running down her cheeks. She apologized. She said that she had heard about the Rangers and now knew that I was one of them. She had made a terrible mistake. It didn't make a hell of a lot of difference to me because I was enjoying lying there on the bunk.

The ward was completely full and the hospital people began doing their work. A young nurse came to me and told me to get out of my clothes. She started to help me. Now, I ain't about to have any girl help me undress. I got my shirt off and dropped it on the floor but I couldn't get my britches off. She took my boots and leggings off and did like nurses do, kind of covered me up and pulled my britches off. She told me a doctor would be there soon to examine me.

I glanced around the room and across two aisles of beds and saw a big soldier lying there propped up. I looked again and then I looked a third time and said, "Hot damn! Get me over there!" She asked what was the matter and I told her I wanted to see that man. It was Butch Bladorn, the guy I had seen on the beach that had been shot in the stomach. The nurse got me a wheelchair and told me the doctor was going to be there in a minute. I said, "Forget the doctor! I want to see Butch!" So she rolled me over there. He was alive. He obviously wasn't going to be doing any running or going back into combat, but he was also obviously going to make it. The nurse then rolled me back to the bed and helped me into it.

The doctor came by and pulled the bandage off my left leg. I tell you it was pretty painful. It had been on there since June 6th. He told the nurse to clean me up and get a stretcher to take me to the operating room. I asked him what he was going to do. He said he was going to cut some of the flesh away from the wound, pull some of the ligaments together and patch me up. I asked him if he was going to take my leg off and he said no. He told me the wound wasn't that bad and that I would be out of there in a short time. This nurse, by this time, had taken me as her personal tribulation, I guess. She cleaned me up and shaved me, although I don't think I appreciated that too much. They took me into the operating room. When I woke up I was back in the ward.

I was still very groggy, but when I came to, my left leg was gone at the knee—there was no question in my mind about it. I propped myself up and looked down. There was no feeling. I reached down and I was convinced my left leg was gone at the knee. The guy in the bunk next to me, an older fellow, told me I was going to be all right and that my leg was still there.

I said, "Don't kid me. I can tell when my leg's gone."

He said, "Well, how many legs did you have when you went in there? Well, you've still got them." We got to laughing at that. His name was Taylor, Lieutenant Colonel Taylor, and he'd been with the engineers. The nurse came over and told me my leg was okay. She pulled the covers down for me to see. Of course I had a nightgown on by then. There was that beautiful leg still there! They had it in a cast up to my knee with a kind of window in it. I asked what about the other leg and she said it was fine. I looked and they had put a band-aid where the bullet had entered and a band-aid where it came out of the leg. A German had used up a whole bullet and it only took two band-aids to fix it.

I think it was about my second hospital day when we got back into the GI way again. Now, at this time, they had not separated anyone according to rank. A full colonel came through, a medical doctor, and he started taking name, rank, and serial numbers. You sure couldn't have officers in the same ward with enlisted men! However, I didn't see any problems with that. We'd been getting along pretty damn well up till then. They took myself and the colonel next to me, and whoever else was commissioned, over to an officers' ward. I hated to move. I was very happy being in the same room with Butch Bladorn.

In about two days I was allowed to get up on crutches. I thought I would go over to the Red Cross hall. When I got outside one of the crutches slipped into a little flowerbed. I put all of my weight down on my right leg, the one not in a cast, and I fell. People came running, put me on a stretcher, and got me back inside. It turned out that they had not paid any attention to the right leg and didn't realize it had been hurt. They x-rayed it and told me the small bone in my leg had been broken. They had to do surgery again to clean out the wound. There were some fragments high up in the leg near my knee. They still bother me today.

June 13, 1944

```
Dear Mother & Dad:

    Well Folks, here I am, still kicking around, in
a minor sort of way, but at least kicking.
    Hope everyone at home is well now. I haven't
received any mail for a while and I guess it'll take
a while to catch up with me now.
    I guess you know all about the big invasion -
probably more about it than I do, as I haven't had
much chance to do any newspaper reading.
    They tell me that you probably will have
received a telegram from the War Department by now,
so to ease your mind from worrying, I'll let you
know just how bad I am - it really isn't very seri-
ous. I'll be in the hospital for about two months,
then I'll be as good as new.
    I caught a few machine gun bullets in both legs.
They're all between the ankle and knee and no bones
broken. Now don't you worry about me. I won't be
crippled or anything else. The doctors say, in a
few months I'll never even know I was hit.
```

Looks like the war will be over before long. The
Germans are on the run now. It can't be too soon
for me. Sure glad I got to help a little. We were
right there in the first assault and the boys did
a great job. I'll write and tell you all about it
as soon as possible.

Incidentally, I've been evacuated from France
and am now back in England. Sure getting swell
treatment. The doctors and nurses treat us like a
bunch of heroes or something.

Tell everyone to write as often as possible.
I'll write whenever I can.

Love all,
          Bob

p.s. Am being awarded the Purple Heart and some
other decorations for bravery in action, etc. If
they knew how scared I was when I hit that beach
they'd change their minds.

p.s.# 2, As you can see, the Red Cross is still
taking care of us.

During my hospital stay, I visited with Butch Bladorn and the
colonel in the bunk next to me. We became very good friends.

While I was recuperating, my comrades in A Company were
busy. Pfc. Morris Prince wrote about their actions:

We were barely crawling along, moving at a snails pace; patrols
were out seeking snipers and other members were left to search out
buildings and areas . . . Intermittent artillery fire also limited our
speed. We had to seek cover several times . . . We knew speed was
essential if we were to aid our brother Rangers on the Pointe. . . .It
was quite paradoxical, as we went along the road, tactically *snooping
and pooping*. We saw the French civilians boldly walking along the
center of the road, going about their chores and business as if nothing
new or different were going on. Most of them hadn't realized what
had actually happened and were astonished and surprised to learn that
we were real Americans. Once they learned and gained our identities,
there wasn't anything they wouldn't do for us. Milk and cider bottles
were brought forth and flowers were thrown at us. That was one day

we didn't go thirsty or hungry. . . .

We were out in the middle of no man's land, all by our lonesome. The troops of the main body had stopped when we had started the fight at the road junction and our tanks had been forced to retreat to the rear due to the seriousness of the situation. There we were . . .sweating it out with shell after shell landing nearby. I don't know how many shells were thrown at us in the short period we were in those ditches, but I do know that when the barrage lifted, I couldn't recognize the immediate countryside as it was so cratered and beaten up.

That night we ate our "K" rations, dug our slit trenches deeper and prepared to pull our guard. We tried to get a little rest . . .We finally contacted our brother Ranger companies. . .They had held the Pointe for three days, fighting off one counter attack after another.

The hospital staff started making decisions about what they were going to do with people. They asked me if I wanted to be Z.I.'d (sent back to the States or the Zone of Interior). I told them the only thing I wanted to do was get back to A Company. I had received some information about who was alive and who wasn't. I made it clear to the doctors that all I wanted to do was recover and make it back to the Ranger battalion. It wasn't that I was so gung-ho to get into combat, but A Company was my company and I hadn't fired a shot yet.

So they started a rehabilitation program. I got the cast off the right leg after a very short time. When they took the cast off of the left leg, I started physical therapy. This was quite an experience. I hobbled on crutches down to a physical therapy room and a nurse, who was a captain, told me to go in the whirlpool and flex and work the leg. The ligaments had to be stretched. I spent a couple of days going in there an hour or two at a time. About the third day, this would be the last of June or first part of July, I went in without the crutches, and went through the exercises. As I started out of the physical therapy room, a nurse stopped me and called me over to the desk. She said, "You're walking on your toe. You're going to be crippled all your life because you haven't got guts enough to put your heel down. I doubted that you were a Ranger when they brought you in here and now I'm pretty well sure you're not. If you don't have enough guts to put that heel down, you're not going back to the Rangers. You're going back to the States."

That was one of the hardest things I've ever done, to put that heel down. But I showed that old biddy that I could walk, and that I had guts enough to stand the pain. Thank God for that woman! She knew what she was talking about. I made almost a complete recovery. There were very few things I couldn't do from there on in until I got to an older age.

June 22, 1944

Dear Mother and Dad,

No news but thought I'd drop you all a few lines to let you know I'm getting along OK.

Hoping to get some mail soon, but guess I'll just have to wait. How's all the kids? I'd sure like to hear from Sam.

I've been outside most of the day - in a wheel chair, but at least I was up - got a nice sun-burn too.

They stitched up my left leg yesterday - it should be in shape to walk on in another week - still have a cast on the right one though.

It sure seems like a long time since I hit that beach. Guessed we missed seeing all the head-lines too. Was there anything in the papers back there about my outfit?

I'm sending some more clippings. Be sure and save them for me.

Must close now. Tell everyone "hello" and write often. Bob

Address - First Lt. Robt. Edlin 0-1293387
Detach - of - Patients - Ward #22, 97th Gen. Hospital, Apo 647 - New York City, NY

Copy of clipping

One of the most daring exploits of the landings was that of American Rangers, who seized a battery of six 155 mm Guns, four of which were emplaced. At least two of the big ships in the initial convoy were ordered to turn the bulk of their firepower on the battery, which commanded the bay as well as the beaches. Then the rugged Rangers stormed ashore, battered their way up sharp cliffs and had captured the battery 15 minutes later. The Germans attempted to recover their strategic battery, but all thrusts were repelled by the Rangers.

From a New Albany Newspaper, Monday, June 26, 1944:

Louis L. Edlin, 605 MacArthur Drive received a letter from his son, First Lieutenant Robert Edlin Monday morning, one day after being notified that the boy had been wounded, in which Robert said he had been wounded in the left leg and had been operated on. The wound is healing nicely, he said, and added that he expected to be able to walk as well as ever when he fully recovers.

The letter was written in a hospital, presumably in England, on June 18. He spoke of seeing S/Sgt. Joe Caufield, New Albany, in the hospital. Caufield is a former stereotyper for the Tribune, and is the husband of Mrs. Elizabeth Caufield. Edlin said Caufield is the first New Albany man he has seen since. . . .

"It took a trip to the hospital to bring us together," he said. He added that he has been decorated with a ribbon representative of the Purple Heart medal, which he will receive later. Only last Tuesday night a number of New Albany people, including Mrs. Bertha Van Pelt, heard a radio commentator in England remark the first two Yanks to embark at an English port upon a vessel headed for the invasion were Lieut. Edlin, of New Albany, and a boy from New York. The boys raced up the gangplank "Rarin' to Go," said the commentator. Young Edlin was a well known amateur boxer here before the war. A brother, Marion, a technical sergeant with the Army in the Pacific was also a boxer having participated with Robert in The Tribune Golden Gloves boxing tournaments several years ago. Lieut. Edlin had been stationed in England training with a Ranger outfit to spearhead the attack on Europe. He was a member of Company D 152nd Indiana Infantry which left New Albany in 1941 for Camp Shelby, Miss. He was transferred later to the Rangers in England.

By now things had got so GI around that hospital, hell, anybody would want to get out of there. We couldn't go to the toilet without permission.

I decided I would like to take a weekend and go visit friends in the 28th Division, the outfit I had been in when I came over seas. I wanted to see my old friend Preston Jackson, who I would later name my son after. I had to get permission from the head of the hospital. Now, why a guy had to get permission to catch a bus and go 30 or 40 miles I don't know. He decided he wasn't going to give me a leave and I told him, "I'm going to go anyway." He told me if I did I would be court-martialed and that if I were court-martialed I would be sent back to the States. There isn't anything too wrong about that, but I didn't really want to get in that mess.

Finally, he said I could go for the weekend provided I would take crutches with me. I got a signed pass, I got out and parked the crutches in a garbage can outside the hospital and got on a bus. I went down to visit Company I and Company K of the 112th Infantry. It took me several hours to get where they were, but I was welcomed with open arms. They hadn't been in combat yet and this was my first chance to be a real hero. I wore my Purple Heart ribbon. You would have thought I had single-handedly captured the beachhead. These men could hardly wait to talk to a seasoned, old combat veteran. I didn't tell them that I'd used up only two bullets.

I enjoyed the visit, and old Jackson and I, as we always did during our wartime service together, managed to get into town. As Jackson said, "If we were out in the middle of a desert somewhere, me and Bob would find some whiskey and some girls."

And we sure did! We probably got a little too drunk. Jackson was a little upset because I had gotten hurt and he hauled off and popped his fist through the hotel window. That isn't something 1st lieutenants and captains are supposed to do. We paid for the window. We got our heads together and got back. I told Jackson I would see him later. I didn't realize what the circumstances would be the next time I saw him. The next time I would see Jackson would be in the Hurtgen Forest.

When I got back to the hospital, I asked for a meeting with the doctor who had been treating me. I told him I thought I was ready to return to my company. He told me I wasn't ready. He said that if I got my leg infected I would have a lot of trouble with it. I told him if he would release me from the hospital I would have the company medic with the 2nd Ranger Battalion look after it. I really wanted to get back because I knew they were short handed. He took me to the head of the hospital. Very reluctantly they told me they would let me go but that my records weren't ready and would have to be forwarded. They said I would catch holy hell from my battalion when I got back because they would think I had gone *over the hill.*

Dave Jacobus Private Collection

Sgt. Klaus dressed as Hitler for a few laughs

Bob Edlin standing next to a trench, part of the coastal defenses in France

9

RETURN TO COMBAT

I don't care about being a captain. I don't care about being a company commander. All I want to do is be in A Company of the 2nd Ranger Battalion.
                                                    –Robert Edlin

They released me from the hospital and I hobbled out. I was more or less on my own. I had to get back to the battalion the best way I could. I got on a civilian bus and went down to the dock area. I checked in with someone who was running the port and they put me on a boat. They said my papers were not in very good order, but since I was going back to France instead of trying to leave, they had no problem with it.

I went across the Channel and landed at Vierville sur Mer, that same hell-hole place. The same pillbox was there, but it was ours now. I hobbled up the beach and up the same cliffs where Sergeants White, Dreher, Courtney, Ray, and all the other guys had done their job. There was still a lot of debris on the beaches. I saw many burned out tanks and the old LCA was still sitting there that the 5th Rangers had used for cover. Of course, the bodies had been removed. I could see an infantry division moving in through the draw. I thought, "Things are under control now."

I caught a ride on a truck and got up near a place called St. Jean de Daye, France. I heard the Rangers were guarding a prison camp there. Here I rejoined part of the battalion. Bill White commanded the company from the time that I turned it over to him on the beach till they got to Pointe du Hoc on D + 2, along with the 5th Rangers. As soon as that battle was over they got back into a rest area, reformed the battalion and brought in replacements.

They broke the battalion into two groups. They made Captain Arnold battalion executive officer to take care of A, B, and C Companies. They made Slater a major in charge of D, E and F Companies.

The American forces had captured the port of Cherbourg, even though it was beat up and useless. Part of the battalion remained there. I got a ride to Beaumont-Hague, where the Rangers were training. When I arrived I was called into battalion headquarters and sure enough, I caught hell from the battalion adjutant because I didn't have the right papers. But he was glad to see me. He was an old friend. The first person he took me to was Doctor Block, the battalion medic. He examined my leg and raised hell with the hospital for releasing me. He told me he wanted me to lie out in the sun two hours every day. He put a solution on my leg to make it heal faster. It worked; it did heal fast. He told me that Colonel Rudder wanted to talk to me.

I went to Colonel Rudder's headquarters. He was set up in an old army barracks. Jim greeted me with a hug and was just as happy to see me as he could possibly be. He said he wanted to talk to me a few minutes before deciding what we were going to do. We sat down at a table, and he poured a couple of drinks. Now, that was just something for me as a junior officer to sit there with that man and have a drink with him. He talked to me as an equal. He asked me to help him make a decision. There had been a problem with a couple of people before the invasion and another problem with something that had happened on the beach. He was undecided at the time as to how to handle it. It was inconceivable to me, but he took the advice of a young, 22-year-old lieutenant. I told him, "Why not just leave things alone? Everybody did the best they could. We were all just doing our best. Let's just reorganize and go forward."

He said, "Well, that's what I wanted to hear." Then he asked what I wanted to do. I told him I wanted to go back to A Company. I didn't ever want to leave A Company. He told me he had put Lieutenant Bob Arman in as company commander. Lieutenant Arman had been in either E or F Company and had earned a Silver

Star. He was an excellent officer. He said, "I can't replace him as company commander. I could move you down to one of the other companies. It might be that you could get promoted to a captain and make company commander there sometime in the future."

I said, "Colonel, I don't care about being a captain. I don't care about being a company commander. All I want to do is be in A Company of the 2nd Ranger Battalion. That's my place. I don't feel I'm qualified to be a company commander." But I didn't mean for the rest of my life. However, I never got promoted after that.

Arman was maybe 26 years old and was from Lafayette, Indiana. He joined Colonel Rudder and I in our meeting. Rudder told him the situation and asked him how he felt about A Company. Arman immediately said he would be glad to go back to one of the line companies if Rudder wanted to move me into A Company as commander. Rudder said "No." He thought he would put me into A Company as executive officer, providing it met with Arman's approval. I liked that. I really thought that's the way one should operate; the company commander should approve any officer or man that comes into the company.

Arman was sincere when he offered to turn the company back to me, but we decided the best way to do it since there had been so many changes and confusion, was for him to remain company commander and for me to be executive officer. So, Bob and I went back to A Company. I was really looking forward to getting back with the guys. I wanted to see my friends there: Whitie, Courtney, Dreher, Klaus and all the others. First, Arman took me in and called in the two new replacement officers that had command of the 1st and 2nd Platoons.

The 1st Platoon was commanded by Lt. Robert Meltzer. He was a well-educated young fellow and a writer. He was very confident and self-assured. I had occasion over the next six or seven days before he was killed to talk with him quite a lot. When Meltzer first came into A Company he had driven around the French countryside and had written several stories that had been published in the *Saturday Evening Post*. I recall reading one of them at a later date. It was called *Calvados Patrol*. Meltzer was a very active and courageous fellow who intended to write the big novel about WWII someday. I'm sure, had he lived, he would have done that.

The replacement in the 2nd Platoon replaced Lt. Stanley White. He was a 1st lieutenant named Sylvester Porubski. We called him "Pop" because he was a little older, probably 28 years old, and had been in the military for 10 or so years. He was a very steady, reliable and quiet soldier. There was nothing dynamic about him whatsoever; he was just a very fine officer.

Arman pointed out where the 1st Platoon was and I went down there. They were staying in pup tents. I found Sgt. White, Whitie, the platoon sergeant, giving somebody a haircut when I walked up behind him. It was a wonderful reunion. Whitie got the members of the platoon together. We had a reunion with the old timers who had been there before D-Day and I met the replacements. There were 20 or so new men. Courtney, Dreher, Whitie, Klaus and some others were there. When someone came up with a jug, we had a few drinks since we were back in a rest area.

We talked about what had happened on D-Day. We went over the roster of men that had been with us on D-Day and I think only about six made it across the beach without being killed or wounded. Out of the first assault squad, Donavan, Patterson, Hart, Ware, and Shannahan were all killed or wounded on D-Day.

We talked about Joe Rafferty, the company commander, who had been killed on the beach.

We talked about 1st Sergeant Ed Sowa. No one saw Sergeant Sowa get killed but his dog tags were found on a grave in a cemetery above Vierville sur Mer. He was a hell of a good 1st sergeant.

Roy Latham was the first man I saw get hit on the beach. He got shot in the cheek. I've never seen him since. After we talked about all these men we started talking about training. Some of the men that were wounded had come back to the company. Everybody was shaping up and ready to go into combat.

I rejoined the Rangers in the middle of July. On the 25th there was a break through at St. Lo. We saw part of the planes going over and we saw the terrible damage their bombs had inflicted. It was like a desolate desert when they got through bombing. We were in a training period about July 26th through August 1st.

At this time, we were assigned to guard and transport prisoners. Morris Prince explains:

> Our prison pen was a plain affair. All it was, was a large open field enclosed by barbed wire fences. At every corner we had a platform where a light machine gun stood mounted and a guard stood prepared to use this weapon if necessary. There also was a lighting system that made our area look like Broadway and Times Square when night fell. This was to mark the place for what it was and to give warning to the Luftwaffe not to bomb their own men. . . .We were on the go from dawn till dark and our battalion of 500 was credited for handling over 25,000 Heinies.
>
> Being we did all of the interviewing and interrogating, we got to learn something of the Heinies, of his thoughts and of his reasoning. We discovered certain bits of information about them. . . .Their ages ranged anywhere from fifteen to fifty...the batches of young men and old granddads we picked up made us wonder how the hell Hitler expected to win the war. In general, these Heiny "sad sacks" didn't like the war or their big generals running the show. They had the greatest of respect and admiration for their Fuhrer, though, and believed him to be the greatest man on earth. They hated the Russians with passion, and feared them likewise. They were deathly afraid that we were going to hand them over to the Russians. Most of them thought that Germany couldn't win the war as they claimed the Reich was depleted from its previous fights, but the younger and indoctrinated Nazi never doubted that the "Vaterland" would emerge victorious. All the Krauts were impressed by our powerful motorized and armored forces and were in full praise for our *Luftwaffe*. They couldn't understand how we had allied ourselves with our fighting comrades, the Russians, and they repeatedly tried to warn us that we'd be fighting them before this present conflict was over. They spoke very little of their own ally, Japan. They seemed to be totally ignorant or very poorly informed on that subject. . . . They weren't dumb though, as every one interviewed asked if it couldn't be arranged to be sent to a prisoner of war cage in America.

The weather was beautiful through the latter part of July and the early part of August. Of course, we were very close to the seacoast at this time. It was here that most of the men in the Rangers and the rest of the American troops became experts in the French language. We immediately learned to speak all the French that was necessary. Things like, "Avevous cognac? Avevous calvados? Vou le vou couche? and Combien?" I think all that boiled down to, "Do you have any cognac? Do you have any calvados? Do you have any eggs? Do you want to shack up tonight?" Needless to say, there was very little calvados, very little cognac, very few eggs, and damn little shacking up at night.

Bob Edlin Private Collection

Bombed buildings, location unknown

Dave Jacobus Private Collection

After mission with Cavalry

Bob Edlin Private Collection

Burby and Klaus, October 1944

Bob Edlin Private Collection

Swedo, October 1944

THE FABULOUS FOUR PATROL
Standing: Bob Edlin and William Dreher
Kneeling: Warren Burmaster and William Courtney

10

THE FABULOUS FOUR PATROL

It was an all star patrol. They were each and every one of them extra special and brave men. All of them were decorated for their bravery.

–Len Lomell

I was a different kind of operator than most of the officers in the Ranger battalions. When asked to go on a patrol, I chose to work with a small group and Rudder went along with it. I never followed the rules in this regard. I would take a couple of guys and we'd go do the patrol because I didn't want to risk more people.

William Courtney and William Dreher, along with Bill White and myself made up a very well-known patrol in the 2nd Ranger Battalion. It all got started late one evening when Courtney and Dreher were on an outpost with a couple of other guys. Whitie, the 1st sergeant, and I went down to check out all the outposts. We stopped to talk to Courtney and Dreher.

I can remember that one of them said, "Hell, there ain't any Germans out there." Courtney laid down his guns and went walking across the hillside. Dreher said he couldn't let him go by himself, so he went after him. Of course, Whitie and I went after them too. We probably walked six or seven miles through the countryside and never came into contact with any enemy at all; there just wasn't anyone out there. That's how the four of us got started.

Dreher, called "Big Stoop," had been a private first class on D-Day and had received the Distinguished Service Cross. He later would receive the Silver Star. He was a big fellow about 6'3" or so, and played football. He was from Cleveland, Ohio. Dreher was just a bundle of fun all the time, but also one of the bravest men I have ever met in my life.

His best friend was Sergeant Courtney. They were two of a kind. They called Courtney, "No Neck." Courtney, a T-5 (technician 5th grade) on D-Day, won the Distinguished Service Cross. Later, he would also win the Silver Star. He was about 5'8" and weighed about 200 pounds. He was from northeastern Ohio and had played football in school.

Bill White, we nick-named him "Whitie," was an ex-jockey from New Jersey. He was around 5'6", weighed 115 to120 pounds and was just a fantastic soldier. In the 2nd Ranger Battalion, Whitie was only one of three to receive a battlefield commission. He was good-looking and seemed to take things a little more serious than the rest of us.

Bob Edlin Private Collection

I took this picture from the lead jeep in a patrol. We found Jerries around the curve and we won the fight.

Bob Edlin Private Collection

Virgin and Hurley. "Two real fighters."

Dave Jacobus Private Collection

Mortar squad: top row; Serrette, May, unknown, Jacobus
Kneeling; Hart and Dassaro

The next day our patrol was assigned to a pillbox mission. The German pillbox had only a few machine-guns and some riflemen, but it had to be taken out. It was surrounded—barbed wire in the front and on the sides and water in the back. This was a pillbox that probably held eighty men.

We tried to move around it and attack from the backside—the waterside. You must remember these Krauts had been there for years and they knew the terrain well. Whitie, Courtney, Dreher, and myself found ourselves pinned down in a minefield. We came across a dead American soldier that had been there for some time. He was all bloated and we could see that animals had been at him. We needed his ammo so we cut his cartridge belt off. I tried to pry off his dog tag, but the Krauts were laying into us pretty heavy at the time. I sure hope someone found him later.

The Germans had us completely pinned down with machine-gun fire. Right there I knew what it was to have fear. There was no way we could get out. I thought, "Boy, if they put a mortar on us, we're whipped!" I was out in front, Courtney behind me, then Whitie and Dreher. We were trying to wiggle our way back out through a little hollow place in the ground. Dreher was trying to lead us by scooting backwards, a difficult task under such heavy artillery fire. If he could get out, he would go for help.

About that time, my platoon sergeant, Bill Klaus, could tell that there was something definitely wrong. (Sgt. Bill Klaus had been wounded on D-Day but had already returned.) He could hear the firefighting and could tell that the Germans were firing in the direction that we went. He could hear my M-1 and Whitie's BAR. He knew we were pinned down and in trouble. He had the mortar section drop smoke in front of where he hoped we were and also in front of the pillbox.

Now, the mortar section could only carry a very few rounds of smoke and they gambled it all right there. They laid the smoke in front of the pillbox. The black smoke flew up and we backed out of there.

As I came out, I went by the American soldier again. I felt very fortunate that four more of us weren't there with him. When I got back to our platoon, about three hundred yards back, I talked with

Captain Arman at company headquarters and he told me to talk directly to Colonel Rudder. I called Colonel Rudder at battalion headquarters and explained the situation. I told him I hated like hell to lose any men, but that I was going to lose them all if I had to take that pillbox. I told him I needed a tank or some artillery to get the pillbox out.

Rudder agreed with me and told me he would get me some help. Just a few minutes later two fighter planes came over. We spread markers on the ground so they could see where we were. They flew over and took a look at the situation, circled back and began strafing the German pillbox. We were less than 100 yards away.

We started moving up. The planes were coming in so low, it seemed like we could touch them. They cut the hell out of that pillbox, but of course, it wasn't hurting them too much. Still, the Germans immediately put up a white flag. The planes let up, waggled their wings, and headed back to where they came from. The Krauts came out and signaled for us to come up and get them, however, we weren't that stupid. So, they came through the minefield to us.

The Germans had a lieutenant there that spoke English. The lieutenant told me we could have taken them; they were ready to quit. He said they were told to quit when we got close. They were putting up some token opposition just to show us Americans how good they could be. Somebody in our group remembered the dead soldier still lying in the minefield and knocked that arrogant son-of-a-bitch on his ass. That German would have been a dead Nazi right then and there if I hadn't stopped him.

Around the 5th we moved to a little town called Mayenne. We relieved part of the 1st Division, again protecting their flank as they were driving toward Paris. We stayed there until the middle of August. Then we traveled by truck to our new mission.

Pfc. Morris Prince describes the reactions of the French to our arrival:

> Our lengthy journey from Mayenne to our new base of operations at Le Folgoet was one of triumph. Although we had to undergo the

discomforts that a trip of such distance entails, we were atoned for it by the hearty welcome and greetings the people threw at us. At each town and village the civilians would line up and down the streets and cheer our progress through their communities. They were heart-rending affairs and did us all good to behold these spectacles. All ages and both sexes enthusiastically waved their hands and jubilantly shouted words of thanks and encouragement to us. Flowers and fruits bedecked our vehicles and every time we halted, the good old cider or wine jug would come into play. In return, we would throw out to the people, especially the younger kids, certain articles from our "K" rations and watch humorously the fighting and scraping that would ensue among the people for the possession of these articles . . .

We . . . noted the similarities and contrasts between Brest and Normandy . . . Whereas in Normandy everything was scarred and shell-marked, in Brest all stood in their picturesque finery, seemingly untouched by the ravishes of war.

After some twenty hours of continual riding with only time out to stop for regassing, we reached our destination at Le Folgoet. We were all tired and fatigued from our journey, but our spirits were never better. This liberation business was a pretty good business. It made us happy in thought that all our strife and fighting were being appreciated, that these people were conscious of the fine meaning of freedom, liberty and democracy and were showing us their approval for our aid in bringing to them these principles and ideals that they had lost four long years ago.

A Company was pulled back into a rest area. Here we picked up five or six replacements for the 1st Platoon. The Brittany Peninsula had been cut off about this time. Patton's Third Army had driven through and was on the way to Paris, but they had left a large concentration of German troops all the way up to the port city of Brest. In addition, stationed there were several hundred thousand Germans, including part of a Paratrooper corps that was a terrible threat to the Third Army. These troops could be supplied through the port at Brest. The submarine pens there also had to be captured. The Allies needed this port for a supply port, even though it turned out later that it wasn't useable.

Over a period of 10 days, Courtney, Dreher, Whitie and myself made an additional 10 or 12 patrols together on the Brittany Peninsula, just west of the city of Brest. We saw little combat but we did pick up a few prisoners and some information. I was called back to the company. Captain Arman told me he had received instructions from Colonel Rudder that I should report back to him.

So I went back to talk to the colonel. He said that my patrol was doing excellent work but there was too much rank in my patrol from one Ranger company. Rudder said, "You're using a 1st lieutenant, a 1st sergeant and two squad sergeants. That's too much. You're going to have to cut down."

He also told me that I could go on all the patrols I wanted and I could take Courtney and Dreher but that I couldn't take my 1st sergeant. He said if we lose a 1st sergeant and a platoon leader at the same time it would be quite a loss to the company. I was pretty upset but I saw the wisdom of it.

So I went back and told the group. Whitie said he was going to ask to be busted to a buck private so he could stay with the patrol. I immediately said he was much too valuable as a 1st sergeant to even consider anything like that. I told him that he owed it to the others to stay on as 1st sergeant.

Whitie said, "You're the boss." From then on he spent a lot more time at company headquarters. Our little group was broken up.

I discussed with Courtney and Dreher about who would be his replacement. I suggested that we find someone who spoke excellent French and did not drink. Of course, Courtney and Dreher understood the French part but they wanted to know why I wanted someone who didn't drink.

"Hell, it's simple mathematics. With Whitie, none of us spoke French and all four of us drank all we could get. Now, if we get a guy that can speak French and doesn't drink, we only have to split the cognac and calvados three ways." They thought I was a genius.

The logical choice was Warren Burmaster, one of my favorites, nicknamed Half-track. Burmaster, from Louisiana, spoke fluent French. He had joined Company A on D-Day + 4. He was a very brave man and he absolutely did not drink! From here on in our patrol consisted of me as the point man, then Courtney and Dreher, followed by Burmaster as the getaway man.

This was a time when A Company really learned a lesson. We had been pretty cocky and pretty lucky since D-Day. On August 21, headquarters ordered a patrol to go out in the vicinity of a place called St. Renan. The mission was to contact the 8th Infantry Division and to scout out an area to their front. They decided to send the 1st Platoon of A Company and, of course, I wanted to take the patrol. Captain Arman and Colonel Rudder told me that I was not the platoon leader. It was time that we let Lt. Meltzer take charge of the platoon if he was going to fight in combat, and combat was coming rapidly to us again.

My job as executive officer was to fight with both platoons as was needed and necessary. I realized this. I realized that it wasn't my baby all the way. But I was in on the planning of it. I told them I thought they ought to take a four-man reconnaissance patrol, including a platoon leader. I told them to take Courtney, Dreher, and Burmaster because they were men with a lot of experience.

They decided to take Meltzer, Courtney, Dreher, and three other men. That was almost enough for a combat patrol! Among the three that were chosen was a medic, Pfc. Roberts. I was pretty upset about that.

I argued, "I see no reason to take a medic on a damn patrol. If you are three or four miles behind enemy lines, you sure in hell don't need a medic. If somebody gets hurt, you either have to pick him up and bring him back or you have to leave him there."

They all left on the patrol anyway and in two or three hours I saw Courtney and Dreher running back over the hedgerows. I was watching for them. I immediately alerted the battalion. We didn't know what was coming behind them.

They had been ambushed and attacked and lost four men. Three of them were killed, including Lt. Meltzer. The medic had been wounded. To me, it was something that should never have happened. It was probably due to the inexperience of some of the men who went. The experienced men returned. When you lose that many people out of a 35-man platoon, it's quite a blow.

The next month in the Brittany Peninsula was a war that's never been talked much about. It was toe-to-toe slugging and battling for the Ranger battalions all the way. For the infantry divisions involved it was a rough time. The weather wasn't bad and the supplies and food were good; it wasn't that kind of hell. It was that the Germans kept on fighting and we were in action almost constantly. There were many small battles and skirmishes that took place that many people have never heard of. I know over those next 30 or 35 days I was in combat every day.

During this time A Company came up to a hedgerow. We were ordered to stop. We dug in and under. That means we dug into the ground and then back in under the hedgerow as far as we could, to protect ourselves from over-head fire. Several shells fell pretty close. This was about the closest combat we had seen since D-Day. The Germans were firing at us from a pillbox located about 200 yards out to our front. I quickly had one of our 60mm mortars fire back. I immediately received a message from battalion to cease-fire.

I was called to battalion headquarters and reprimanded for firing at the enemy without orders. Someone, not Colonel Rudder, told me that arrangements had already been made for the Krauts to surrender. They wanted to fire a few rounds at us to save face; then they would quit. That was okay with me but someone should have told the troops about it. Also, the German gunner didn't have to get so damn close.

This was my first contact with the political part of warfare. We were supposed to let the damn enemy shoot at us until they were ready to quit, stick up a white flag and surrender. We didn't get a chance to get our licks in. That didn't seem quite fair.

Dave Jacobus Private Collection

Lt. Wilson, Capt. Arman, and Lt. Porubski

Dave Jacobus Private Collection

White and Fronczek, Landerneau, France, September 1944

Our battalion about this time began to break down into small units. Each platoon, no doubt, could tell some wild tales about this period. We were assigned all over the countryside—all over the Brittany Peninsula. Sometimes I would go three or four days without seeing anyone except people in the 1st Platoon.

During a period of 15 days, Courtney, Dreher, Burmaster, and myself made 17 patrols and every one of them was potentially dangerous. Every one of them was behind enemy lines. We were unbelievably lucky during this period of time. We never had a loser.

I remember one patrol mission in particular though that could have turned into a disaster. It was also one of the funniest. I believe it was one of the first times that the four of us were out on a patrol together.

Our job was to locate an enemy battalion headquarters. We started out. I led the patrol across the enemy line into "no man's land." After crossing a small road we came up to a hedgerow fence, and we could hear the enemy moving beyond it.

We knew we were near their battalion headquarters by the way they had it outposted. We had been in a firefight earlier in the morning, so we were out of grenades. I looked up over the fence and on the other side, covering a roadway, I saw a German lieutenant with a light machine-gun and a couple of crewmen. When he saw us, he threw a "potato masher" grenade at us. It took those things about five seconds to go off. So I picked it up and threw it back.

I waited a few seconds but it never exploded. I figured, well, it must have been a dud. I jumped across the hedgerow. I planned to jump on top of the gun. Instead, I landed right on top of the sergeant's back, a German sergeant's back! He had heard us and was crawling around trying to get in behind us. When I landed on his back, his helmet fell off. I hit him over the head with the butt of my knife but I didn't really want to kill him. Then I banged him on the head with my Tommy gun. That knocked him out.

There were two more Germans with him. The other German machine-gunner was lying there scared to death and a German lieutenant was lying beside him with a great big knot on his forehead. The grenade I had thrown back had missed his helmet, missed his gun, and hit him in the forehead right above the left eye. The grenade still hadn't gone off but it knocked him out. So we took them prisoners. I sent them back with Burmaster and Dreher and threw the machine-gun out. That was one of the funniest times we had on a patrol.

Courtney and I went probably another two hundred to three hundred yards and I heard a machine-gun open up. This was a traversing machine-gun that continues to traverse as you are putting a new belt of ammo in. I was behind Courtney and he was looking up over a wall. I saw the machine-gun start probably about 20 yards to the left of where Courtney was standing. When it got to within just inches of him, the belt ran out of ammunition. It continued traversing while they were feeding a new belt of ammo in and started firing again just about six or eight inches on the other side of Courtney. He stood there during that whole period and didn't realize that they were shooting at him. How can you beat that for luck?

I yelled at him and we dropped down. We came around the edge of a hedgerow to a small clump of trees. We could see telephone lines and we could see radios set up. We realized that we were not at a battalion headquarters, but probably at a regimental headquarters. This information would be very valuable to our headquarters so we just hauled ass out of there.

I talked to Courtney later that day and also in later years. He still can't believe that the machine-gun had come that close to him and he had not seen it! It's hard to believe just how incredibly lucky you have to be, to get back from behind enemy lines all in one piece.

Actually that was the most dangerous part of the patrol. Our own troops would know there was a patrol out but they wouldn't know where or when to expect us back. They were also familiar with the fact that there may be German-speaking patrols in the area. So, they were very cautious. When we approached our own line, it was just as dangerous as when we approached the German lines.

I'll let Burmaster tell about another patrol we had:

We were given the job of finding small German robot-like tanks with explosives. They were used to run under American tanks. With the punch of a button on a hand-held device, the Germans could easily destroy the American tanks remotely. We were told that this was a patrol with very little chance to come back. We accepted and started out. We had gone about a half-mile through some woods and came out onto a large field with no cover or even grass for a long ways. Edlin led out and the rest of us followed at quite a distance apart. I remember we were halfway out and Courtney yelled, "Mines!" We stopped and looked down. With horror we could see little wires near our feet. We were in a minefield! Lt. Edlin said to retrace our steps. He said to walk back in the same footprints.

If the Germans were in front of us they did not fire. The lt. took us back to our area and reported the minefield location. We never did find any small robotic tanks.

Burmaster recalls another experience involving Courtney on the Brest Peninsula:

While near the French Coast, we came upon a deserted German tank. The track was shot off. Courtney decided to learn how to shoot a German 88. He entered the tank and by hand turned the 88 gun to the coast and shot three or four shells at a buoy out in the channel. He didn't hit the buoy because it was too small. Then he found a German bazooka and wanted to learn how to fire it. He asked me to load the shell and connect the wire. When it was ready, he laid it flat on the ground and fired at the tank. When he turned around, his face was all bloody as he did not have the screen on the bazooka. We wiped his face and took him to the medic to clean him up. He was satisfied then that he could handle German equipment.

I had my first experience with the FFI on the Brest Peninsula—the French Force of the Interior. They were not the experienced guerrilla freedom fighters but just an untrained group of villagers and farmers.

My platoon was assigned a defensive position along a ridgeline. I was given one of these makeshift units of about two hundred fifty men to use as I saw fit to hold our position. I assigned a Ranger to every ten or fifteen French soldiers. Hell, I felt like a general with all these troops under my command. Two hundred and seventy-five men for a 1st lieutenant are a lot of people. Every thing went well all day long. I got them about 0600, had them all day and they were doing a fine job. The Krauts behaved themselves and we had a pretty quiet time.

About a half-hour before dusk the French commander came up to my CP. I got Burmaster there; he was my interpreter. He informed me that they had to leave. They had chores to do and their families were expecting them back. Besides, they said, they didn't fight at night. Anyway, away they went. So much for feeling like a general! We had to regroup and sweat out the night. I never saw those guys again.

The weather was really beautiful the whole month of August in 1944. Bright sunshine and brilliant blue skies. The days were hot and the nights were getting pretty cool. The air was full of American fighters and bombers; we had complete air superiority. My platoon had been in action about 15 days and hadn't had a single casualty.

I realize that the 2nd Rangers were just a very small part of the overall picture. We were with the whole VIII Corps under General Middleton. We were frequently assigned missions for the 29th Division and one of the armored divisions. It seemed like the Ranger battalions were just about everywhere throughout the peninsula.

Around August 20th things began to heat up a little bit. We were getting up close to the "hurting part" of the Germans. If they were going to stop us, it had better be now. We were reaching their stronger outposts and roadblocks. Our freewheeling days were just about over.

A Company was now part of a small task force along with B and C Companies of the 2nd Rangers and three or four tank outfits. Our attacks were being coordinated with planes, artillery, and tanks. Major Ed Arnold of the 2nd Ranger Battalion commanded it. Captain Bob Arman was commanding officer of A Company now. Captain Sid Salomon had B Company and Captain Ralph Goranson had C. All of these officers were D-Day veterans and were all top-notch individuals.

About dawn of a very cool morning, the 1st Platoon of A

Company was leading a small force, comprised of the tanks and all the 2nd Rangers, down a hard top road. We were supposed to make contact with the enemy. When we made contact, the larger force would mount an attack that would carry on through us and up to the Le Conquet Peninsula. The point was comprised of two scouts a few yards apart. I had two excellent scouts in front of me moving up the road. I was just a couple of yards behind them. When they hit something, I wanted to be there.

It was getting light enough that I could see the bend in the road, right after the false dawn. The sun was not quite up yet but I was able to see if any figures were moving—I began to see objects. I could see a bend in the road about 75 or 100 yards ahead.

All of a sudden I heard a voice screaming in my head, "There's something wrong! There's something wrong!" I didn't know what it was but I signaled the scouts to drop to the ground. The second scout crawled back and asked me what was the matter. I told him I didn't know and to just stay quiet for a minute.

A short time later, Captain Arman crawled up with Major Arnold and wanted to know what the hell was wrong. "Get moving!" I told them I knew there was something wrong. I didn't know what it was but to just give me a minute. These men respected my judgment as well as I respected theirs. They quietly moved back—Arman back to A Company and Major Arnold back to the tanks. They told me to move as soon as I could. Colonel Rudder would be climbing the walls, but he'd want me to make the decision.

I still couldn't put my finger on what the problem was. Courtney crawled over to me and said, "What in the hell spooked you?"

I thought, "Damn, I've got it!" I said, "Do you see that pile of human crap in the road?"

Courtney said, "Sure."

I said, "It's steaming. We're the point and there's nobody in front of us. Get Dreher and Burmaster up here."

Then, I wondered, "How far does a man go from his foxhole to take a crap? How far out will he go when he knows the enemy is near?" I figured, he'd probably go thirty yards, where he had some privacy and where he wouldn't foul his own area. So, the four of us, Courtney, Dreher, Burmaster, and myself, crawled up to the bend in the road.

There they were—four Germans sitting on a hedgerow. The sun was almost over the horizon and they were more or less silhouetted. Their backs were turned to us. I could see an anti-tank gun behind the hedgerow in a barricade. I knew they would have automatic weapons on each side. I wondered how strong the point was.

I signaled Sergeant Courtney to report back. He needed no instructions whatsoever. He would go back and notify Captain Arman. The message would get to Major Arnold, then to Colonel Rudder, maybe all the way back up to Eisenhower for all I knew. I raised my M-1 rifle and Dreher, Burmaster, and myself fired at the same time. We took out the anti-tank crew. Then all hell broke loose.

German "burp" guns opened fire from both sides of the road. Burp guns were like American Tommy guns though smaller and had more rapid fire. This German group wasn't very strong or they would have had heavy machine-guns there. The fact that they had burp guns meant that it was just a small detaining force.

A Company immediately moved around, through, and up over them. The 1st Platoon ran directly through the roadblock. I turned and saw Major Arnold. I told him that it was just a small outpost, an anti-tank gun and a few infantrymen. Most of them were dead now or prisoners. B Company moved through us and Sid Salomon's Company took over the point position.

I went over to look at the man I had shot in the back. I rolled him over. He had a picture in his hand. I wondered then and I wonder now what happened to the beautiful little boy and girl in the picture that their proud father had been showing to his friends. I see his face sometimes now at night, even after fifty-six years.

A few miles up the road we came to another strong point. A small gun emplacement was positioned on the next ridgeline. It didn't amount to much. I was told it was just an old French pillbox left over from the last war and to take the 1st Platoon across the field and knock it out.

We were about a hundred yards out from the pillbox when we were ordered to stop. There was a small sunken road running parallel to us. I knew that a German gunner had this road taped to the inch. We took cover.

I radioed back to company headquarters and asked, "What the hell are we stopping for? We're just a hundred yards out and we're sitting ducks here!"

Someone at corps had information from the FFI that the Krauts were going to surrender. I'd heard that bull before! I didn't trust the Germans. You learn to go with your instincts. In the end, it's all about self-preservation. We dug in and under a hedgerow.

Then it came! About thirty rounds of "token opposition" from a French 75 (a type of gun from WWI) dropped on our small infantry platoon. I wished that person from corps had been there then. Lieutenants and sergeants should have run the corps and then we wouldn't have had this bullshit. I swore some of those shells landed right on top of the hedgerow we were dug under. Shrapnel, stone, dust, noise, and smoke were everywhere. Hell had to have been better than that. After about twenty minutes it let up. I ran from hole to hole expecting to find my whole platoon shot to hell. They were dazed and nearly speechless, but had survived. Several of them were digging their way out; they had been completely buried. Others were digging deeper!

I got to the last hole and Sergeant Weir, a D-Day veteran, had taken a hit and had a piece of shrapnel in his upper forearm. He was calm and collected and told me not to worry, he'd be okay. A message came from battalion telling us to go on into position. The Germans had put up a white flag.

We went on up and the Krauts came out grinning. They had kicked the hell out of us and when we got near enough, they quit. If there hadn't been so many people watching us from the rear, we'd have taken those grins off their faces. But we abided by the rules of war.

Dave Jacobus Private Collection
Fronczek and Burmaster on homemade double bike

Dave Jacobus Private Collection

Dave Jacobus Private Collection

Burmaster, Ware, and Serrette

These actions that I'm talking about were isolated incidents by one platoon of A Company, 2nd Ranger Battalion. Both Ranger battalions and several infantry divisions were going through the same thing all over the peninsula. Small skirmishes and small battles were leading up to, no doubt, what was going to be the big one.

On August 30th, early in the morning, we were the point for a task force which included A, B, and C Companies of the 2nd Ranger Battalion along with a platoon of about four tanks. Our job, again, was to contact the enemy.

We were at a little village in France and came to a crossroads with a tavern on the corner. Battalion sent us a message from the company and battalion to hold up there and regroup. I sent an outpost to the front on the road and another outpost down the other road about 50 or 60 yards. Two or three men were to notify us of an attack. However, there's not much danger of an attack when the enemy's in a defensive position as the Germans were at that time.

Of course, Courtney, Dreher, Burmaster and I had to check out the tavern. It had a small stock left. We went up to the top floor, way up in the attic. There we discovered a hole in the roof where a shell had hit. I pulled a chair up to the hole and looked out with binoculars. The rest of the story you are going to find very difficult to believe, but it is true.

About five hundred yards away I spotted a farmhouse in a grove of trees. I could see activity there. I saw a German heavy machine-gun nest. An anti-tank gun was located on the other side and it seemed to be a fairly good strong point.

Just joking, I told Courtney, Dreher and Burmaster, "I believe I can hit that German officer looking over the fence with my M-1 rifle."

They got up and took a look and said, "There ain't no way!"

We all wrote down our estimates of the range and it averaged out to be 475 yards. I picked up my M-1 and set the range at 475, climbed up on a stool, and stuck my rifle through the hole in the roof. All I could do was just grip the trigger because I couldn't get my shoulder in behind the stock of the rifle. So I watched. This old boy over there was sticking his head up with his field glasses every 30 seconds or so trying to trap some American soldiers coming down the sunken lane there. I watched him with the field glass and had my right finger on the trigger. The next time he popped up, I pressed the trigger and he dropped.

I quickly jumped off the stool and told the guys with me, "I hit that guy in the right temple and I dropped him!"

Well, that started it. They began hollerin', "How could you hit him?" They took bets. So I reported the situation back to the company and on back to battalion. I asked permission to check out this strong point and see how strong it was.

Major Arnold came up and asked what the gunshot was for. So I told him.

He said, "Hell, you don't want to find out how strong it is. You just want to find out whether you hit the guy or not. Well, let's go and see if we can get a prisoner. This looks like the last strong point before we get to the Lochrist Fort."

We started down the sunken road. I took a four-man patrol, Courtney, Dreher, Burmaster and myself. The 1st and 2nd Platoons were behind us with Major Arnold and two light tanks. When we got down to the farmhouse the Germans had backed some distance away. They had picked up on our tanks from a mile back and started throwing pretty heavy artillery in. We got into the strong point and had a small firefight there. We captured the rest of the Germans, knocked out the anti-tank gun, and located the German 1st lieutenant. Sure enough! He had a bullet hole in his right temple, exactly where I had said it was. I can't really say that I hit him. Somebody else might have hit him at a later time. But anyway, the story was and still is that I hit the lieutenant from five hundred yards out. Those that know the M-1 rifle can appreciate what a shot that was.

We started back. Artillery was coming in heavy with the tanks drawing heavy fire. We started down the sunken road with the 1st Platoon out front, then a tank, followed by the 2nd Platoon, then the 2nd tank, and then Major Arnold with two prisoners. Courtney, Dreher, and myself were behind Major Arnold but he didn't know we had stayed to protect his back. I could see him slapping the prisoners across the butt with his .45 trying to get them to run. The 2nd Platoon was between the two tanks, which was a mistake. A

German 88 at that point was fanning the rear tank pretty close.

The second tank driver thought a bazooka might hit him, so he kicked it up to about 10mph and closed in on the platoon that was between him and the lead tank. Of course, the lead tank sped up, and I swear, when they came around that bend in the road, they must have been doing 15 mph. The platoon of infantrymen in the middle was fighting mad.

When the guys in the tanks pulled around the corner behind a hill where they couldn't get hit by fire, they boiled out of their tanks. They wanted to fight the 1st Platoon because they'd run off and left them. I wanted to fight them because they'd run off and left me. We were supposed to be behind them to protect them from bazookas. The guys in the middle wanted to fight them because the second tank almost ran over them. The guy in the lead tank wanted to fight the guy in the second tank because he got too close to him. It was probably just a beautiful well-coordinated attack up until we were out-gunned by the 88s. We found out later that we had captured about 50 prisoners, killed 25 to 30 and knocked out three machine-gun nests. Not bad!

It was now around the 1st of September and the weather had grown cool. A Company was operating strictly as a unit on its own, just two platoons of thirty-five men each. We were patrolling to the right of the 116th Infantry Regiment, part of the 29th Division. Their job was to protect the right flank of the 29th. The divisions on their left, which were bearing straight up the Brittany Peninsula, straight toward Brest, were probably 10 or 15 miles from Brest about this time. A Company was just almost strictly alone.

Captain Arman, Lieutenant Porubski, and myself were called back to battalion headquarters. We were advised that the higher headquarters had formed a task force called *Sugar*, named after a Lieutenant Colonel Shep, from the 175th Infantry and commander of the force. We could expect to join up with them at a later date.

Colonel Rudder gave us all the information he had. D, E, and F Companies had already joined the force along with part of a cavalry reconnaissance squadron and a cannon company. We were told to continue patrolling, protecting the flank. We would move all the way up to Le Conquet Peninsula to the battery at Lopres and then on into Le Conquet protecting the flank of the larger forces on our left.

When we rejoined the company we were given the job of taking over a small town. That meant we had to back up several miles because there was a strong point that hadn't been taken out yet. This mission was assigned to the 2nd Platoon under "Pop" (Lieutenant Porubski). We would visit each other in the foxholes to discuss strategy, how to protect each other's platoons.

"Pop" had been in a lot of combat in the last few days and I had had a lot of opportunities to really observe him. The reports on him had been real good—his men were happy with him and Captain Arman said he was doing a wonderful job. So, he and his platoon were assigned the job of coming up the draw and taking out a pillbox sitting on top of the hill, probably 45 or 50 feet high.

My platoon's job was to give him covering fire from atop an adjoining hill. Company headquarters was there and included Captain Arman, 1st Sergeant Bill White, and a radio man. That's all that makes up headquarters in addition to a runner. I had my platoon scattered around the hillside. When Porubski got probably two hundred yards away, the enemy opened fire with machine-guns and mortar-fire.

A German officer, popping his head up from a little observation post near the pillbox, was directing the fire. We could see him about eight hundred yards away. Our sniper fired at the man several times and missed him. I took the sniper's rifle and from a range of about 800 yards drew a bead right in the middle of his forehead, squeezed off the shot, but he didn't flinch. "Pop" continued to have a lot of German fire directed at him. I fired I think three more times at that German officer. I didn't know if it was the rifle, if it was me, or if it was the other sniper that was trying to hit him—but we just couldn't get the job done. They were taking a hell of a pounding down in that draw.

I called to the mortar sergeant to fire on them. The gunner's name was Frank Knight. At a later date he asked me why he never got promoted. I told him that I couldn't afford to promote him. His situation was the same as a lot of people's. He was just too damn good a gunner to be anything but a gunner. I told him about our present situation. He took one look and dropped a round of mortar-fire. He dropped it directly on the observation post and destroyed it with one round of 60mm from a range of approximately eight hundred yards. This allowed the 2nd Platoon to get up and move forward. Porubski got up to within 30 feet of the pillbox. He showed as much courage and guts as anybody that I've ever seen in combat. He just walked directly into it. The Germans came out with their usual white flag and gave up.

We were almost like spectators, standing up to cheer when the 45 or 50 Germans came out and surrendered. Porubski got the Silver Star for that. Probably more men in his platoon should have been decorated at the same time. ("Pop" later died while serving in the Korean War receiving the Distinguished Service Cross posthumously.)

We were pretty much responsible for our own supply, ammunition, and food, whatever we might need. Every day, of course, we sent a patrol back to battalion. Sometimes we didn't know for sure where they were, but we would locate them and pick up C-rations or K-rations or whatever was available. We couldn't get any hot food from the battalion kitchen because they didn't know exactly where we were or what we were going to be doing. However, the battalion staff itself always knew.

We were operating pretty loosely. We lived off what food the countryside gave us, whatever vegetables or food we could find in the French gardens, along with the C-rations. Maybe a chicken or two would viciously attack somebody and we would have to kill it in self-defense. That's a joke. We ate well, and the combat episodes only lasted 30 to 45 minutes at a time. We would capture the prisoners and send them back to battalion. If there were no other enemy in the area we could do pretty much as we wanted until we were assigned the next mission. Around the third of September we joined up with the rest of the 2nd Ranger Battalion. It was the first time we had been with the whole battalion in three weeks or so. Of course, it was good to get back to battalion and have a hot, good meal fixed by our own battalion cooks.

Dave Jacobus Private Collection

"Jake" Jacobus
Mayenne, France
September 1944

Another good patrol story involves Burmaster. He remembers a patrol that took place when Dreher, Courtney and myself were home on leave in December. It's the darndest story so I thought it should be told.

Here's Burmaster's tale:

On December 14th, our patrol was broken up when Edlin, Dreher, and Courtney had enough points to get a pass home to America. I was given a pass to Paris. When I returned to the front lines, the Rangers went on the defense. We had had about two feet of snow on the ground at the time in our area. One day Lt. Porubski told me to make up a patrol and to go through the German lines to see what this particular pillbox ahead of us was made of. We had been blasting it with artillery for three or four days and they still continued to "blaze" us. I pulled together some volunteers and I told them to put white sheets on so that we could blend in with the snow. I also told them to remove any noisy items that they might have had on their bodies. I told them to check their rifles and to pick up two grenades each. The lieutenant told me to take the point and he would follow with the rest of them. During the day I picked out a route to take through *No Man's Land*. I was given a password and checked out each man covered in his white sheet, even his weapons.

About 2200 we started out and proceeded into the *No Man's Land*. I took a sharp right and walked across the front of both lines. Moving slowly and quietly we finally came to a hard black-top road exactly across from the German bunker. We laid down with our white sheets over us. Our job had been to get to the bunker without letting the Germans see us. Just about that time the sound of German boots marching down the road was heard getting closer and closer. We froze. I remember from where I was lying as the lead scout, I could literally reach out and touch the road with my hand. Thirty or so Germans came marching down the road four abreast with the leader out in front. They stopped in formation directly in front of our patrol. Our hearts were pounding. Their leader gave a command. All of the men, to our good fortune, went to the opposite side of the road and entered their bunker and foxholes nearby. Not one German came to our patrol side of the road except for one. The last man to leave the road needed to relieve himself. He walked over, so close to where I was laying, that when he relieved himself on the side of the road it sprayed up onto me. After about 15 minutes I crawled back to the lieutenant. Lt. Porubski told me, "Let's get out of here. I've seen enough." We retraced our steps back but somehow ended up taking a wrong turn. When we were near the American lines I gave the password but heard no response. Finally I used the word *Halftrack* and got permission to enter. We were glad to return that night!

There was more to Company A than this small patrol of Courtney, Dreher, Burmaster and myself. There were many other patrols led by many other people. And I might add that most of the fighting and note-worthy battles were done by platoons and company units rather than just patrols. Our "fabulous four" patrol just got lucky as in the case of our next assignment—to conquer the Graf Spee Battery at Brest, an important seaport and submarine base at the tip of the Brittany Peninsula. To do that, we had to topple a German garrison stubbornly fighting to protect their submarine base. Our little patrol was to be called on yet again!

Brest 'Fool' Comes Home

Lt. Edlin Had Big Role In Fall of City.

Designated as "the fool lieutenant" when his daring obtained the surrender of a 41-year-old Nazi lieutenant colonel in the fall of Brest, Lt. Robert T. Edlin, 22, was at home in New Albany today after 18 months at the battle front in Europe.

The citation with the Distinguished Service Cross awarded to Edlin for his feat stated:

* * *

"On LeCouquet Peninsula, France, Edlin, leading a 4-man patrol, captured one of the outposts and moved into main enemy positions. Taking one of his me̶ ̶with him to aid as an int̶̶ ̶e reached the command̶̶ ̶ce. Here he pulled the ̶̶ ̶in from a hand grenad̶̶ ̶olding it against the ̶̶andant's side, called upo̶ ̶ surrender or die.

"The commandant capitul̶ ̶rrendering an entire bat̶ ̶nsisting of four 280-mm. g̶ ̶pporting small arms, positi̶ ̶rracks, pillboxes and appro̶ ̶ ̶ately 800 prisoners."

* * *

Edlin, member of the famou̶ ̶ ̶ Ranger Division, reached the̶ ̶emy position while other Rangers were cautiously creeping ̶hrough hedgerows to the objec̶ ̶ve. An observer a mile away ̶elephoned the company commander, "That fool lieutenant of ours is up there already; you might as well go in."

Edlin returned to this country recently in a group of three officers and enlisted men of his outfit for a 36-day stay.

* * *

Edlin has three Purple Hearts for a serious wound received on D-Day, and slight wounds September 7 in France and November 22 in Germany. He also participated in a Presidential Citation awarded the 2d Ranger Battalion for its achievements on D-day.

He received a Silver Star for individual outstanding performance during the invasion of France. In addition, he wears a Combat Infantry Badge awarded when his outfit stopped a German counteroffensive with a force that outnumbered the Rangers two to one.

* * *

Edlin is the son of Mr. and Mrs. Lee Edlin, 605 MacArthur Dr., New Albany. He was New Albany's 1940 Golden Glove tournament champion in the lightweight division.

Americans Win Strongest Fort Guarding Brest

'Fool' Lieutenant' Reaches Bastion, Holds Grenade to Nazi Colonel's Midriff

By Lewis Gannett
By Wireless to the New York Tribune
Copyright, 1944, New York Tribune Inc.

LOCHRIST BATTERY, Le Conquest Peninsula, east of Brest, Sept. 9 (Delayed).—This strongest of Brest's defenses fell to American Rangers today. Its big 14-inch guns had not been fired since yesterday afternoon, and the Rangers were crawling through the hedgerows from all sides when an observer a mile away telephoned Lieutenant Robert Armon, of Lafayette, Ind., company commander: "That fool lieutenant of yours is up there already; you might as well go in."

Armon took his company up and found Lieutenant Robert Edlin of New Albany, Ind., standing in the door of the casemate of the biggest gun holding a hand grenade at the slim stomach of a precise forty-one-year-old lieutenant colonel, comander of the fort, shouting at him in English, which the colonel did not understand, to put up a white flag. An understanding soon was reached; ̶̶̶ ̶̶̶ ̶̶̶ ̶̶̶

Edlin named "Fool Lieutenant"

11

THE GRAF SPEE BATTERY

That fool lieutenant of yours is up there already; you might as well go in..
—An Army observer

The Rangers used to say that the 280mm guns of the Graf Spee Battery "sounded like a boxcar going sideways through the air when fired." These guns, according to the information we had, had been taken off the battleship Graf Spee and were being used by the Germans at their largest fort on Brittany Peninsula to protect the French city of Brest.

Brest, the principle submarine base for the German Navy, was the second largest port in France and contained some 80,000 people. It was one of the main outfitting and supply bases for German U-boats preying on convoys bringing supplies from America. The Allies desperately needed a deep-water seaport; they decided that Brest had to be taken at all costs.

The Germans had occupied Brest and the Brittany Peninsula since June 1940. They had built concrete submarine pens as well as concrete fortresses throughout the peninsula area. One of these fortresses, the Graff Spee Battery, located ten miles from the coast near the little town of Lochrist, was an intricately large compound with the fort in the center. That's where the guns were. On top of the fort! It had many names: Lochrist Battery, Graf Spee Battery, Le Conquet and the Germans referred to it as the Man-made Mound.

The 280mm Graff Spee guns could fire 10 miles in any direction. Sgt. Burmaster remembers well: "When they turned the guns on us we could see the shell coming and when it exploded, it made a hole so large we could run five or six trucks in and not be able to see them."

The mission to take the fort had become almost as important as the attack up the draw to Brest, the city itself. Now the taskforce for the mission had been reinforced considerably. The latest information we had from Colonel Rudder was that the taskforce now included units from the 116th Infantry, several battalions from the 116th and 175th Infantry Regiments, 29th Division, the 2nd and 5th Ranger Battalions, part of two other tank battalions and all the supporting forces, FFI and some Russians. It had also been joined by an entire field artillery and part of another field artillery battalion making this a very sizable force. These units were all under the command of the Assistant Division Commander of the 29th Division, Troy Middleton. Three thousand men were going to attack the fort.

During the days and nights of the 7th, 8th and 9th of September, we were under very heavy artillery and shell-fire from the Graf Spee Battery.   It was the worst artillery-fire that we had had up until that time.

The 344th Bombardment Group had been flying over, bombing vessels and strong points in this area during August and September. The 29th Infantry Division also was helping to bring them to their knees. Nobody knew for sure, but we thought they were ready to quit.

Colonel Rudder was planning for a dawn attack on the 10th. But prior to that, a couple of patrols would be used to locate the minefields surrounding the fort.

I was told that I would lead a reconnaissance combat patrol of the entire 1st Platoon as near to the fort as possible. I went back to my platoon and informed them of the mission. I picked Courtney, Dreher and Burmaster to take with me.

We were to spot pillboxes, snipers, whatever we could identify and chart a way through the minefield. If we had the opportunity, we were to capture some prisoners. We wanted to find out the state of minds of the Germans in the fort.

The plan called for the bombers to start hitting at midnight. The fighter planes would come in just before daylight. The artillery would open up a half-hour before the attack. At 0600 the two Ranger battalions and the 116th Infantry would launch a frontal attack through the minefields and take the fort. We were going to be under heavy gunfire. We knew that the big guns couldn't be turned to fire on the assaulting forces; they would be too close. But the 88's, machine-guns, mortars and whatever else they had in there, could be.

At dawn on September 9th, Dreher, Courtney, Burmaster and myself moved out of our positions and came up to probably within 200 yards of a German pillbox. It was a large pillbox, one of the largest I had seen, but of course it was no comparison to the fort itself. We were now so close that we were under the guns looking up at them.

The fort, located in the middle of the compound, looked like a skyscraper about five stories high. They told me later that it was also nine stories deep into the ground. I don't remember any trees inside the compound, just a lot of buildings, such as ammunition warehouses, a laundromat, liquor warehouses, a blacksmith's shop, automotive shops, and repair shops. Everything. There were even streets. It was like going into a little city but with no civilians. At the peak of the fort's activity, they probably had a couple thousand Germans in there.

We used a diamond patrol pattern when we went in. I was out in front, Dreher was to my right, 10 yards over and back, and Courtney to my left. Burmaster was behind, the getaway man. The pillbox was about 150 yards to my left. At each corner of the complex, probably 200-250 yards from the fort, were large pillboxes. The one to my right was probably 500 yards away.

"Achtung Minen" signs for the benefit of the German soldiers and French civilians were in the area. I wish they had also pointed out the path through them. My platoon was sitting back there with their mortar set up and smoke shells ready to go. If they heard gunfire they were going to drop the smoke so that one or two of us might get back.

We'd gone probably 50 yards and were scared to death. We

expected to be fired on right away; my stomach felt like it was in my throat. I could almost feel the bullets hitting my stomach. Every step we took could have triggered a mine and caused us all to be blown to hell. I had more than I could deal with; I was ready to quit. I was thinking, "I'm through."

I was turning to say, let's turn around and pull back, when I heard Courtney say in a very quiet voice, "I see a way through the damn minefield!" He took off at a dead run. We weren't supposed to go through the minefield, just find a route through it.

I heard Dreher yelling, "Stop, Courtney! Stop!"

I said, "Let him go! Come on, Dreher!" What Courtney had seen in front of him and what I could not see, was a path where our bombs had exploded the mines. I jumped over to the path that Courtney was on and followed him. Right behind me was Dreher and right behind him was Burmaster. With blind faith we followed Courtney through the minefield. We came up directly to the mouth of the pillbox.

If you can, imagine this. The sun was up and it was cold. September in France can be cold and miserable. The ground was wet, almost freezing! We lay there, flat on the ground, listening to the Germans talking in the pillbox. There was no activity anywhere. They hadn't even fired a round at us yet. I should have realized then that these people were ready to quit. The pillbox door was open and nobody was guarding it.

I don't remember this but Burmaster has told me: "By the front door (of the pillbox) we could see a German soldier hanging by his neck. To get in you would have to push his body to one side. He was a deserter and provided a reminder of what would happen if any other German tried it."

I knew if we took this pillbox we wouldn't be able to get out of it; we would have to stay there until the next morning. I made the decision to go for it.

I didn't have to talk. I didn't have to say a word. I looked at Courtney and he nodded his head. I looked at Dreher, he nodded his head. Burmaster dropped back about 10 yards. If we got busted in the pillbox, he would hopefully be able to report back to the battalion what had happened.

I eased over in front of the door. I would go in first. That was my job! I dove in onto the floor with my Tommy gun ready to open fire. Dreher dove in on my left and Courtney dove in on his knees to my right. The three of us were in there! The lights were on and it was bright. About twenty Germans were inside. We all hollered, "Hande hoch!" All their hands went up. Nobody reached for their guns. They just stood there. Their weapons were there—laying on the floor and stacked in the corners. Machine-guns were mounted in the pillbox facing out towards where we had just come from. These were some of the toughest German forces, Ramke's Paratroopers, and they just quit.

I told Courtney, "Talk to somebody. See who's in charge here." Courtney, in his high school German, started to talk.

One of the Germans said, "Sir, I speak fluent English. I went to college in America."

I asked him, "How do we get into the fort from here and to your commander?"

He said, "I can take you to the fort commander."

What a hell of a spot for a 22-year-old lieutenant to be in. I was sitting there with prisoners in the shadow of the strongest emplacement on the whole Brittany Peninsula. Should we attempt to take the fort? It was a decision that I had to make. I knew if I asked Colonel Rudder, he would very likely say no. It would just be too much of a risk to him.

I said to Courtney, "What do you think? Are you game to go with me?" I would have been a damn fool if I didn't ask my men. I was putting their lives on the line, too, and they might have had an idea that I hadn't thought about.

I remember Courtney saying, "Well, I don't see anything else to do right now."

I told Dreher to stay with the prisoners, Courtney and myself were going into the fort with the German lieutenant. I called Burmaster in and told him to get the radioman to radio Colonel Rudder to lift all fire on this fort—all artillery fire, all planes, all bombs, all fighters—lift everything. They would radio Rudder and tell him that I was going into the fort.

Lewis Gannett, a famous reporter from a New York newspaper, corroborates my story in an article he wrote. He was standing next to Rudder and Len Lomell, the battalion sergeant major, when the message came into battalion. He wrote in a newspaper story later:

It's big 14-inch guns had not been fired since yesterday afternoon, and the Rangers were crawling through the hedgerows from all sides when an observer a mile away telephoned to Lieutenant Robert Arman, of Lafayette, Ind., company commander: "That fool lieutenant of yours is up there already; you might as well go in."

Dreher was now left in command of the pillbox. I had a lot of confidence in Dreher. He would have taken down a raft of them if he had to. We threw their guns out the door. None of this was preplanned.

Courtney and I took the German lieutenant and moved up through the minefield. In the wide-open daylight we walked together, no white flag, a German officer walking alongside two Americans. I had my Tommy gun on my shoulder and a fighting knife on my side. Courtney had the grenades and he had his Tommy gun. We slung our arms together because we didn't want it to look like we were taking this man prisoner. We talked all the way. We talked about where he went to college in the States. We talked about where Courtney and I were from.

There were obvious pathways that had been used over the years and we moved directly to one of the entrances of the fort. The fort looked like a modern-day amphitheater. We went in down through a tunnel, much like the huge tunnels that football players use to enter an NFL stadium today.

As we got close to the large doors, they opened. They were electric; maybe the first the world ever had. The Germans were that advanced. We walked into the hospital section, big enough to hold three or four hundred patients. I saw an operating room and white-clad doctors. Nurses and their patients were everywhere. Here we were, two American uniforms with guns in our hands creating complete turmoil.

Courtney yelled, "Hande hoch!" All their hands went up immediately.

The German lieutenant asked us if he could talk to them in German and I said, "Yes, but talk slow. I want Courtney to know what you are saying." Courtney was translating to me as he talked. The German lieutenant was telling them to remain calm and to sit down. He was going to lead us to the commander of the fort to possibly negotiate surrender so there would be no more casualties.

Then we started up the stairs. I remember even seeing an elevator. We passed several German soldiers on guard at cross-corridors. The German lieutenant would speak with them in German and they would immediately lower their weapons. Courtney translated what he said. He told them he was taking us to the commander and not to cause any trouble or problems.

Then we came to a door. The lieutenant said, "This is the commandant's office." He started to knock on the door.

I told him, "Don't knock. Don't touch the door. Just step back." I shoved the door open and dove in. I was across the desk and shoved my Tommy gun at the commander's throat. I said, "Hande hoch!" He put his hands up. The commander was sitting behind his desk, a big mahogany desk, in his swivel office chair. Courtney was behind me and closed the door behind him. It was just Courtney, the commander, and myself in the room.

Without taking my eyes off the commander, I said, "Courtney, tell him who we are."

The commander, Colonel Fuerst, was surprised when we walked through the door, although he was calm and the smoothest character I ever saw.

He walked over to a table and poured out a drink and said, "What do you want?" Courtney started to say something in German when the colonel said defiantly, "You don't need your interpreter, Lieutenant. I'm fluent in English. I speak excellent English."

I said, "Fine. Why don't you just surrender the whole fort and all your prisoners and get this whole thing over with."

Fuerst replied, "Well, why should I do that? You can't capture this fort and you can't take Brest Peninsula." He was very hardnosed and arrogant. His attitude was that he wasn't going to quit. The thought came to me that he probably would surrender but I had to help him save face.

"You're completely surrounded. There's Rangers all around you. And the Air Force is going to bomb you. You're going to lose every man that you've got." I had no idea! "Why don't you do the right thing and save not only your lives but save the American lives too."

Fuerst responded, "Well, I'm not going to surrender. I'm going to use my telephone. I'm just going to call my outpost." I told him to leave the telephone alone. He said he was just going to see how many Americans were there.

He picked up the phone and spoke in German. Courtney told him to talk slowly.

He hung up. "They'll call back in a few minutes."

Colonel Fuerst then carried on a regular conversation with us. He even went so far to ask us if we would care to have a drink. I couldn't have had a drink. My stomach was too upset. My heart was pounding. I don't know who was more scared, Courtney or me. We were in a position that we couldn't get out of. If he surrendered, we'd have done a great job. If he didn't, then we were obviously going to be prisoners. In just a couple of minutes, which seemed an eternity, the phone rang. He answered and talked in German on the phone. Courtney looked over at me and shook his head.

I remember Colonel Fuerst saying, "Aaaw." He hung up and said, "I found out that there's only four of you. You two here and two in the pillbox. Those are the only Rangers here. You're my prisoners now."

"No sir! We'll never be your prisoners." My thought was, if we had to, we'd kill him and drag that desk up against the door. Courtney and I would lay back on the floor with our Tommy guns and the hand grenades. We would fight them off as long as we could.

I don't know where it came from but I remember next saying, "Courtney, give me a hand grenade." Courtney unhooked one and handed it over to me. I pulled the pin on it and as most stories say, rammed it in his stomach, but it was lower than that.

I threatened with as much bravado as I could, "You either surrender or you're going to die right now."

I remember the colonel saying, "Well, so are you."

I had had enough of this bullshit by then. "I'm going to count to three."   I had already pulled the pin and released the lever, it would flip over and ignite the fuse and the thing would blow up in three seconds. Forty-eight pieces of shrapnel would explode out. I said, "One, two . . ." I started to say three.

Then Fuerst conceded, "OK."

I very gingerly pulled the pin up and stuck it back into the hammer. He had surrendered. I knew he was going to. I could see it in his eyes. All he was doing was saving face. He stuck it out to the bitter end. The man was a brave man.

Now the party was over except for the incidentals. I told the colonel to get back on his P.A. system and tell his men that he had surrendered the fort completely to the Americans. I told him to tell his men to fall out with their arms and line up in the courtyard outside the fort. He did. He picked up the microphone and spoke in German. Courtney understood what he said. It was plain and clear that he had ordered his people to lower their arms and not take any hostile action against the American forces.

The colonel told me he would prefer to surrender to a higher-ranking officer than a lieutenant in the Rangers. I told him I didn't give a rat's ass *who* he surrendered to. "We'll take you to our battalion commander."

I thought there would be a couple hundred Germans in the fort. I looked out the window to watch them coming out. It seemed like there were thousands! I couldn't believe it! The final count turned out to be over eight hundred. I saw them begin to line up in their ranks, in military manner, and to stack their arms.

I turned to Courtney. He was using the telephone. I said, "Who the hell are you talking to?" The colonel, at Courtney's request, had connected him to General Ramke, the commander of all the German forces at Brest. Courtney was talking man to man with Ramke in German. He was giving Ramke the opportunity to surrender full fledge—to surrender the whole peninsula. By this time they were surrounded by probably 50,000 American soldiers, tankers and artillery.

Patton had broken through the German lines and was halfway

to Paris. The nearest German troops to be of any help were 300 miles away. The Brittany Peninsula was cut off and isolated. Obviously they were going to have to give up sometime. If we could have talked Ramke into it, then ten more bitter days of fighting would not have had to happen. He did not go for it and as a result, thousands of German and American soldiers were killed.

At this point, understand that a four-man patrol couldn't accomplish this surrender by itself—not even with luck. The fort and these men we captured had been under heavy bombardment from the Air Force. They had had heavy artillery fire for several weeks. They had been in a hopeless position with their backs to the water and no way to get out. The history books will show that they had been ordered to hold out as long as possible. I believe at this time their commander had been the only thing holding them together.

When I came out of the fort with the colonel, there were army people everywhere. There were photographers and newspaper reporters. The whole 2nd Ranger Battalion were just outside the fort. They had gotten word as soon as the Germans made the surrender announcement. By that time I had a radioman there. He contacted Colonel Rudder. The radioman, nicknamed Wild Bill, was assigned to A Company for this particular mission. I came out and the radioman walked up to me and said, "Colonel Rudder wants to talk to you." I picked up the phone. I knew I was going to catch hell. I realized also that we had accomplished something here that the world wasn't going to believe.

Rudder said, "I'm coming up to accept the surrender. But I want you there. I want you to get credit for the surrender."

"Yes, sir. I will be there."

That was one of the stipulations that the fort commander made. He didn't want to surrender to a lieutenant. He wanted to surrender to a man of equal or higher rank.

Rudder went on to say, "Get Courtney, Dreher and Burmaster there. I want all of you there."

We were getting ready for the formal surrender ceremony. Everybody knew about it. The word was back to corps. Maybe it was all the way back to the Queen of England! I went to find the guys. I found them in one of the liquor warehouses.

The liquor warehouses were buried underground. The beer was stored in two or three warehouses in big wooden castes—50-gallon kegs. The cognac was in another warehouse and the wine was in another. In the wine warehouse I remember that there were thousands of bottles of wine in racks. These warehouses were as big as my auction house or maybe even bigger—all underground. They were dark and cool, dusky cellar-like places. I remember that they were so cool that you could see your breath. I went in one of them and found my men happily drinking beer and cognac. Some were using their helmets to drink out of. Somebody handed me a canteen full of German beer and I thought, hell, this wasn't going to hurt.

Sgt. Klaus, my platoon sergeant, had been on a patrol when I was in the fort. He told me later how he got picked up by Colonel Rudder on his way to the fort for the surrender.

"That day I was on a small patrol of my own checking out a village. I had three or four men with me. There weren't any Germans in the town so we went on through the town. Then we continued on further to see what was beyond.

"Just about the time we approached a cemetery on the right side of the road, we heard a vehicle coming. We jumped over the wall into the cemetery, out of sight, and prepared to see what the car was going to be. As it got closer we saw it was a German car with camouflage paint on it with somebody sitting on the fender.

"We were ready to blast the thing when we recognized the guy on the fender was an American. So we stopped the car and it happened to be Lt. Col. Rudder in the car with a couple of other Americans. He told me that the fort had been captured. He said, "Have your men jump on here—anywhere." So we jumped on the car to go up to the fort with him so he could accept the surrender of the Germans. As we progressed up the road a ways, we came to an intersection. The colonel said to me, "Drop off one of your men here. There's some Germans supposedly coming up here to surrender." I dropped a man off named Hoff. I didn't see him the rest of the day.

"We went on up to the fortification. I met Lt. Edlin up there and some of his patrol. It was quite a day. I remember the German commander of that fort. He was absolutely immaculate. He looked like something out of Hollywood. He had his best uniform on, all polished up. His facial features reminded me of a famous comedian of that

time, Joey Brown. He had a huge mouth. I remember that to this day.
He was of average height and good-looking. I remember his appearance because he looked so sharp. The rest of us looked like bums.

"Another sergeant and myself went into the fortification. We were hungry. They had every facility that you could mention in there. They had a hospital and a kitchen, everything they needed and safely underground. We headed for the kitchen. They had a big pot of stew simmering on the stove. We helped ourselves and it was great stuff! We were quite hungry anyway. It was a great day.

"Hoff, the man that I dropped off at the intersection, was a replacement after the D-Day invasion, a recruit from Iceland. When I saw him later I said, "Hoff, what happened to you?"

"He said, "Boy, about 50 Germans came up there. I herded them into the barn. They had about 25 *ladies of the evening* with them." I don't know who they were, French girlfriends or what. He told me that one of our other companies came through the area. One of the men from this other company picked up one of those girls and took off. Then another man did the same. He said that shortly he didn't have any more ladies with him. He was standing, alone, watching the Germans. Then, an artillery barrage came in. He said he had to jump right into the barn with the rest of the German prisoners. However, they were ready to give up. They weren't going to cause any trouble. As time went on the ladies started drifting back and finally they all came back. So, I don't know what happened to them later. He was relieved of his duties and the prisoners were taken away. I thought it was kind of funny.

While I was in the fortification that Edlin captured, a lot of us had loot on our minds. One of the first things I saw in one of the German officer's rooms was a nice little folding alarm clock. It had a leather case and it folded together and zipped around. That looked good to me. I thought I might need that somewhere. So I put it in my shirt pocket.

"Shortly after that I was called to go across the road and defuse another part of the fort. While we were over there we got things calmed down. There was a minefield there and they had a couple of strands of wire across the top of the hedgerow. On the other side I happened to glance down and saw half of a pistol that one of the Germans had taken apart. I had picked up the other half somewhere. On the wire fence were several *Achtung Minen* signs. I kept looking at that pistol. I had half of it in my hand that I had just found and the other half was over there. I thought, 'Should I jump over that row and into that minefield and get that other piece of that pistol or not? What the hell. The odds are that I won't land on a mine.'

"So I got on top of the hedgerow and jumped into the field that said, *Minen*. I no sooner hit the ground and that damn alarm clock in my shirt went off. I almost had a heart attack. I think my feet touched the ground and I flew right back over the fence. It scared the hell out of me! I'll never forget that as long as I live. I think that was one of the worst scares I've ever had.

"Then I found an underground bunker. I walked down into that place. It was just a hole in the ground about eight feet deep. It had a table with a candle and a couple of cans of sardines on it. I sat down and ate the can of sardines.

"Up above ground I heard a shot. I thought, 'Oh man, the war's starting again.' So I came whipping up out of that hole. There was Sgt. Dreher. He had shot a huge pig. I don't know why he shot the pig. I don't even remember eating the pig. Maybe the Frenchmen came in and got it. I was quite relieved that the war hadn't started again.

"During those times, if we took out a German position, the French would come out of the woodwork. They would loot the place and take everything they could. I've seen a Frenchman take the shoes off a German before he had even quit kicking. They would grab anything they could. They had reason to hate the Germans, I guess. They had it tough for five years.

"After the fort was captured, I did not talk to Courtney about whether he was scared or not. I don't believe that Courtney, Dreher, Edlin and Burmaster had fear of anything. I'm sure they had some butterflies, but they never showed it. Looking at them you'd never know. Nothing perturbed them at all. It was great for the rest of us. We'd see them and want to be like that. I wondered about myself a lot of the times. I'm sure a lot of the men did. Like whether we could be that way. When we were quaking in our own boots and then we saw somebody else calm—it just had a calming effect on everybody I think."

Rudder accepted the surrender—a real formal ceremony. It was the way the Germans wanted it. We were still trying to help the German colonel, Colonel Fuerst, to save face. It was like an old-fashioned thing that you'd see in the movies. The four of us were the guard of honor. Rudder was standing in front with Lomell to his left. Rudder's staff was on the other side. There were four or five companies lined up behind him with the presentation of arms. The Germans were standing there with their arms stacked at parade rest. Their colonel walked out in front of them and called them to attention. Rudder called his troops to attention. Colonel Fuerst walked forward to withdraw his firearm and present it to Colonel Rudder. Colonel Fuerst reached for his pistol and found it was missing. He didn't have it. I had it! I had taken it earlier from Colonel Fuerst inside the fort, of course, because I was afraid he'd shoot me. Besides, I thought, "What a hell of a souvenir this will be." I could have gotten four or five bottles of whiskey for it.

Colonel Fuerst didn't know what to do. Rudder turned to me and said, "Where's his pistol?"

I said, "Right here, sir."

I handed Rudder the pistol and he gave it to the colonel, who put it in his holster and then pulled it out again to present it to Rudder.

After the surrender ceremony, the newspaper people were talking to Rudder. The papers came out and said that Rudder took the German colonel back to his dugout. The paper showed pictures of them going into the dugout as they were talking. What they were talking about is none of my business. I'm sure Rudder was still trying to convince this guy to do anything to keep the attack from happening on the city of Brest proper. And they were working on it. People were coming down from the corps and there was a big turmoil. All the Germans were standing together.

Before I turned to go back to where the beer was, Rudder said, "Wait a minute. I want to talk to you."

I said, "Yes, sir." I knew what was coming.

He started in on me. "You're the dumbest . . . You risked the lives of you and Courtney. You risked your own life." And he went on and on. He called me every name in the book. He finally shut up.

I said, "Are you through, Colonel?"

"Yes, I'm through!"

I said, "I just want to ask you one question. What would you have done if you were in my position?"

He looked at me with big tears running down his cheeks. "I hope I'd have had nerve enough to do what you did." He hit me on the back, "Get back there and drink that damn beer." And he walked away from me. That was the greatest medal I ever got in my life.

All of A Company was relieved that the battery had been captured and the guns were silenced forever.

Prince later described in his manuscript, the guns up close and personal:

Those 280mm guns, which had caused us those endless and worrisome nights, were found to be of immense stature. Their gigantic structure and encased concrete homes had made these giants immune to our shelling and bombing. Their large muzzles easily contained our helmets in their openings and the size of the shell was equivalent to a good-sized bomb. These huge masses of steel even dwarfed the 155mm guns at Pointe du Hoc making them look puny in comparison!

The rest of the battalion was going to move in and take over the fort. Rudder wanted us to just sit down and do whatever we wanted to do. Probably none of this would have amounted to anything except that there happened to be a news reporter there, a gentleman by the name of Lewis Gannet.

I never talked with the man, never met him. I later read a story that he had written that he had seen the capture of the fort and had talked to Colonel Rudder. Some of the details were left out but I didn't mind. There was nationwide publicity about the capture of the fort, and of course, the story came out about four Rangers capturing 850 men and four guns. I appreciated the publicity, but I think the men of the 116th Infantry and 175th Infantry Regiment, and the Rangers of the 2nd and 5th Battalions, and Air Force, and the artillery unit, and the chemical warfare units, and the engineers that had all fought their way up that peninsula and were prepared to assault the fort, contributed just the same as my patrol. Four men didn't do a thing but get lucky.

Americans Win Strongest Fort Guarding Brest
"Fool Lieutenant" Reaches Bastion,
Holds Grenade to Nazi Colonel's Midriff
By Lewis Gannett
By Wireless to the Herald Tribune
Copyright, 1944, New York Tribune, Inc.

LOCHRIST BATTERY, Le Conquest Peninsula, east of Brest, Sept. 9 (Delayed), — This strongest of Brest's defenses fell to American Rangers today. Its big 14-inch guns had not been fired since yesterday afternoon, and the Rangers were crawling through the hedgerows from all sides when an observer a mile away telephoned to Lieutenant Robert Arman, of Lafayette, Ind., company commander: "That fool lieutenant of yours is up there already; you might as well go in."

Arman took his company up and found Lieutenant Robert Edlin of New Albany, Ind., standing at the door of the casemate of the biggest gun holding a hand grenade at the slim stomach of a precise forty-one-year-old lieutenant colonel, commander of the fort, shouting at him in English, which the colonel did not understand, to put up a white flag. An understanding soon was reached; the white flag went up, and hundreds of Germans began emerging from the network, of underground passages where they had hidden.

A thirty-four-year-old Texas colonel soon arrived and took Lieutenant Colonel Fuerst blind-folded to the command post in the vain hope that he could persuade the German officer to bid all his men on the peninsula to give up the suicidal struggle.

Captives Exceed Attackers

I saw 400 German prisoners at task force headquarters by 2 o'clock; 300 more along the lanes leading to the fort and 300 more sitting in a potato field atop the fort when I arrived with an artillery colonel who had been firing on Lochrist for ten days and wanted to see what his guns had accomplished.

"It looks like more prisoners than you had men to take them with," I said to Lieutenant Arman.

"That's right," he said. "We had fewer than 1,000 out here and we threw in everybody we had."

By midnight the total of prisoners had touched 1,400.

A Nazi lieutenant was the only artillery officer left in the fort. He said the American artillery had done his guns more harm than the constant air bombardment. A 280 mm. Gun which the Germans said had been taken off the Graf Spee had been sheltered under ten feet of concrete but had been knocked out of action. One of its gunners remained beside it and blew out his own brains as Lieutenant Arman entered the position.

Expected More Guns

The Germans said a 14-inch "G-3" gun, which had a 360-degree traverse, had been frozen in the air three times but always had been repaired. It was still firing into the area of an adjacent American division two nights earlier. The Americans believed the battery contained more big guns than it did. What they thought were .88s were French .75s with added muzzelbreaks.

Twenty feet underground was a modern hospital with an operating room, X-ray and dental chair. The electricity was still functioning and there was an excellent stock of Bordeaux wines.

The main attack was made by American Rangers, but one company of infantry and considerable forces of fighting French and more than 100 Russians, who had previously served in both the Red and German armies, co-operated in the attack. All agreed the Rangers were the toughest of the lot, the Russians next.

Bulldozers in Action

When I returned from the fort late in the afternoon bulldozers already were smoothing over shellholes in the approach roads and engineers were neutralizing mines so that trucks could move up to take out the German prisoners. The lanes and hedgerows still were filled with Rangers greedily cooking their first hot food in three days and discussing the operation and debating when they would get home.

Ivor Jones, of Johnsontown, Pa., was telling Neal Berke, of Dundee, Ill.: "Me and Bill hopped one fancy hedgerow last night and heard fancy German voices. We sneaked back up the fancy road and damned if the next thing he heard wasn't a fancy French buggy driving right into the German lines. You can't beat those fancy French."

He has seen the same buggy since, as French peasants are everywhere about the fort.

There was frost on the fields about Brest this morning, but the chilly Americans were creeping in from all sides. Some pockets of resistance persist on the point, but the main area has been reduced to the arc of a circle five miles wide and two miles deep.

That was the end of the combat on Brittany Peninsula for A Company. The following day we were in reserve behind everybody but the nurse's corps if there happened to be any of them there. We sat there for several days without any action just watching what was happening across the channel from us. But the fight for the city of Brest was not an easy one.

Tech Sergeant, Thomas Hughes, 116th Infantry describes what

it was like:

The German defenders were backed up as far as they could go; they either had to surrender or die. Most of them chose to die. It was not pleasant or pretty. Fifty-five years later, watching the last battle in the movie, "Saving Private Ryan," reminded me all too realistically of how we fought in the ruined town of Brest. The horrible scenes in that movie of a wounded soldier, screaming, with his insides spilling out, are not a movie director's fancy. I saw those things. I don't want to talk about it.

When Brest fell, the city had almost been completely demolished. The seven-week siege cost the Americans 10,000 lives. The Germans at Brest surrendered to the Allies on September 19th. The victors marched into a smoking ruin. Seven thousand of Brest's 16,500 homes were destroyed. Five thousand more were so badly damaged they had to be demolished. The U-boat war was also at an end. The last submarine left Brest on September 4, 1944.

The war now was 650 miles away. For the time being, we were out of it. The units on the Brittany Peninsula were ready to move forward. Some of us hoped the war would be over for us. But of course, that wasn't the way it was to be. The Third Army and the First Army had moved all the way past Paris by this time. We had a leisurely 15 or 20 days there.

                                                    Sept. 13, 1944

     Dear Mother and Dad:

          It is sure swell to take a bath again and change
     socks after three weeks and not have to sleep with
     your boots on.
          Hope this finds all of you feeling good. I have
     never felt better myself.
          I am sending a box of souvenirs. You should get
     them in a few weeks. Just some stuff I picked up.
          Have had a lot of interesting things happen in
     the last campaign. Guess I was pretty lucky. I will
     try to tell you a little bit about it. You may have
     seen some of this in the papers before you get this

letter, as a couple of reporters were around today.

Anyway, I was out on patrol and managed to slip into a German garrison with a couple of men. I shoved a grenade into the stomach of a commander, and he surrendered his position to me and told me where I could find his colonel. It wound up that myself and three men captured a peninsula, 850 Germans and a bunch of big guns, etc. I know all that sounds hard to believe. I am still dazed about it, but that is the way it happened, or at least all I can tell you about it. I am sending the case of the grenade home. Please keep it for me. If any of that is printed in the papers at home, send me a copy, as the reporters were from a New York paper, so I don't know if you will see it or not.

Well, I guess I had better close as I have a lot to do. Please write often and send me a box of candy bars if possible.

Love to all, Bob.

P. S. I have been recommended for DSC. Expect to receive it next week. Hope this doesn't sound like I am bragging, I am not. I was just lucky as the devil and I will admit I was a very scared boy.

We moved on foot for a short way and then we got on trucks and traveled back down the roads we had come up at a bitter cost.

The French people were everywhere. They were alongside the roads and when the trucks went by they were throwing flowers, offering anything they had to offer, food, drink, just like a victorious march. I don't know what the victory march was like through Paris or Berlin or anywhere else but I know for three or four days we experienced just a tremendous feeling of gratitude.

After about the third day we stopped in a rest area. We had a battalion meeting and the whole battalion was there. We were in no danger, assembling all together like that, as we were so far from the front. Rudder had nothing but good words for all of us. The casualties had been fairly light for the whole campaign.

However, he was very upset and very livid about a newsletter that the 29th Division put out a couple of days later that read: "29,

Let's Go", and then told the story of the 29th capturing the Graf
Spee Battery, completely ignoring the Ranger battalions.

Colonel Rudder went directly to the 29th Division Commanding
General and to the Ninth Army Commander and complained about
it. The next paper that came out printed a different story and gave
the credit to the 2nd and 5th Ranger Battalions.

In none of the histories that I've read of that campaign since
then, have they ever mentioned the actual units that captured the
fort. I've always felt that they did that because they were upset at
Colonel Rudder for screaming at them. It's pretty hard for a lieutenant colonel to give a major general hell, but evidently he did.

We were in a rest area and the sun was shining. Rudder was trying to show people that officers have some advantages, so he had a
mess tent set up for officers only. Usually we just ate out of mess
gear like everyone else. I went back to the officer's mess to eat.
We were all eating. I noticed that people were kind of remote to me.
They didn't seem as friendly and joking, like slapping me on the
back or making jokes about me. So finally I asked one of the other
lieutenants, "What is the matter? What's wrong?"

"Nothing, sir."

That's the first time that anybody had called me sir in a long
time. I said, "What's the matter with you, calling me sir?"

"Just a story I heard."

Frank Kinnard came over to me. He said, "Well, I guess you got
the report. You're being recommended for the CMH."

I said, "What's a CMH?" That's how stupid I was.

"The Congressional Medal of Honor."

I said, "Awh, bull!"

He replied, "Rudder is going to take you back to corps."

I learned later that Rudder had recommended me for the citation and all the guys had put their names on it.

Rudder, Courtney and myself, went up to VIII Corps
Headquarters, to General Middleton's office. He looked like God to
me. He was probably about 55 years old, but he looked like 110. I
was only 22. At that age we didn't talk to generals; I still don't very
often.

He read the citation out loud. He looked over at me and said, "Is that the way it sounds to you?"

I said, "Yeah, pretty much. I think that's about the way it went. Courtney here was with me."

He said, "I'm going to question the others separately." He asked Courtney and the jeep driver to leave the room. We talked about it a little bit. General Middleton said, "There is no question that you'll get it. If I send it up in this form, you will get the Medal of Honor. There are a couple of things that you need to know. The first thing is, I talked to General Darby." (This was a couple of months before General Darby was killed.) He had read the citation to General Darby on the phone. Darby had said that there was no question in his mind that I should have the Medal of Honor. This is what Middleton told me. He then said, "The fact is, no Ranger from World War II has ever received the Medal of Honor. There are guys who were in Sicily and Italy that did some tremendous things along with the guys on the beaches of Normandy. Not one has received it. The second thing is that you're not going back to your outfit. You're going home today. We can't take the risk of a Medal of Honor winner being captured. They could use it as a propaganda thing. If they caught one of the great Rangers that had been decorated with the highest award, they could then drag him through the streets."

I looked over at Rudder. "Colonel, I don't want to go home."

He said, "Well, Bob, you understand what the Medal of Honor is?"

I said, "Yes, sir, I know that it is the greatest honor that you can get in the Army. I'd love to have it. I wish that they could give it to me after the war is over, but if I have to go home and leave A Company, I just flat don't want it."

"Well, I think you should go ahead with it. I agree with how Darby feels. This is an exception."

I said, "I don't think that it was any greater than what you all did up there at Pointe du Hoc when Lomell knocked out the guns." I thought to myself, "Who am I?" I was a 1st lieutenant sitting in a room with a colonel and a general. I said, "That's it. I don't want it." I got the DSC instead. There was some talk about a CMH when the war was over. Five or six years ago someone brought it up again. But it's too late.

RESTRICTED
HEADQUARTERS NINTH UNITED STATES ARMY
Office of the Commanding General
APO 339
29 October 1944

AWARD OF DISTINGUISHED-SERVICE CROSS. By direction of the President, under the provisions of AR 600-45, 22 September 1943, as amended, and under authority contained in Circular No. 32, Headquarters European Theater of Operations, United States Army, 20 March 1944, as amended, the Distinguished-Service Cross is awarded to:

First Lieutenant Robert T. Edlin, 01293387, 2nd Ranger Infantry Battalion, United States Army, for extraordinary heroism in connection with military operations against the enemy. On 10 September 1944, on Le Conquet Peninsula, France, Lieutenant Edlin, leading a four man patrol, captured one of the outposts and moved into the main enemy position. Taking one of his men with him to aid as an interpreter, he reached the commandant's office. Here, he pulled the safety pin from a hand grenade and, holding it against the commandant's side, called upon him to surrender, or die. The commandant capitulated, surrendering an entire battery consisting of four 280mm guns, supporting small-arms positions, barracks pillboxes and approximately 800 prisoners. By his ingenuity, personal courage and willingness to sacrifice his life, Lieutenant Edlin brought about the surrender of the most important enemy installation in the sector. His extraordinary heroism and courageous actions reflect great credit upon himself and are in keeping with the highest traditions of the military service. Entered military service from Indiana.

Dave Jacobus Private Collection
Courtney with pockets full of grenades

Edlin and Klaus reading letters from home

12

REST AREA

We got duded up because it might be that Dinah Shore was going to look at us;
that's the way we thought back then..

–Robert Edlin

W ord came down that Dinah Shore was going to be a featured performer in a USO show. It was to take place fairly close to us. When the Brest campaign ended we had gone into a rest area and had been sitting there out in the country for four or five days, not in combat.

We got duded up because it might be that Dinah Shore was going to look at us; that's the way we thought back then. We started to walk up the road to the show when Colonel Rudder came along in a jeep.

"Hold it. Everything's off," he said. "The trucks are going to be here in about ten minutes to take us to the railhead around Reims." Patton had broken through there. "We'll be moving out in about a half-hour."

So we didn't get to see the show. We packed up and were moving up the road. Here comes Dinah Shore, riding in a jeep, pulling up alongside each of our vehicles and singing parts of songs. She stopped to talk and shake hands with us Rangers. I remember that well. We were just thrilled to death.

The 5th Rangers missed the show too. When we left the Brittany campaign at Brest, we never saw the 5th Rangers again till the war ended. We knew what they were doing; we heard stories about them. But after that we were about five hundred 500 miles apart.

At the railhead, we boarded the old French boxcars called 40 and 8s. A French boxcar could hold either 40 men or 8 horses. That's how the French did it in WWI. It was a very slow moving train.

Pfc. Morris Prince wrote a good description of that train ride:

We were tightly crammed and packed into these old and decrepit French boxcars, commonly referred to as 40 hommes et 8 chevaux (40 men and 8 horses) which had seen better days in World War I. . . .the cars were filthy and dirty before we entered them and by the time we ended our travels a pig sty would have appeared to have been a place of sanitation in comparison. The only compensation we got from this trip was the excellent opportunity to view first-hand the landscape that is beautiful France and to derive the experience that only such a journey could entail. . . .The more crowded we became the more we joked, the dirtier we got, the more we laughed and the more we traveled the better we liked it. . . .There wasn't an inch on the floor that wasn't covered by someone or a part of someone's anatomy. A mortar base plate was turned into a pillow and a "K" ration box, miraculously enough became a bed. What a life and what an ordeal, yet an experience we wouldn't want to have missed for a million dollars.

This was a five or six day trip. It was not a comfortable trip. We had our own mess kitchen on the boxcars and we would stop alongside the tracks for meals. With 35 men to a boxcar, it was pretty crowded. We couldn't play leap-frog or anything like that. In the daytime we took turns sitting at the doors of the boxcar, looking at the French countryside. Naturally, there was a crap game going on somewhere.

Every time the train stopped, the French civilians were everywhere. They were screaming and yelling, treating us like we were conquering heroes or something. A lot of trading went on for chocolate bars, chewing gum or cigarettes, whatever we might have for vegetables or fruits or whatever the French had available. Altogether, it was a pretty nice trip. We enjoyed it. Or I know I did.

We always had several people with our unit that could understand enough French to carry on a conversation, and there were always a few French people who spoke English. About the third day we passed through the outskirts of Paris. We saw some of the towns we had read about in history books and heard about all our lives. We didn't get the opportunity to go through Paris at that time; that came at a later date. But we did see the Eiffel tower off in the distance.

After 750 miles on the train, on October 5th we arrived in Longuyon, France. We loaded onto trucks and moved to a rest area inside a large forest around Arlon, Belgium. It began to get pretty chilly along about this time.

We started training and got the replacements in we needed to bring the companies up to strength. We did five to ten-mile hikes. We did a lot of athletics and played a lot of football. I want to add a story here about a football game. I've told it to my children so many times that I still remember it well.

The 2nd Rangers were playing a corps headquarters football team. It was a pretty close game; the score was tied. They were a lot bigger than us and had a lot more men to draw from than we did. About 30 seconds were left to play in the game when our quarterback faded back to throw a pass to me in the end zone. I went wide and could hear the crowd roaring. If I caught the ball we were going to win the game. About that time the pop of the timer's gun was drowned out by the flat crack of a German Mauser rifle. All hell broke loose. The corps headquarters people stood in amazement while the Rangers hit the ground, most of them jerking out weapons and firing at a tree. A German sniper fell out of the tree and hit the ground. Some person shot the football just as I was reaching up to catch it and pop went the football. Needless to say, that ended the football game and the German sniper. Courtney, Dreher, and I ran over to the tree. Courtney said, "Look at that. Somebody hit him right between the eyes." Dreher said, "Yeah, but we would have won the football game."

I don't remember where this next incident took place. It really doesn't matter. Places run together. We were back in a rest area and I was in the mess hall. There was a good-looking kid there and a newspaper lying close by, *The New Albany Tribune*.

Dave Jacobus Private Collection

Serrette and Jacobus, Schmidthoff, Germany, 1945

Dave Jacobus Private Collection

Burmaster and Serrette

Dave Jacobus Private Collection
"Jake" Jacobus and Bob Edsall

I reached over to pick it up and he said, "That's my Tribune, sir."

"I don't care who's Tribune it is, I'm from New Albany."

He replied, "Well, I am too. Hot damn! You're Bob Edlin."

"Well, how'd you know that?"

"My mom has been talking to your mom. Have you gotten any letters yet?"

I said, "No, I haven't gotten any mail. You guys back in head-quarters get it before we do."

He said, "Yeah, Mom told me that your mom and her are good friends. They live in the same housing project, about three or four houses apart. I guess they sit and talk about us everyday."

That's just another example of a small world.

Next we traveled to our new campsite, an orchard just outside Eupen, Belgium. Eupen and Esch, Luxembourg were the most Americanized places that I saw anywhere in Europe. Most of the people seemed to speak English in both places. They had ice cream parlors similar to the ones we had back in the States. People were very compatible, just fine people.

While here, a young second lieutenant and I went into a Corp Officer's Club in Eupen. They were kind enough to open the hospitality room to the Ranger battalion. Of course, that didn't last too long.

The first night we were there, we noticed a lieutenant colonel from corps headquarters dancing with a young nurse. The young lieutenant with me, Ed, decided he would like to dance with the nurse. I encouraged him to go ahead and cut in on the officer. That would be the normal thing to do.

So, he tapped the colonel on the shoulder and they talked a minute or two. He came back and said, "That joker wouldn't let me dance with her. He's not letting anybody cut in on him."

Now, we'd had a couple of poppers by that time and I got a little upset. I said, "Ed, I'm going to go out there and talk to that guy and see if I can't convince him to be a little more courteous to combat people."

So, I went over and tapped the colonel on the shoulder and he said, "Well, what do you want?"

"I really don't want anything. I kind of thought maybe you ought to let that nurse dance with the lieutenant if he wants to."

"You Rangers are causing enough problems around here. Why don't you and I just step outside."

So we did. He began to tell me how he was a boxer at West Point and an officer and a gentleman and why didn't I just take off my coat and we'd settle this thing. I started to take off my coat and when I got it about half way down my arms that cutie sucker punched me. There were four or five people gathered around and I heard somebody say he hit me with a flashlight. I don't know what he hit me with but he whopped me upside the mouth and knocked me back against a jeep. I was about half out. By the time I'd recovered the M.P.s were there and asked me if I wanted to file charges. I said, no, I didn't want to file any charges against a lieutenant colonel. It would just cause a lot of trouble. They took me to the hospital where I got seven stitches in my upper lip. I can feel that thing right now. Then I had to go back to the battalion and suffer all the joking and kidding about what happened.

We had a meeting the next morning about a training program and Colonel Rudder asked me what happened. I told him that it really wasn't our fault but we had run into some smart alecks. He asked, "Are you going back to the officer's club tonight?"

I said, "I don't particularly want to go back to the officer's club tonight. I'm not in much of a partying mood."

He said, "Well some of us are going, so you're going."

That night several of us went back. I don't remember how many, but we went in and the manure hit the oscillator. The colonel hit the colonel and away we went. After the fight was over, we pulled out and went back to the rest area. The next day Colonel Rudder called a battalion officer's meeting and said that the officers of the 2nd Ranger Battalion were restricted from the Corps and Army Headquarters Officer's Club in that area. I guess oil doesn't mix with vinegar too well.

FOXHOLE LIVING

It was starting to turn really cold. The temperatures were getting down below freezing. When we slept in foxholes, usually we put three men to a foxhole. Our body temperature would get the place warm after a while. However, sleeping between two lovely young ladies would have been a lot better than sleeping between Courtney and Dreher. Many a night they told me to get in the middle. They wanted to get me warmed up first. The lieutenant is in charge and responsible for getting food; he's responsible for getting ammunition; he's responsible for going up front and checking the line out and taking care of his men. An enlisted man, if they had a good leader, whether it be a platoon leader or a company commander, would take care of him because they wanted to keep him; they didn't want him to get hurt.

I had to wake up every two hours to go out and check the line. We had outposts. In a foxhole we had two or three men; two men were sleeping and the other was awake. The foxholes were five or ten yards apart. If no one was alert, the Germans could come creeping in and take out the first foxhole. Then a guy could have the enemy coming at his back; he wouldn't think it was the enemy. Then the enemy could take two more men out. Then they're 30 yards into your line. So every two hours I had to get up and go check the lines. I won't say that I did it every time. Klaus checked for me a few times. Courtney did and Dreher did. Most of the times, at least three or four times in a night, I was up there to let the guys know that I was not back in a castle somewhere taking it easy.

We talked in the foxholes, but not a lot. I talked with the guys about what we had done that day, how we could do it better, and what we might have to face the next day. We'd say things like, "Bill down there, how's he holding up? Are his feet all right? Joe, down there on the right hand side of the line, wasn't he down there on the end last night by himself? Let's get somebody down there." Stuff like that. Somebody might say, "I got a letter from my mom yesterday." We might talk about our moms awhile. I don't recall a lot of talk about girlfriends. There was some I guess. Guys kept that pretty personal. I talked to some officers about their wives, about how they worried about them. You can't worry about your wife, you can't worry about your girlfriend, your mother or anybody else. You've got to keep your head open. All the way. We were there for one reason. To get the damn thing over with so that we could all go home. The obstacles were not only the enemy; the obstacles were our own people sometimes.

The Third Army had driven up almost to the German border and supplies were very short. Oil was short, gas was short, everything was short except cold weather and there was plenty of that. I decided, while we were still in the rest area, to take a trip to visit a friend I had met when we had been stationed in Wales. He was now in the 28th Division. I went up to visit him on the Sigfried line; they were located just where the "dragon's teeth" were. I got to regimental headquarters of the 112th and they directed me up to where K and I Companies were.

I found them very down in spirit; their morale was very low. I wanted to crawl up to the top of a little hill there to take a look into Germany, since that would be my first look at it. The company commander, a friend of mine in the past, wouldn't help me go up there. He was afraid I might draw fire on them. I said, "What the hell, that's what you're here for, to draw fire and to fight back." I went to battalion headquarters and a fellow, who had graduated at the same time I had from OCS, was now the battalion commander. He looked like he was forty years older than he ought to be. It finally dawned on me, they had had a hell of a fight through the Normandy country up to where they were now. They were one of the units in WWII who were probably punished as much as anybody.

When I got back to my Ranger battalion, I was so happy to be with people who were there to fight and were not afraid to risk their hide a little bit and didn't want the war to end with them laying on their butt in a foxhole somewhere.

After the Brittany Peninsula campaign, we were at a rest area about three hundred yards behind the front lines but close enough

Dave Jacobus Private Collection

Virgin, Sargent, and Taylor

Dave Jacobus Private Collection

Burmaster on left

Dave Jacobus Private Collection

Sgt. Bill Klaus and Lt. Bob Edlin

for artillery fire to hit us. Once a week the intelligence officer of the battalion had to get together the companies and give then a lecture on current events, the story of how things were going in the war and how things were going back in the States. They did that regularly.

On one particular day, C Company was gathered under a tree like it was a Sunday afternoon for their briefing. A and B Companies had already been briefed. Morrow and Middleton, also from New Albany, had joined the Rangers in the States before me, and had landed with C Company on D-Day. I'd see them every day and they were under the tree with the rest.

I was in a fox-hole probably 40 yards away. I remember glancing over at them. The sun was shining, a little breeze was blowing and it was a little chilly. Lt. Heaney was giving them the story. Goranson was there. I was looking down when I heard a crash and I knew it was a shell. It had hit that tree and tree burst followed. The shell burst to the ground.

To this day nobody knows if it was one of our rounds or a German round that hit the tree. I heard screams. Immediately I was out of my hole at a dead run. I heard Klaus holler at me, "Don't go, Bob. Don't go. There might be another one."

It didn't register on me. I looked back and there was 10 more guys coming too. We got up there and it was desolation. There were guys everywhere spread around. The first man I grabbed was Oscar Morrow. He looked up at me and said, "How bad is it, Bob?"

"It looks like it's your right shoulder. You're going to be OK, though." I hollered at somebody, "Put a tourniquet on him and stop the bleeding right now."

Aid men were starting to come, but in the first few minutes the guys took care of themselves. Somebody put a tourniquet on his shoulder. I turned to the next one and it was Ray Middleton. They had been sitting next to each other, of course. Old buddies.

He said, "God, Bob, it hurts."

I looked down at his leg, I think it was his left leg, and I knew it was gone right above the knee.

He said, "How bad is it?"

"Ray, it's badder than shit. Let me do what I can to stop the blood. I'm going to put a tourniquet above the knee and stop the bleeding."

By that time an aid man was there and said that I had done the right thing. He said, "What now?" I said, "Well, can't you somehow bandage that thing and hold it together and get him back to the hospital with the leg?" He said, "Hell yes."

He made kind of a sling contraption. His leg was just holding on by two fibers. Of course, he lost that leg. They couldn't do anything for him. Doc Block told me later that there wasn't any need even looking at him because his leg was gone. He had to be taken out of there.

Much later, it was Easter Sunday, 1945, my mother sent me a picture out of the local newspaper showing a veteran at the church services. He was praying for his brother Rangers that were still in Europe and might be going to the Pacific. It was the most heartrending picture I'd ever seen. It was Ray sitting there with the Ranger patch on his shoulder, some ribbons on his chest and his leg gone with the flap up on the seat. I showed it to some of the guys and I took it over to C Company. They actually cried when they saw it.

The next clue we had that we were going into a tough battle was when they gave a number of us three-day passes to Paris. It was a long trip back, but what a thrill! A chance to see this famous city.

I saw it all right! I checked into a Red Cross billet. It was a hoity-toity kind of place. You were not allowed to do any drinking in the building—a ping-pong and chess type deal which didn't set too well with most of the Rangers. I got a hot shower, clean uniform, good chow, and was out on the streets to see the Eiffel Tower, Arc de Triomphe and the great museums. But I never saw any of it. I had gone to Paris with a group of Rangers, but I kind of lost them somewhere. Among the mass of dog faces in the street came a familiar figure, John Leone, last seen by myself at Camp Shelby, Mississippi in 1941. John, now in a combat engineer battalion, had left with our original unit from New Albany.

We howdied and shook hands. Johnny offered to show me around what was at the end of the museum trips. We discussed old times over some strange liquid stuff till we ran out of money. That was my sight seeing trip to Paris.

MEETING EISENHOWER

The first president that I ever met was Dwight D. Eisenhower when he was Commander-in-Chief of the Allied Forces. I remember he came down to a bivouac area in Eupen, Belgium. It was cold, rainy and wet. There were about 150 Rangers gathered around him and he was talking and laughing and joking. A perfect gentleman and just a fine guy. He asked the question, "Is there anything that you men need?"

Somebody spoke up, but it wasn't me, "Yeah, how come you're wearing a boot pack to keep your feet warm and dry and you don't get out in the rain or anything and we don't have any."

The boot pack was a kind of an overshoe they had just started issuing. One of the other men in the battalion yelled out, "Well, everybody back at headquarters has got them."

Which was true. Back in Army headquarters, and corps and division headquarters, everybody was wearing their boot packs, parkas, and warm clothes and we were still wearing summer clothing and the temperature was now down in the low thirties and high twenties. The good stuff doesn't go to the front line troops first; it goes to the rear echelon and headquarters' troops and slowly works it's way down to the line troops that really need it. They get it last.

General Eisenhower said, "That will be taken care of." God rest his soul, it was. Evidently he went back and caused a ruckus because it was only a few days later that we received supplies and boot packs and even wristwatches. Stuff that we never had. He must have raided the whole headquarters unit to get enough for one Ranger battalion.

ARMY ATTIRE

I liked the German helmet better than the American helmet; it covered the back of the neck better. However, our helmets were more than just something to cover our heads. It was also a cook pot, something we could make soup in. In a rest area we would shoot some rabbits or one of the guys would make a trap and catch a rabbit. We had guys that could do anything. Then we'd have rabbit stew.

We also used it as a wash basin to take a bath in. In dire emergencies we also used it for sanitary use. If we were in a foxhole and under heavy artillery-fire, bowels have to move regardless. We couldn't get out of the hole if we were under heavy artillery fire. The assault might have continued for 48 hours. As a final resort, we would fall back on the helmet.

In the beginning we had been issued raincoats. In the summertime they kept us hot and in the wintertime they kept us cold. They didn't keep out much rain but they helped some. We used them on maneuvers in Louisiana and England. I remember we had a pack with our rolled blankets at the bottom. There was a flap on the back of the pack where the mess gear would go and a carton of cigarettes or whatever. Straps came down and attached to the cartridge belt. Then across the top we had our raincoat or overcoat, if we had one, rolled up like a blanket roll, and strapped down. If it started to rain we had to take the raincoat off and put it on over the pack. I would say, most of the time after a while in combat, we got rid of them. They just weren't very good. When we got into the combat part, we couldn't burden ourselves with everything.

The overcoats were the same thing. They had the ones that came down to our ankles if it was GI issued. They were comfortable and warm, but if they would get wet, we could never get them dried out again and they became very heavy.

We had to carry our pack, our rifle or some kind of weapon, and we had to carry ammunition. We also had to carry rations. When we went in on D-Day we were lightly loaded, but we still had packs that weighed 50 or more pounds. Well, a guy like me that jumps in the water carrying 50 pounds will be dragged right on down. So a lot of us, including me, dropped them pretty quick. I dropped my gas mask right away too. I figured I'd rather be gassed than drown. That's the way I looked at it.

WEAPONS

I had two guns during the war. The Tommy gun and the M-1. I liked the M-1. I'll tell you what happened to me that happened to so many other guys. I carried a Carbine at first. It's a smaller gun, semi-automatic but it still shoots a .38, a smaller shell. However, it wasn't as accurate and didn't have any range to it. We got rid of those. Going in on D-Day I carried an M-1. The M-1 weighs over nine pounds. Most officers carried Carbines but in the Rangers we could carry whatever we wanted. So I carried an M-1. Then when we got in to close combat, within 30 to 40 yards, even though the M-1 is semi-automatic, for close-up work a Tommy gun is 100% better.

Early on in the war, if the enemy was over 200 yards away, I was carrying a Tommy gun and then I couldn't reach him. If I was 30 yards away I was carrying an M-1 and I didn't have the fire-power. So I started carrying one on each shoulder. Several other people did that too. I would do that as often as I could.

After we captured the fort at Brest, I took my Tommy gun and I started to carve "Fool Lieutenant" in it. I thought it would be easy. I didn't get very far, however. Whitie did a little carving in it and I guess everybody else did too. But then I did a foolish thing and let it get away from me somewhere down the road. Somebody, some-where might have it.

PRACTICAL JOKES

In the rest areas we always played jokes on each other. Enlisted men and officers in the Regular Army were not very close, but the Rangers were different.

Klaus remembers some of the pranks I used to pull:
> We had a couple of days off. We were in a German house. He and I were in a room and the door was closed. He was writing a letter and I was bugging him. If I was to threaten him his favorite thing to say was, "There's nothing stopping you but your nerve." He threatened to hit me and I said, "There's nothing stopping you but your nerve."

About half a second later I wound up out in the hallway lying on top of a door. He was so quick that I didn't know what was happening. I must have gone backwards, hit the door, the door came off its hinges and I wound up in the hallway on top of the door. I started laughing. He didn't mean to hurt me. We were just being playful.

RATIONS

The water bag, which is the most important piece of equipment in the army, was on the water trailer. They'd bring up the water trucks with a water bag that we called lister bags. These were big bags that looked much like a punching bag. They were back at battalion headquarters somewhere around the mess hall. We would go back and fill up our canteens or if we were on the line we'd fill up a five-gallon water can. I'd drag a can over to three or four holes to see if they needed water. Then I'd have one of them take it on to three more holes until we all got water.

The basic ration was the D-bar. The D-bar was a fortified solid chocolate candy bar. D-bars were used when we were on a quick mission and they didn't expect us to be out for very long. It was appropriate when we couldn't carry very much. We were only supposed to eat one D-ration bar a day.

The next ration up the line, was the K-ration. When we went into combat we carried three K-rations in our packs. K-rations were the size of a box of popcorn. The breakfast K-ration might have scrambled eggs in a little bitty can, some biscuits, a package of coffee, sugar and maybe four cigarettes. For lunch, it might have a little can of Spam and a cookie or whatever; supper would be a small can of pork and beans. I'm talking smaller than any cans you can find in a store. It was just enough to sustain you for a few days.

C-rations were what we ate when we were in a foxhole. Maybe once a day, two or three guys would go back to battalion and bring up some C-rations. The C-rations contained an average size can of corn or peas and a can of Spam.

We went from foxhole to foxhole distributing the C-rations so everybody could get a hot meal. A patrol would go back to the battalion and pick up four or five packages of C-rations. Most of them had a little table that we could light. It would come out a real blue hot flame. We'd dump all this stuff in our mess gear and set it down on the top of this fire. The trouble with it was, if we got our food hot enough to eat, we burned our hands.

The mess gear was just a plain dish on the bottom with an aluminum top that had divisions in it. They would fit together so we could hold them in one hand. Along with that, we had our canteen cup. At breakfast time, if we weren't under artillery or machine-gun fire, runners would carry up a five-gallon water can of coffee. The runners crossed along the hole and would fill the guy's coffee cup. That's the way we did it.

Then we had the 10-in-1 rations. The 10-in-1 means 1 package will feed 10 people one meal. So the can might have a three-pound ham in it. We didn't have our battalion cooks there. We just had our platoon. So, three of those 10-in-1 rations would feed a platoon. A couple of guys would cook the meal and then the rest of us would go back one by one to get our food.

Officers in combat are supposed to eat last, always, but I had my meals handed to me. They would bring it to me and say, "This probably isn't done or you probably won't like it, but we have to get rid of it." That's the way they treated me.

If we got closer to the battalion in a rest area, then we would have battalion meals. If we got lucky we would have beef. Wild steers or wild cows, it seemed, were always attacking Ray Charles. He would have to shoot them. And then after they were shot, the logical thing to do was to strip the animal down, butcher it and eat it. So that's where we got our beef. In order to stay out of trouble with the high brass, we'd say, "Well, this cow went crazy, so we had to shoot him."

Then we'd run into wild chickens. They would be cackling and giving our location away to the enemy. We'd have to grab them by the throat and squeeze them. We figured since they were dead, we might as well eat them. Usually this was not something that was official. Nobody told the battalion commander about it.

Depending on whose turn it was to go rustle up some food, they'd go find some vegetables and some meat or whatever. Or fish.

Sometimes we would drop a grenade into a river. The explosion would stun the fish and they came to the top. Then we'd eat fish.

It didn't matter if we had two cows, which would give us all the hamburger and steaks we could eat, or 50 chickens. We donated it all to the company mess and the whole battalion ate on it, because the next day, some other outfit might get lucky and we might not. So that's the way we did the big meals. I do remember at times being very hungry. But sometimes I was so scared, I didn't know whether I was hungry or if it was my stomach tightening up with fear.

When on a patrol in the lead position, it can feel like suicide. And then the stomach really tightens up. When I was lead man, if I came to a bend in the road, I could feel the bullets hit my stomach. A guy could stand no more than a half-hour of this torture. The guy just behind usually wasn't too anxious to get up there either, but if he was a good man, he was watching the front guy. There would be no set time to rotate, but if he saw the point man begin to hesitate a little bit, then he would go up and relieve him. That front guy then would normally go to the rear of the platoon.

We were usually following five to seven yards apart. If the whole platoon had been used up taking the point position, then we probably had covered five or six miles. So the first platoon then dropped all the way back to the rear of the 2nd Ranger Battalion. We kept rotating the point position that way.

In the regular infantry, they had guys that just couldn't pull it. I can't fault them. I can't recall one time, though, that a guy didn't take his turn at point in A Company. And I never heard about anybody in any of the other companies. There was just too much pride not to.

When someone was the point man, he was crouched down, like he's snooping in poop. He would move as low as he could and stay very, very alert. If we were moving down a road, we had patrols out on the flank. We were looking for any clues, like a hawk or buzzard circling. Maybe there was something dead up ahead. I don't think we were taught this. We didn't have any instructors that had been in that type of combat. We just figured it out. But I haven't seen a modern field manual. I don't know if present day Rangers are teaching that kind of stuff or not. Our manual was dated 1914 and covered only the basics.

When we moved down a road, let's say in France, and there were civilians alongside the road waving at us, "Vive le Americans," we could bet that the Germans were at least three or four miles away. There were also the Free Forces of the Interior, the FFI or the French guerrillas. On a patrol, if they dropped off to the rear and the civilians stopped showing up beside the road, then we knew we'd better hunker down a little bit and increase the gap between men. If it was night, we might have to keep the gap pretty tight. The Germans could grab the guy in front and we'd think he was still out there. They could continue and get the second guy and kill him. Or we could move our whole battalion through the German lines and they could attack us from the back. So we had to be constantly alert.

SINGING SONGS

We sang songs as a morale builder. We sang when we were walking along the road, when we got drunk, or when we passed a column of regular infantry. We wanted to let people know that we were Rangers. This was, of course, done behind the front lines. I remember a couple of songs we sang. *We are Rangers true to the red, white and blue. We'll fight for the wounded we adore. Give a battle cry, ringing through the sky, bringing freedom to every shore. We are Rangers true to the red, white and blue. We'll fight till the last man is down. Keep your eye on the grand old flag.*

Another verse, *When the Rangers come there's no beat of the drum, just the flash of a cold steel blade. . .*something like that sang to the tune of the *Grand Old Flag*.

I don't know who made the songs up. I know I didn't, but I sang them all the time.

V-MAIL

We sent V-mail home and didn't have to pay postage. The folks back home paid postage when they sent letters to us though. The 1st sergeant would get all the mail.

When I wrote home I stayed away from telling about the combat side of it. I tried not to say too much. Our folks would send us packages. Sometimes I would write home to ask them to send some cans of salmon, if they could get it, and cookies. We could make salmon sandwiches that were nice.

After D-Day, when the first mail came in, there were bunches of boxes of stuff. For those that were dead and received packages, the decision was made not to send the boxes back to the families. We opened them up and distributed them amongst the rest of us. The letters were returned however. Some of the *Dear John* letters came after the guy was dead. That's the way life goes. When someone got killed, the company commander or the platoon leader sat down and wrote a letter to the person's parents, when we had time.

I wrote one to Shireman. Earl Shireman was from Corydon, Indiana, 20 miles from New Albany. He got drafted and joined the Rangers and was in A Company when I got there. I was a 1st lieutenant and he was a buck private.

He came up to me one day and said, "You know, we didn't live too far apart. I'm from Corydon." So we'd sit and talk about that quite a lot. It always meant a lot to me that he was only 20 miles from my home. Unfortunately, he was killed on the beach. I wrote the letter to his family.

FRENCH-GERMAN FRATERNIZATION

The Germans had been living there for four years. The French knew where the Germans were. Anybody that thinks there wasn't any fraternization between the French girls and German soldiers, they're crazy.

We heard about some of the Germans that were living with

French women just as if they were husband and wife. We would hear about German officers living with the mayor's daughter. It happened.

I can remember one little town on the Brittany Peninsula. Some outfit had taken the town and we were moving through it to attack the next town. There was a big commotion in the town square. We stopped to look and saw three or four women down on the ground having their heads shaved. The other men and women were holding them down and shaving the women's heads. These women had been fraternizing with the Germans probably for years. The town's people, who knew about it and hated them for it, were getting even with them. Everybody knew they were German sympathizers or prostitutes, whatever you want to call them. That was the first time I saw that.

HYGIENE

Sometimes we would be in a foxhole and feel absolutely filthy dirty, just crummy! If the firing let up and it wasn't too bad, we would get a helmet full of water and take off our shirts. This would be, of course, in July, August or September. We would take our dirty socks and rinse them out and use them to wash up under our armpits and clean ourselves up a little bit. If we could get the water halfway hot, we could possibly get a shave. We'd cut ourselves pretty good but we'd get somewhat of a shave and feel 100% better. Then we would wash our socks and let them dry out. That's the best we could do. We didn't have towels or washrags.

But we didn't take a bath every day. Sometimes we went two or three weeks without a bath. If we were lucky, we would come upon a stream or river that we could use to bathe in. We needed to be sure of what we were jumping into, though. The first thing we did was send a patrol out and check each bank to be sure there weren't any mines or booby traps. Then we'd move the patrol back a half-mile or so both ways. When we were sure it was clear, we would set up an outpost maybe two or three hundred yards across the stream. Half of the guys then would take off their clothes and get in the water, play and jump around all they wanted to. When their time was up, whoever was in charge would yell and those guys would come out and get dressed. They would pick up their weapons and take over the job of guarding while the other half would go in. But that was rare.

In Germany there were separate latrines for the officers and the enlisted men. That was an old thing. You have to keep some distance between rank because if you don't there's a lack of respect. When I was a sergeant I had a great deal of respect for officers, lieutenants, captains, and colonels. Then when I got to be an officer I lost respect for some of them. I got closer to them and I found out they weren't the guys I thought they were. They were just people like the rest of us.

Dave Jacobus Private Collection
Jesse Serrette taking time for a quick shave

Rangers traveling by truck to new mission

THE GREEN HELL OF GERMANY

To the guys that were at the Hurtgen Forest, it was worse than D-Day.
–Robert Edlin

W e pulled out of the rest area and went forty or fifty miles towards Germany in trucks. Our next mission was to go into the Hurtgen Forest to capture the Roer Dam. I believe the plan was for the 4th and 28th Infantry Divisions, plus an armored division, to come through the town of Aachen. From there they were to move through the Hurtgen Forest and the town of Schmidt to take the high ridge there. The danger was that the Germans could blow up the dam and flood the Roer Valley making it impossible for the American troops to get across and advance forward into Germany. Our job was to capture the dam. We were to team up with a cavalry unit and do a quick raid on it. As it turned out this never came to pass because the 28th Division, the 4th Division and I think a total of four or five armored divisions, for various reasons, were unable to get their job done.

The Hurtgen campaign started in October with the capture of Aachen. We arrived in November. The months of November and December were terrible for us; it was the worst winter that had ever been and one of the most terrible battles that you could ever imagine. To the guys that were at the Hurtgen Forest, it was worse than D-Day.

The 28th Division and the 112th Infantry were on the ridgeline at Germeter. Heavy German forces releasing heavy artillery fire occupied the high ridgeline of Schmidt. When we arrived we found that the 28th Division, also known as the "Bloody Buckets" because their losses were so great, was nearly decimated. At least three infantry divisions had been almost wiped out in the fighting there. Some of them actually dropped their weapons and ran in retreat. Some of them surrendered. When we were brought in, it was a last resort. The battalion that we relieved had a thousand men and we were only 500 Rangers.

We drove up to the fringe of the Hurtgen Forest, just 30 miles from Aachen.

The Hurtgen, a 50-square mile area, is a tremendous wood with big trees. Dense! One could hardly walk between the trees.

Capt. Ralph Goranson, C Company, remembers that one of his men had a special talent, particularly when we were in the Hurtgen:
    "The Germans had a habit of freshening up with 4711. It's an aftershave that was very popular in Europe. It still is. This one ser-geant that I had would be like a pointer in the morning. Like a dog, sniffing. Especially in the wintertime. He'd say, "They're over there. I can smell them." The Germans, not knowing we were close, would be freshening up. Instead of shaving, they'd wash their hands and have something to eat and then they'd put a little aftershave on. That smell would come with the breeze. That's when we were in the Hurtgen forest—the green hell of Germany!"

It was cold and just coming on toward dark. The mud was ankle deep. It was snowing so we were wearing overcoats. A ridge-line ran from Germeter to Vossenack and then there was a valley. As I started up the hill I encountered an officer from the 112th, my friend Captain Preston Jackson. He told me, "Bob, that is the worst fighting that I've ever seen in my life up there. I wish you would-n't go. I wish you'd just flat tell them you're not going any fur-ther."

I said, "Jack, is that the condition of the 112th Infantry?"
    "It is." He told me that there were men up there that I would-n't believe would ever lose their nerve and they had gone com-

pletely blank. "They absolutely can't hold out any longer; it's the most miserable thing that you've ever seen in your life."

"Well," I thought, "we'll calm things down." How I thought five hundred men could do what four infantry divisions couldn't, I just don't know. But, you know the funniest thing about it was that eventually we did just that.

A Company was to take the town of Germeter, C Company Vossenack. Part of B Company was in Germeter and part of it was to go to the left of Germeter.

The hill leading up to Germeter was almost more than we could overcome. It was a terrific hill—almost like climbing the side of a mountain. We were following what looked like a fire trail. The snow was coming down and it was getting on towards dark. Artillery fire was breaking on the ridgeline. Jeeps were stuck and couldn't get up the hill. Nothing could move.

I was at the rear of my platoon since I had stopped to talk to Jackson and the platoon was beginning to straggle a little bit. I was trotting, trying to catch up to my company. However, I was carrying a light pack where these men were carrying a full load. They were carrying full ammunition, bazookas, mortars or whatever, and they were having a terrible time staying up with the front of the line. The enemy realized that something was happening and were throwing 88 shells and small arms fire on top of us. After seemingly hours, we finally reached the top of the hill. We came to an intersection we later called "Purple Heart Corner." I guess there were more Purple Hearts earned there than most corners in the world.

We reached the town of Germeter. We were to replace the 112th Infantry here. When the soldiers were coming out of the houses they had just occupied, I saw that the last guy out was a company commander from my hometown of New Albany. We chatted for a minute or two. He said he knew the Rangers were coming and he was hoping to see me. He told me that this was one hell-hole and if I could get out, to get out anyway I could.

I went into the first house on the corner, which was the house we were to take over. This was mistake number one that I made. Now I know: don't ever take the first house on the corner; get down in the middle of the block.

We went down into the cellar of the house. The 2nd Platoon had gone into the house next to us. I told 1st Sergeant White to put a man at the top of the stairs and a couple of men out at the front, where I knew there was an outpost, a listening outpost, to talk to battalion if I needed to. I hunted up Captain Arman, our company commander. We got together with Major Arnold, who was more or less in charge of A, B, & C Companies at the time. We decided all we would do was hold the ridgeline. Our mission was only defensive and we expected the Germans to counterattack. The 3rd Division had moved out and was gone. The 4th Division, on our left, was to be here just a couple of days more. We were told to just hold our line.

We went back to our little shanty on the hill. The guys that had been there before us had charcoal fires burning in tubs. It was smokey down there but warm. I said, "What the heck is wrong with this? It's warm, comfortable. We've got a roof over our head. There's nothing wrong with this." We ate some rations and rested up. All we had to do was leave a guard at the head of the stairs and an outpost once in a while. We put in a telephone line, which was promptly knocked out.

An idea occurred to me. I don't know where the idea came from. I said, "Let's go outside and act like we're digging a foxhole. They're going to know that we're changing troops in here anyway." The Germans usually welcomed new reinforcements with more artillery and tried to beat us down. So we threw some dirt up there and acted like we were digging some foxholes. The idea was for the Germans to shell the foxholes instead of shelling the house. The rest of A Company saw us digging and they went out and did the same. B Company's commander, Sid Salomon, told his men (I heard later), "I don't know what that 'dumb-ass Edlin' is doing out there, but let's go out there and do it too." Then we went back into the basement.

When daylight came the German artillery just beat in there where those foxholes were. The barrage woke everybody up; it brought us to our feet. Periodically during the day they would fire heavy fire on the trenches to pin down the troops they thought were in there but we were safely in the cellar, still keeping up the charcoal fire. For 10 or 12 hours they shelled those holes and we sat back and laughed at them. If you've ever heard a car crash or a plane wreck, the sound was minor compared to the artillery that poured in on those positions. Round after round punched, beat, and slapped the ground. They completely tore those foot trenches apart.

One of the young fellows, a platoon runner, saw a wild cow running down the street. He was afraid it would hurt somebody and he shot the cow for safety's sake. Then somebody in the group, who had been a farmer or a butcher, cut the cow up and hung it out for a period of time. The steaks were delicious with a little bit of potato wine. I don't give a damn where you go—some Ranger some place will find some cognac, some vodka, or some potato wine. Man, I'm telling you the 1st Platoon of A Company was eating high on the hog that night.

Then the Germans wised up and got mad, I guess, and all of a sudden the artillery started coming in on us—mortars, 88's, and tank fire. We were in the basement and they shot the house down around us. I'm telling you, it was the purest hell I'd ever been through. It was round after round of crashing and smashing, beating on our heads until we thought that there was no way we could stand it. I was lying on my back on the floor and the only way I could keep my sanity was by joking with the men. Guys were all around me, just lying there. I started saying, "Well let's see, if I would be directing that artillery fire . . ." I'd say, "Up 100 yards. Right 100 yards. Fire two." I was trying to relieve the tension. Then I'd say, "Left 50 yards, open her up. You're right on the house." I was telling jokes, you know. I was just trying to keep the morale up. Most of them realized it. Then one guy looked at me and said, "You're directing them to shoot right on us, Lieutenant!" Another guy said, "You damn fool. He's just playing, trying to make us relax."

We went through another hellacious shelling with several more casualties. The first one hit the basement. It went off. That was a terrible moment. An artillery round came into the cellar and exploded. I heard Sergeant Fronczek, a staff sergeant, moan. When I got to him it was the most terrible looking wound I had ever seen. His jacket and shirt were ripped apart. I pulled his shirt open. Shrapnel had torn across his chest. His lungs were exposed. He had a pack of cigarettes in his pocket and I could see the tobacco shreds being sucked into his body as he struggled to breathe.

I hollered to Klaus, "Do we have any contact on that radio?"

He said, "I can't get the company right next door, but I can get the battalion."

I said, "Just as quick as they can, tell them to get some medics up here and get this guy out of here. He's going to die." In only a few minutes two guys and a medic came in under heavy shellfire like you wouldn't believe. They came down into that basement and put him and a couple of other guys on a stretcher. They carried them upstairs to a jeep and they were gone in two, three minutes time. Shells were breaking all around them. How those guys had the nerve to come up there in a jeep, I'll never know. Within half an hour we had word from Doc Block, our battalion medic that he would make it. And he did.

We stayed in there. We had 30 men to start with and came out with only 13.

When the artillery lifted, we found Major Arnold and had another meeting. Major Arnold and Captain Arman came over and told me Rudder needed me to take a patrol to Schmidt. The town of Schmidt was the high point in that area. The high ground is where the artillery observers can observe down during the firing. So in combat the high ground is the ground you've always got to take. The major said, "Bob, we're not going to tell you how to do it, we're just going to tell you to find out if there is any enemy infantry in Schmidt. We need to know if there is going to be a counter-attack because we've only got 240 men between here and Brandenberg. I don't want you to risk any body. Take just a couple of guys like Dreher, Burmaster and whoever you want."

THE TRAP

I took Courtney, Dreher, and Burmaster, just a four-man patrol. We started out across that frozen wasteland that ran probably three miles down through the valley and up the hillside to the town of

Schmidt. As usual on a patrol, we rotated the point man as much as possible. This was open area; we could stand on the hill at Schmidt and look down at Germeter and Vossenack in the valley and see a flea move during the daytime. Now it was dark and snowing again. The snow was probably eight or nine inches deep and we were moving along a road. I was afraid to get off the road because this had been a battlefield. I figured there were minefields everywhere. I told Courtney and Dreher, instead of fanning out into a diamond patrol as we usually did, I would go out in front about 75 or 100 yards and then they were to come together behind me. Burmaster was another 50 yards back as the getaway man. These men were so good that immediately they took issue with it; all of them wanted to lead the patrol. I reminded them that I had been ordered to take the patrol to get the information and also I had the rank and we were going to do it my way.

We moved up the hill. It was quite a climb. It was as bad a climb going up to Schmidt as it was going up the Germeter hill, except now we only had light weapons. I think we were carrying Tommy guns and fighting knives. We didn't have helmets; we didn't carry anything else at all since we were not up there to get into a fight, but merely to get information. Not only was it physically trying but also mentally trying. We expected gunfire at any time. We had been receiving heavy artillery fire from this area now for two nights and two days.

We came up to a black top road and moved to the edge of town. Everything was quiet. There was no artillery fire; there was nothing. I knew that the 28th Division had captured Schmidt a week before we got there and then had been driven out. Then they captured it a second time. We looked down the streets of the town of maybe ten thousand people and found it deserted. I brought Burmaster up. I told him we were going to check through the town a little ways. "Hold here and if you hear any gunfire, take off at a dead run, get back to the battalion and tell them that there were no troops or anything until we hit the first building." A premonition came to me—a warning that I guess comes to a lot of combat men. I told Courtney and Dreher to wait there also. "I'm going through the town."

Dave Jacobus Private Collection

Dave Jacobus Private Collection
Jacobus and Klieve

They said, "No way."

"There is no point in risking all of us. I think it's a trap." I left Courtney and Dreher there and moved into the town by myself, probably 50 or 60 yards, cautiously. I was sneaking around the buildings. Absolutely nothing. There should have been some self-propelled weapons in sight, some activity somewhere. There was absolutely no sound. Even though it looked like it was a wide-open town, it smelled like a trap. The same thing had happened to the Rangers at Cisterna, Italy. The Germans let two battalions go right through their lines and then closed in behind them and annihilated them, wiping out the 1st and 3rd Ranger Battalions. I thought this was going to be the same thing here. Of course, we'll never know.

I got up to a big building on the corner, kind of a barn. I heard some voices. American voices. I thought, "What the hell is this? This really smells bad to me. I'm supposed to jump into this building to see what's in it." Instead of that, I crawled around to the side and listened. I could hear American voices and then I could hear German voices. I thought, "These guys are prisoners of war in there." The Germans were telling them something. I found out later they were telling them to keep talking English, keep talking English. They knew that I was in the town. They knew where Courtney and Dreher were.

I had had enough. I pulled out and went back and told Courtney and Dreher, "Let's get back to battalion as quick as we can." I didn't want to put this information on the radio because the Germans might be listening in. We picked up Burmaster and went back under shellfire.

When we got back, Colonel Rudder was sitting at the command table. I told him that I had gone all the way through the town without any firing. He listened to me. For a colonel to listen to a 1st lieutenant when somebody is pushing him to do something is really something.

"Colonel, it isn't what I saw, but what I didn't see."

He said, "That's what I'm interested in. What did you *not* see?"

"I did not see any Germans. We could walk right through that town." Then I told him about the prisoners.

He said, "You think it's a trap?"

I said, "Yes, sir. I think it's a trap like the 1st Ranger Battalion experienced at Cisterna."

He said, "You're a smart lieutenant. We're going to up grade you about one rank and down grade you about two. Why didn't you get your butt out of there sooner?"

So, here is the real end of that story. Twenty-five years later I met a guy by the name of Patterson, a judge down in Kentucky who had gone to OCS with Jackson and I. He had been a good friend of ours. He came up to me at a Ranger meeting. We talked. He was one of the troops who had gone into Schmidt and was captured there. He told me that he had been held prisoner in Schmidt, in a large barn along with some fifty other American soldiers. They had been held there for three days before they moved them back to a prisoner of war camp. While Courtney, Dreher and I had been standing outside the barn debating on whether or not to advise our higher headquarters that the place was open to attack, he was probably inside that barn. He had heard American voices. Patterson swore that he was in that building. But he hadn't known that it was me outside. He was told, however, that there was a Ranger out there. At that Ranger meeting, a quarter of a century later, we sat and hashed it out and it all fell together. I truly think that he was in that building.

We went back up the hill again. Mud, sleet, snow, ice. Then the temperature was probably two above zero. But, you know, every year and every beer it gets colder and colder. We got back in the basement with the other 13 Rangers and had been gone about 12 hours.

In the Hurtgen, we went 30 or 40 days without a shower. We were in combat almost constantly. No bath. We had to get water brought to us. The odor of a man that hasn't had a bath in 30 days, well, there is no odor because you smell the same way. We continued to change our socks every day, though. We carried two pairs of socks all the time. We might have only had them on for four or five hours. We would take them off and wash them in snow. Then we put them under our armpits to dry them and they would dry in about an hour. It would freeze our butts off to start with. We were careful. As a result we didn't have much frostbite in the Rangers.

Those times are difficult if not impossible for people to grasp. I heard Lomell make this statement, "These guys that write the books and people that read newspaper stories, they just cannot understand what it was like. They nod their heads and say, 'Is that right? Boy, that sure is something, ain't it!' But they don't know."

Now I'm quoting me. I don't see how anybody, my mother, my son, my dad, or anybody could understand what it was like to be up there with the temperature ten below zero or even ten above zero. It was colder than hell. It was snowing and sleeting for 30 days in foxholes and the basements of houses without a shower and very little hot food and very little of anything. I mean minute after minute, day after day. Constant artillery fire falling on us. Guys screaming, people getting hurt. Ten replacements come up and we didn't even know their names and the next day only two of them were left. We didn't know if they were dead or where in the hell they were. We just didn't know. Then when we'd gone through all that and try to tell about it to someone else, it's pretty hard for them to grasp what we are getting at. It was the most horrible thing to ever have happen to us. But all of this didn't break the Rangers. Honest to God's truth. It's been published in many books. The only reason that I can see that it didn't break the Rangers is that same old thing—our fellow Rangers needed us.

Of course, this was also a time when we weren't getting any letters from home. When we were in active combat and in a foxhole, nobody was going to bring us a package with cookies in it with mortars falling all around and machine-guns and snipers firing. We also wouldn't crawl back to get it. We didn't need it that bad to risk our lives for it. Good food was scarce also. Every once in a while we would send a detail back to drag up some hot food of some kind. But mostly it was C-rations and K-rations. We had been in the Hurtgen Campaign for 40 days. A Company was the first company up the trail into the Hurtgen Forest to relieve the 28th Infantry Division.

B COMPANY TRAPPED IN MINEFIELD

We were one "beaten down" little platoon now. The only connection we had with the rest of the world was by radio. I knew the 2nd Platoon was still in Germeter; I just didn't know where the rest of the battalion was. I guess that's what you call *battlefield isolation.* We were just 13 men now against the whole German Army. Bill Klaus, Gabby Hart, Courtney, Dreher, and I huddled together. Someone said, "Let's don't panic. The whole damn U.S. Army is around here somewhere." We got ready to settle in for another night of hell when I got word to report to battalion headquarters. Not a patrol, just me. I told the guys, "Hang on, we're probably being relieved. I'll be back in a half hour or so."

Carroll, my runner, and I took off down that terrible fire trail past "Purple Heart Corner." All the way, the steep trail was frozen and the snow was now asshole deep. I didn't even know where battalion headquarters was. We were slipping and sliding. They could probably hear us in Berlin.

We finally came onto an outpost of the battalion bivouac area. They were expecting us. It was early evening but darker than the inside of a black cat. I told Carroll to rustle himself up some hot chow and wait at the mess tent.

I finally located the battalion headquarters. Someone told me Colonel Rudder himself wanted to see me. I knew then we were not being relieved; I didn't need to see the colonel for that. Rudder was billeted in a small building sort of like a hunter's shelter about the size of a small bathroom. In it was a little kerosene stove, table, a couple of chairs, and a double bunk bed. Captain Arman, A Company, was sitting on the bunk. Colonel Rudder was huddled by the stove. "Big Jim," as we called him, was only about 35 years old, but he looked like a tired, worn-out old man. I had never seen him this way.

I started to report in a military manner, but he just said, "Sit down, Bob." I did and he handed me a cup of hot coffee. He looked at me for a minute and said, "Arman is here to make arrangements to relieve B Company, but we've got a problem. I heard from Sid Salomon a short time ago. B Company is pinned down in a minefield. They're under heavy artillery and machine-gun fire with a lot of casualties."

He continued to talk and I learned that B Company had been pulled out to a gap in the woods between the towns of Germeter and Bergstein. They had sent what was left of B Company, about 50 guys, to fill the gap and patrol between two infantry divisions. About two miles into the woods they got into a minefield.

Sid Salomon, B Company Commander, tells about his ordeal better than I can. In 1987 he wrote these words:

B Company moved into the Hurtgen Forest area it had been ordered to hold, advancing a couple of hundred yards forward from where the divisional company CP had been located. The going was difficult. The divisional company had not provided the Rangers with a guide. The night was black, few stars were out. The forest was littered with fallen tree limbs and leaning trees as a result of the devastating artillery barrages from both sides. The lead platoon of the Rangers walked into a German minefield in the pitch darkness of the forest, probably just short of the German front lines. Several mines were set off by men stepping on them, low moans ensued as the Rangers attempted to stifle their cries of pain in order to protect the rest of the company. While the men of the lead company held their positions to avoid setting off other mines, the other Ranger platoon dug foxholes for themselves and their lead platoon associates. The aid man, in the black of night, did his best to attend to the wounded and performed admirably.

They were trapped in the minefield. B Company couldn't find a way out. They didn't lose anybody, but if they took a few steps they could be blown up. So they dug in. The ground was frozen so they couldn't dig in very well but they did the best they could. The rest of the battalion had already pulled out of Vossenack and back into a rest area.

Rudder continued talking. "I need a volunteer to take a patrol in to find a way to get to them, make arrangements to relieve them, and try to bring out some of the wounded. The patrol needs to go in now. A will relieve B tomorrow night. I'm not going to ask you to go, but that's the situation."

The picture ran through my mind like a kaleidoscope. I thought, "I can't take any more of this. I'm tired and scared. This would be pure hell and I can't stand anymore of my platoon getting slaughtered."

But we went. Courtney, Dreher, Burmaster, a driver, a medic, and myself made up the group. We started up there in a jeep and rode about a mile down the road with artillery all around us, stopping at a point where we thought B Company was located. It was hard to believe what we saw. The trees were knocked down by shells. Big trees. I thought to myself, "B Company must be taking a hell of a beating." We got out and I told the medic, "Grab a stretcher. Courtney, grab a stretcher too and we'll go in there and get out a couple of the wounded anyway."

The driver said, "I'm going with you, Bob."

"No. You've got to stay here and watch the jeep."

He replied, "Do you think somebody is going to steal it?"

I couldn't argue with him there. So he came with us. He didn't have to go in there. He was a very brave man.

The first few yards off the hardtop were not bad, just slippery ice and snow. Then we were into the trees. It was so dark it was impossible to move with a potential mine at every step. The trees were down as if a mad woodcutter had been through there with a giant buzz saw. I thought, "Shit, I forgot the marking tape, we'll have to go back."

Courtney sensed my thoughts, "We've brought the tape and we're marking the path."

I prayed, "Lord, just give me the strength and guts to make a few more yards, then we'll rest a minute." A shell landed 30 yards away. "Damn that was close." A few more yards, I heard a German machine-gun and not too far ahead. The snow was falling so hard that it was almost blizzard conditions; we couldn't see the guy right in front of us. A German flare lit up the bizarre scene. The flare showed uprooted trees, dead American and German soldiers, twisted bushes. No satanic artist could have dreamed up such a sight.

I didn't think I could make another step. Then a big hand clutched my shoulder. Sergeant Dreher. "Drop back behind Courtney and I'll get it for a while."

Courtney was 10 yards behind Dreher. I heard him say, "What's the matter, Lieutenant? You volunteered for the Rangers, didn't you?" Burmaster was there too. We all took turns with the lead. Except the medic and the driver. These guys were important and had to take care of the wounded. We, however were just foot soldiers. Another few hundred yards. The artillery was heavy and then machine-gun fire rattled through the trees like hail.

I heard a quiet voice challenge us from the B Company outpost. Geez, we didn't know the password. The voice asked, "What's the lieutenant's first name?"

Courtney answered, "Bob."

The voice replied, "Come ahead. I'll lead you to Captain Salomon's CP. It's under a small bridge by a woodcutter's trail."

Sid was sitting there. I could hardly see him but I said, "Sid." We hugged. He thanked us for coming. I told him we would take out the worst wounded now but we had marked the path and A Company would be in at 2000 hour tomorrow night to relieve them. The B Company medic, Clark, would help us get the wounded out.

Artillery was still coming in and there was an occasional machine-gun fire. We decided to carry out two wounded at a time. The jeep driver and Courtney started back with the first litter following the luminous tape. The second medic, William Geitz, loaded another litter and picked up the front end. However, he was standing on a mine and didn't know it. He wasn't big enough to set the mine off, but when I picked up the other end of the stretcher all the weight went to Geitz. It exploded. The last thing I saw was a silhouette of the man on the stretcher, his body going up into the air. I learned later that man died but the heroic medic, Geitz, survived but lost a foot. Fitzsimmons, a good friend of mine, was hit in the face. The blast of shrapnel knocked me into a tree. I thought I was gone. I must have been unconscious for a moment. I became completely blind and deaf. Then I reached over and couldn't feel my left hand. I thought, "It must be gone at the wrist. I'm going to die right here in this damn German woods." Strong arms picked me up. Dreher threw me across his back and on a dead run, ran all the way back to the jeep. He ran past Courtney and the other guy. He laid me down in the jeep. When the jeep driver got there he told him, "Get him to the hospital NOW. This guy we don't want to lose." That's what the jeep driver told me later.

I woke up lying on a stretcher. I wasn't blind. I could see a dim light and I could hear Doc Block's voice. "Wash his eyes out with Boric acid. It's just dirt and mud." I had some hearing in one ear. I could hear Doc say, "Take him back to a hospital."

"Wait a minute Doc, how bad is it?"

"You're not hurt bad, *gold brick*. A little shrapnel in your hand and face. They'll fix you up back at a field hospital, it's mostly shock and some mud."

I asked someone else in the aid station about the others. All they told me was everyone was okay.

I was put into an ambulance along with several others. I learned later, the medic who lost his foot, rode with us. I don't know what route we took, but the German artillery chased us a good ways. It ought to be against the rules to shoot at you when you're leaving somewhere. The morphine took effect and I woke up being lifted out of the ambulance. It was still dark. Someone told me we were at a field hospital. I was taken into a brilliantly lit tent. My vision was getting better. A doctor told someone to clean me up. They worked on my face and hand. He came back and told them to get me ready to move back. They acted like I was a number. I yelled out, "Wait just a damn minute."

A nurse came over and told me, "Calm down, soldier." I told her, "I ain't no damn soldier. I'm a lieutenant in the Rangers. Get your ass in gear and get your commander over here." That got their attention.

A major came over and explained they had no time to treat the slight wounds. We had to be sent to the rear and the field hospital had to treat the severely wounded. I told him, "I know that, but isn't there some one here that will listen to me?"

"All right," he said, "I'll listen, but you are no better than the rest."

"Major, there are about 50 men from B Company still in that woods. About the same number from A company are going in to relieve them. I know the path into that death trap. If you'll clean up my eyes and hearing, I'll take them back up there. Then you can send me where you want, I don't care."

"Lieutenant, if that hand gets infected you will lose it."

"I'll trade a hand for 80 men." That's the way the Rangers were in 1944. The doctor told me he would take care of me at lunch time since he had a free hour then. He sent an order to the mess tent for breakfast. I had four fresh eggs with bacon and toast, the first good food in a long time. I asked the cook if they ate like this everyday. He told me that the doctor and nurses had given me their weekly ration of fresh eggs. I felt bad for about 30 seconds.

About 12 noon the doctor, nurse, and several large aid men came in. The doctor told me he could not use anesthesia or I would have to stay over night. He pulled the crusty bloody bandage off my hand. That hurt! Then I found out what the big aid men were for. One held my legs and one my right arm. The nurse held my left arm. He took a pan of hot soapy water and a scrub brush and went to work cleaning my hand. I was screaming, it hurt so bad. "The hell with A & B Company and the rest of the Rangers!" I never thought it could hurt so much. After this short period of torture, he took a knife and some tweezers. I remember he said, "This is really going to hurt." He was right. They counted 48 pieces of shrapnel that they removed plus whatever shrapnel stayed in there, put a bandage and sling on my arm and patched up my face. The doctor said, "You're on your own."

I knew he would be in trouble about the paper work. I asked him if he had any children. He said his wife and two boys were back home. "They can't wait for pop to come home and tell them all the stories about the war, especially about the Rangers."

I took out of my pocket some German money that a German soldier had loaned me. That's a joke. The German was a dead German. I gave them to the doctor and told him to send it to his kids. He was quite a man and one fine doctor.

I looked for a way back to A Company. It was November 23rd when I left the hospital. Cold rain, sleet, snow, and mud were everywhere. I went around the corner and saw a 2nd Ranger Battalion water trailer picking up water. I asked for a lift back to the battalion. The driver asked me why in the world I was going back.

I asked him the same question. "We can both just take off over the hill."

He thought about it a little and said, "Yeah, but the guys up there need this water. That's why I'm going back." Well, that's how I saw it, too.

It was nearly dark when we got back to battalion. I knew better than to go to headquarters. Doc Block would kick my ass, so I took off up that same Germeter trail again. It hadn't changed, it was slick, slippery, and slimy. I was dragging when I got past Purple Heart Corner. It was one dark, cloudy, snowy night. I heard shell fire in the distance. No one challenged me as I got into our beat up old house. It was empty. The charcoal fires were out and my platoon was gone. I realized they had gone to relieve B Company without me. It had been 24 hours since I left.

My hand and face hurt. I still couldn't hear, and I'd had about all I could take. I wondered, "Should I go on into the forest or go back to battalion? Lt. Arman and Lt. Porubski are up there with Klaus, Courtney, Dreher, and the rest. I can't stay here. I might get captured." So back down that hill I went setting a speed record on the way.

At battalion headquarters I found out Rudder had been called back to headquarters. Someone told me to take the colonel's bunk for the night. Someone from battalion mess brought some hot food, even cut it into bite size pieces and offered to feed me. Someone else from headquarters briefed me on the situation and told me the company was okay and would be withdrawn in a couple of days. About 30 men of A Company were the only members of the 2nd Rangers still on the line.

Dr. Block came in and checked my hand and face and read me the riot act for not going to the rear. "Doc, if you'll give me something for the pain, I'll go on back up to the company at daylight."

"Boy, you ain't going anywhere. Get your butt in that bunk and stay there." I agreed that I didn't feel so good. I would just rest a little while. When I awakened it was still dark but it was 24 hours later. Colonel Rudder was dozing in a chair while I was using his bunk. They just don't make colonels like that anymore!

After rejoining A Company the morning of November 28th, we were relieved by units of the 8th Division and joined the rest of the battalion in a rest area. We went back and started training to get replacements. We trained men in squad maneuvers and such. All the other infantry units were exhausted and resting but the Rangers were up doing bayonet training. The guys in the Rangers just wouldn't quit; they kept going!

Dave Jacobus Private Collection
Sgt. John "Dusty" Donovan leaning on top of truck

Dave Jacobus Private Collection
Lansome and Hurley

Dave Jacobus Private Collection
Bob Edsall and Dave Jacobus in
Arlon, Belgium, December 1944

14

HILL 400

Now they had taken that Hill in half an hour. They just walked up there with pure guts and gunfire and took it.

–Robert Edlin

About six nights later, December 6th, we got the call to hit the road. This time we were to be on the offensive. We could always tell when we were going to hit the road because just before, we always got a good meal. Our new objective was Hill 400, so named as it was 400 meters high. (Pointe du Hoc was only about 40 meters.) The Germans called it Castle Hill. This was the high ground and very important to the Germans. Sid Salomon, B Company Commander, 2nd Ranger Battalion explains: "The Germans were tenacious in their defense (of Hill 400), the ground which they were defending was to be the pathway for the projected German offensive, personally engineered by Hitler." Now if you can believe this, a total of six thousand men had tried to take the hill. Not all at one time, but various groups. And they were wiped out. They couldn't take Hill 400.

It was night—dark and snowing. We were going up to Brandenberg, Germany, and then on foot to a little town called Bergstein, which had been captured by an infantry outfit.

Pfc. Prince describes well our ride that night:
> Our mission was to take Hill 400, which lay about one half mile east of Bergstein, which was then our Army's farthest penetration into the east. We rode our vehicles in complete silence and darkness. We were huddled together like little lambs at the slaughter house. A cold

wind plus a slight drizzle were dampening our spirits and soaking us thoroughly, making our very existence miserable. We detrucked at a turn-about, which was a good four miles from the actual front. The reason was that any further progress of the vehicles would come under enemy shelling range and give our entry away. We wanted our entrance to be of a secret nature, so as to effect a surprise attack.

It was cold sleet, snow, and mud as we moved up the hard top toward Bergstein. Artillery shells were beating the road around us. I wondered, "Are the damn Krauts as tired as we are?"

About five rounds hit the road in front of us. I yelled at the platoon to hit the ditches. "That deep ice cold water should wake you up." We crawled for several yards over and around bodies, American or German, we didn't know. Actually, we had been in combat practically two and a half solid months by then. I got callused—hardened. Seeing wounded men didn't bother me. I'd just call for a medic.

Back on the hardtop, someone bumped me from behind. Geez, I had gone to sleep walking. More artillery! I thought, "I can't stand any more of this. Well, it can't get any worse." I moved back down the line, talking to the platoon. "Wake up you lazy bastards. When it gets too rough for everyone else, it's just the way we like it." They pepped up a little.

We learned that we were to go into and through Bergstein. D, E and F Companies would go up and capture the hill. A and B Companies were to go around and protect the flank of the hill so that the Germans couldn't counterattack and come in behind them and capture them. We were to act as an outpost to keep the Germans from getting up that side. I don't know where C Company was but B Company was next to us with the same mission.

As we moved up the roads, we were still under heavy shellfire. I was kind of crawling through ditches part of the time. The platoon was with me and the rest of A Company. I didn't know how the rest of them were distributed, but when we got up into the town of Bergstein there were American tanks burning, and bodies and slaughter everywhere. We passed on through that. A Company was assigned to outpost, or defend, the right flank of Hill 400 going up it.

As we were coming up the hill to Bergstein I saw a guy standing in the road shaking hands with everybody. I thought, "Who is that fool standing right in the middle of a crossroad shaking hands and I'm crawling through the ditches afraid that I might get hit?" I stood up and walked over and there was Colonel Rudder shaking hands and telling everyone goodbye and good luck. He'd been transferred to the 28th Division to become the commander of the 109th Infantry Regiment. His leaving was probably the greatest loss we Rangers suffered during the war.

When I got up to him, he put his arms around me. I was kind of his baby boy. He said, "Bob, don't take any chances. Quit taking chances."

I told him, "I'm through taking chances."

Sid Salomon puts Rudder's transfer into perspective:

A civilian does not understand this. Rudder turned down a promotion once. But the Army was in such desperate shape— Rudder was almost forced to take this promotion and then became a full colonel. It was a most inopportune time. It could not have been anymore inopportune than when it happened on December 7, which was almost as severe for us as June 6, 1944. The timing was just very poor on the Army's part, but the Army doesn't think of the small unit. They're thinking of the so-called big picture. Which is understandable. It's how it should be. But consequently we suffered a lot of casualties. And one of the reasons was the change of command at such an inopportune time.

Mrs. Rudder, whom I still stay in touch with, remembers that time when he left our unit also:

I didn't hear from him for six whole weeks. He had been given command of the 109th Infantry Regiment on the 8th of December and on the 16th is when the Germans came through in force and started the Battle of the Bulge. He wrote to me:

January 6, 1945

My Darling,

Note my new address because I am no longer with the Rangers. It was with a heavy heart that I went

away from them. No commander ever had the privilege
to command a finer bunch of men than they are. They
gave their all so freely as good soldiers should.

However, the unit I now command is a true
American fighting outfit. And their manner of performance in the recent crisis was something to
behold. It is unbelievable that men will withstand
the hardships they do and still give their all for
God and their country.

Love, Earl

We found some foxholes. One of the guys said, "Lieutenant
Bob, there's some foxholes here."

I said, "Well, they're German foxholes and they're probably
booby trapped. Go careful and look for booby traps." So they
checked out all the holes. They were all clear so we took advantage of those holes. They were dug deep and probably saved a lot
of lives.

Sitting on the bluff, we could hear the artillery fire coming in.
It was terrible and it was starting to come in on us too. It was worse
than the Hurtgen Forest. The history books say it was the greatest
concentration of artillery fire that has ever been. And we laid there
and took it. Along about daylight, the Germans sent a patrol
towards us. We defended the position pretty well. Someone made
the comment that the only thing warm on that hill was the BAR barrel; it was pretty hot.

Hill 400 jutted out from the ground like the Grand Tetons, flat
land and then all of a sudden there loomed a big hill. If I recall
right, there were trees all the way up to the top of it.

Then I heard the attack. I heard the American fire start. I heard
D and F Companies going up the hill.

In 1987 Sid Salomon compiled the 2nd Rangers' memories of
the Hurtgen Forest and Hill 400. Each man remembered it as if it
were yesterday:

(D Company's story) The 1st Platoon leader assembled his patrol
. . . and proceeded at about 0330 to make the reconnaissance of Hill
400. After climbing the steep hill, the patrol successfully gathered the

desired information...D, E, and F Company Commanders...quickly reviewed their plans for the assault...The assault of Hill 400 was to take place at 0730. D and F Companies were to move quietly to their line of departure by 0700 and be in a position to take off on the run at precisely 0730 . . . hooting and hollering all the way up the hill . . . As daylight dawned, Hill 400 loomed 400 meters high (1,312 feet), at a 45 degree angle, and thickly wooded with evergreens concealing a very important OP on top. It was actually a beautiful sight as dawn arose. One of the men commented, "Here we go with the old *King of the Hill* game." He was so right. A German artillery barrage started just as D Company began the assault. It was 0730 when the Rangers spread out and started to run . . . yelling as loud as possible and firing at random up the hill. This daring charge, carried out on the dead run into the small arms fire coming from the Germans on the Hill . . . resulted in a quick success . . . They continued running forward over the crest of the hill to their preplanned positions. One section sergeant took a patrol forward down the hill, almost to the Roer River, chasing the enemy all the way...heavy enemy artillery barrages rained down upon the Rangers almost continuously for the rest of the daylight hours . . . shells detonated immediately upon hitting the trees, causing the trees to come crashing down along with a shower of shrapnel; only a very few Rangers escaped being wounded by it; it was horrendous...The fire fights and assaults were at close range and from time to time resulted in hand-to-hand combat . . . Of the 65 D Company Rangers who had started off on the assault, only 55 men made it to the top of the hill, and then only 15 of that group walked away when the battle was over . . .

(F Company's story) All men armed with rifles were to fix bayonets, and all weapons were to rapid fire randomly up the hill. At the start of the attack, everyone was to yell as loud as possible . . . A several minute heavy artillery barrage (American) pounded Castle Hill . . . F Company took off and started to run up the incline shooting and shouting . . . Shortly up the hill, the CO and a squad of men ran into a pillbox, a complete surprise as intelligence information had given no prior knowledge of any pillbox . . . An outer steel door of the pillbox was partially ajar. As one F Company BAR man fired a burst into a gun port, another kicked the partially ajar door open still further, threw in a grenade, and quickly pulled the door closed. That created the desired effects as cries of "Kamerad" were heard, and out came a

Dave Jacobus Private Collection

Sgt. Bill Klaus

Dave Jacobus Private Collection

Dave Jacobus Private Collection

dozen or so stunned and wounded Germans. Some of the F Company men had already attained the top of the hill. . .It was now 0830. . .The F Company CO had already been wounded and before proceeding back to the battalion aid station, proceeded to call out coordinates to his radio man for close artillery support. The radio man was instantly killed by artillery before he could relay the artillery support request to the Bn. CP and the CO was again wounded. Radio communication to battalion was now lost completely. Two walking wounded were sent down with requests for reinforcements, more ammunition and additional medical supplies. Another German counter attack was repulsed by the remnants of F Company. In order to get reinforcements, the Company Commander started back down the hill towards the battalion forward command post. He did not get far. Along the way he apparently made the wrong turn amidst the fallen trees and debris. . .and ran smack into another pillbox loaded with Germans who overpowered him and took him prisoner.

We could hear the artillery and we could hear the American gunfire as they progressed up the hill. I heard them open fire with the BARs and the American Tommy guns and rifles. I heard the German small arms fire going off, there was a difference in their sounds, absolutely. I heard the American sounds get to the top of the hill in half an hour. Now they had taken that hill in half an hour. They just walked up there with pure guts and gunfire and took it. Casualties were terrible. They were just about wiped out. I think Len Lomell was leading what was left of them and they were almost slaughtered. But they held on.

I got an idea. The thought just kept coming into my mind. "If they counterattack again, why don't I take this platoon and slip round the hill behind them and come in with open fire from the back. Then they'll think they're surrounded and maybe they'll break and run and leave D, E, and F Company alone. Maybe we can pull the fire from them and then we can run." What I was going to do was leave my position at the outpost, move in behind the attacking Germans and open fire on them. Then I would slip back over in our holes again. I knew I could do this. I needed permission. I radioed back to battalion to the new battalion commander. Rudder was gone. A captain had been promoted that night to major. His name was Williams. My request was denied.

I went back to the basement of the house. We were under heavy shelling there, I guess everyone was. I hadn't been there fifteen minutes when I heard a crash. A shell had come in through the roof and was teetering at the top of the stairway leading into the cellar. We were afraid to touch it for fear it would go off. We were like prisoners. When we left the cellar, we had to slip around it.

Shortly after that, an infantry battalion came in to relieve us. Then they pulled D, E, and F Companies off the hill, what was left of them, which wasn't very much.

Sid speaks today about Hill 400:

Many years later, I and my oldest daughter, were trying to follow the combat trail of the 2nd and the 5th Battalions. We got to Hill 400 and climbed it. That was the first time that I had been back there since December of 1944 when we had our Hill 400 battle. My daughter and I climbed up on the fire tower up on top. Then I realized why the Germans so desperately wanted that hill. We stood up there, on the fire tower . . . that was there in 1944 and it's still there today. We could see for miles all around. It was a superb observation post for their artillery. It's understandable why they controlled that area. As long as they had the hill, they controlled the area. That's why our battalion took that hill. When I look at maps now, I realize some things. I've spoken to my good friend Frank South, and have said to him, "Holy Christmas, look where we were back then!" We didn't know it, but we were surrounded by the Germans. Remember, we didn't have the maps that are available now or the maps that divisions had. Being a separate battalion, we were like the runt of the litter. I guess that's the best way to describe it. We didn't get everything because the Army was not geared to a small independent separate battalion. They were geared to deal with a division strength. Remember a division in WWII had 15,000 men as compared to our battalion which had 500 men, and the 5th Rangers also. During our combat time, which was just under a year, we were probably attached to eight different divisions, and only about two or three of those divisions knew what to do with us. The top military commanders weren't familiar with Rangers.

I got orders to report back to battalion headquarters and get back as quick as possible. I thought there's no way I can make another patrol. I'd had just about all I could stand. I just walked down the road to battalion headquarters. I didn't care about artillery or anything.

Captain Block had just been killed by an artillery shell. This was another tremendous loss. It seemed like the whole battalion was getting tore up. I went in to headquarters and said, "Somebody called me back here, said they wanted to see me. I guess you got another patrol."

"Nah," he said, "you're going back to the States. You're going back to the States for a thirty-day rest and recuperation leave. Twelve are going back out of the Rangers."

A new policy had come down from Eisenhower. If a man had been decorated twice and had been in the campaign for at least six months, active combat, then he was eligible. I told them I didn't want to go. He said, "Well, you're going this time. You're going and Courtney and Dreher are going, and Len Lomell."

There were about 12 of us. He said, "Go back up and get your gear and get Courtney and Dreher and get back here. There will be a jeep waiting for you. Oh, and before you go, battalion sergeant major wants to see you."

So I went over to where he was. Sergeant Rubenstein was the sergeant major. "Yeah, I got your orders here and Courtney and Dreher's. You have a good time back in the States and don't come back."

"Well, I don't know about that."

I started leaving. Then he said, "Wait a minute. You've got some medals here." He went into a footlocker and it was full of Purple Hearts. He pulled out a citation and a DSC in a box and handed it to me. "That's yours."

A lot of people have told me in the years since that they would like to have a picture of me getting decorated. Well, there wasn't a formal ceremony. It was only Rubenstein handing me a medal and telling me to get my ass out of there and get back to the States. That's how I received the second highest award that the U. S. Army can give a soldier. I'm about as proud to have been decorated that way as anybody can be. That's maybe the way it should be.

I didn't walk, going back down the road; I crawled down through the mud. My hand was still hurting pretty bad, still had a bandage on it, but it was out of the sling. I got back and got Courtney and Dreher. I told Gabby Hart that Sgt. White had been promoted to a lieutenant and had moved up to D Company. Hart was the platoon sergeant. I told him that we were going back to the States but I didn't want any of the rest of them to know about it. "Hang on and maybe they'll get the rest of you out of here."

AMERICAN RED CROSS
CONTINENTAL HEADQUARTERS
— PARIS —

WELCOME TO PARIS!

LC · № 00003

Date 1 NOV 1944

1st Lt.   *Robt. E. Edlin*   O-Ð43382
RANK / GRADE   SIGNATURE   ASN

Upon presentation of this ticket at the Reception Desk

A. R. C. Lafayette Club
37, Avenue de l'Opéra, 37

arrangements will be made for your eating and sleeping.
    Since all our facilities and rations at other American Red Cross
Clubs have been reserved by the military authorities for other men on
leave. This ticket is not valid elsewhere.
    Do not lose it because it must be presented at each meal provided for you.
    The ticket is not transferable and can not be duplicated.

LUNCH	DINNER	BREAKFAST	LUNCH	DINNER	BREAKFAST

L C

15

ON LEAVE HOME

*There ain't no cab fare for people like you. You've done paid all the cab fare
you'll ever pay with me.*

–Bertha Webb

W e went back and there was a jeep waiting, sure
enough. We made it to the train, boarded and were on
our way home. It had been two and a half years since I had seen my
family.

I don't know how far we went on the train but soon the train
came to a stop. We heard rumors about a big battle taking place.
The Germans were coming through Malmedy, counterattacking in
a battle that would later be known as the Battle of the Bulge. We
were not too far from there. There was some talk about forming up
into squads, getting arms, and going back to aid in the battle. But
that never happened.

So we kept going on the train back to Paris. I have a picture
somewhere of Len Lomell and I in Paris celebrating.

```
EUROPEAN THEATER OF OPERATIONS
UNITED STATES ARMY
Office of the Commanding General
```

```
                                         APO 887
                                   December 1944
```

```
TO: Officers and men returning to the United
States.
```

GENERAL EISENHOWER has approved the return to
the United States for a thirty day furlough of a
limited number of personnel. It is right and proper that the first men granted this privilege should
be chosen from amongst those actively engaged on
the front. You have been selected by your Commander
as the most deserving from your outfit.

As Commanding General of the Communications
Zone, ETOUSA, I welcome you here to Paris; I assure
you that I, as well as all other members of the
Communications Zone, wish you God speed, a pleasant voyage and a. well earned vacation on our home-
land. During your absence we shall continue to do
all within our power to support your comrades who
are carrying on until you return.

                    Faithfully yours,

                    JOHN C. H. LEE
                    Lieutenant General,
                    U.S.Army.
                    Commanding.

Finally we got back to England. We shipped out January 1,
1945, later than planned due to the Battle of the Bulge. We were
on the *Acquatania* five days back to New York.

When we got off the ship, there were crowds welcoming us
home. Dances were held in our honor. There were newspaper
reporters scrambling for interviews and photographers taking our
pictures.

We went by the Red Cross tent. They gave us bottles of milk to
drink, the first fresh milk that we had had in about two years. Some
of us not for four or five years. I myself had never seen milk in a
bottle. All we had over in Europe were cans of condensed milk.

Old Bob Fitzsimmons was on the trip home also. He and I
decided to see what New York was like at night. We wound up on
Times Square, both of us still pretty beat up and wearing bandages.
We went into Jack Dempsey's place and as I recall we didn't buy

anything. We didn't need to. Jack Dempsey said we couldn't spend any money, not our own anyway. Everybody was buying for us. We learned that our fighting troops were in trouble with the Battle of the Bulge.

Then Courtney, Dreher, and myself, were sent to Camp Atterbury by train, nonstop straight through. They processed our papers there.

We were in somewhat of a dilemma. We didn't have any money. I asked someone, "How can we get some money?" We hadn't been paid for ages it seemed.

He told us, "When you get to your home towns, go to the army facility and they will give you partial pay."

When we got to Atterbury, I took a train to Jeffersonville, about five miles from New Albany. I got off the train and got on a bus to New Albany. There I found a cab. I really didn't know how people felt about returning soldiers. I walked over to the cab and there was a lady cab driver. This was unheard of to me. I asked her how far it was to MacArthur Drive. I didn't even know where my family lived but I knew the address. She said, "Oh, it's just a little ways. Jump in. I'll get you over there."

I said, "Well, I don't have any money. I don't know how much it costs."

She said, "We'll work that out later."

She put my baggage in the trunk and took me over to my home. She got out and got my bag out.

I said, "I can carry this."

"You've only got one hand. I can carry it."

I said, "Wait one minute and let me borrow the money from my mom for the cab fare." She proceeded to tell me, "There ain't no cab fare for people like you. You've done paid all the cab fare you'll ever pay with me." She got in her cab and left. Her name was Bertha Webb. I'll never forget her.

I had called Mom from New York and told them I was coming in. Dad had taken off work and he was there. The whole family was there. There was hugging and kissing. They told me Mom had gotten the telegram that Marion had been seriously wounded in action. She got the second telegram when I got wounded in action. Then

Bob Edlin Private Collection

Part of Ranger
battalion on
leave in Paris,
December 1944

Bob Edlin Private Collection

Sgt. Klaus kneeling in center

Bob Edlin Private Collection

Rangers on leave after Hurtgen Forest in Paris
Len Lomell, center, leaning on post

she got the telegram that Sam's submarine was missing. That worked out all right, but all together she had received five telegrams about her sons. I could see she had aged considerably.

```
                                 Saturday, Jan. 27
                                 Germany
Hello Bob:
     Well! Are you there? Hope so and hope you've
still got just about 30 days left in your furlough.
Well! You must have just got home today.
     Sure would like to have gone with you, but! The
guys who were really deserving are the ones who went
and I mean - you - Court and "Big Stoop." I'm damn
glad that you fellows got to go. I was nearly as
glad about it as you all were.
     Today it snowed again but we were pretty well
set up in houses. The news looks good over here and
it may be over soon - but who is getting optimistic,
not me. Sure would like to make the Derby this year.
I guess the tracks will be open by then.
     It wouldn't be so good for me, being home - no
races. We are doing some stiff training and a lot
of hoping that the Russians get to Berlin in a
hurry. Them boys can really scrap, I guess - must
be most all like you and Courtney and "Big Stoop"
and your boy "Half-Track." He's tops - all of you
are in my estimation, but probably more so in mine
than anyone else's.
     Bob, you are the best soldier - officer or oth-
erwise that I have ever known. I mean it. I toss
bouquets only where they belong where I toss them.
     Don't worry about the boys - nothing has hap-
pened since you fellows left except a little more
artillery absorbing - a long stretch of it this
time. We are all back and okay. Lt. Porubski has
done some swell work and Lt. Arman and all the boys
too.
     So long and have a good time. I'll see you some-
time. Best of luck.
                                 "Whitie"
```

My time off went quickly and was just great. When the 30 days leave was over I got back on the bus and went back to Camp Atterbury. Courtney and Dreher were there but I didn't see anybody else.

We got back to the ETO and found the 2nd Ranger Battalion. This was probably the middle of February. We pulled into battalion headquarters and found the commanding officer, Colonel Williams. Things had changed considerably; it didn't seem like the same old Rangers to me. But when we got back to our company, then it seemed like the same old Rangers. They had been through some hell at Simarath and had lost Half-track, who had been seriously wounded, along with some of the other guys.

Even we could tell the war was coming down to the end now. We did some more skirmishing and were assigned to be with the 2nd Cavalry Division, an armored reconnaissance outfit. We'd fly up the autobahns at 40 or 50 miles an hour or more and covered 50 miles a day. We moved across the Rhine.

I remember the next excursion. We'd only been back a couple of days. We were sitting outside of a little German town. Arman was there and we were talking. Everybody was gathered around. I said something about the big cliff across the road. "How long do you think it would take to get to the top of that thing?"

Some of the younger guys said. "Oh, about three or four hours."

Courtney said, "I think we can make it in about half an hour."

They started laughing.

I said, "Well, let's go!" Courtney and Dreher and I took off. We brought a flashlight so we could flash it at the top of the cliff when we reached the top. We were up there within half an hour. We flashed the flashlight and came back down, but everybody had gone to bed. They didn't even wait to slap us on the back or anything. But we enjoyed the challenge.

Though things were simmering down pretty much, we had a little combat along the way. One man got wounded pretty bad.

For our next mission, my platoon was attached to a tank outfit. We reported to a full colonel. We were ordered to put a stop to the *Werewolves.* The *Werewolves* were a group of young German soldiers that had deserted from the regular army and were acting as guerrillas. Orders had come down all the way from the Supreme Allied Command that these young men must be stopped. We heard they were stretching piano wires across the highway, cutting the heads off of jeep drivers. They were stopping supply trucks bringing supplies to the American soldiers as well as the German people.

The tank colonel told me he wanted us to take our platoon through a woods to flush them out. We did this but didn't find a single soul. He was pretty upset. He said, "Well, my orders are to get them any way we can get them. Go get them. That's your job, you go figure it out. I want them turned over to the American authorities." Then he added, "I'm not going to accept any responsibility. If there's any problems, they're yours. I'll deny that I ever gave you an order."

I went back and talked it over with Gabby, Courtney and Dreher and the other guys. We all agreed he was right 100%; we had to stop them. So we went into a little town there. I've never talked about this much. It's very distasteful to me. We gathered the townspeople together. There were a couple hundred people in the town square, men, women and children. We lined up 12 or 13 young German men from the ages of 14 to 18 which I suspected were the *Werewolves*.

I had an interpreter. I told the mayor of the town that we were going to shoot these men one at a time until somebody told us who the werewolves were. "We've got to put a stop to this, here and now." I explained to him that nobody would be harmed if they turned themselves in. They would then be turned over to the military authorities. They would be fed and clothed and taken care of the way they should be.

Not a word from anybody. I raised my weapon and one of the guys there in the platoon gritted his teeth and said, "I'll do it," and he fired a round. He was so shaky that he missed and hit a guy in the shoulder. Down he went. A woman came running and screaming, "Don't do it! Don't do it! That's my son!" The interpreter got the information from her that these guys were the *Werewolves* and where some more of them were.

My platoon immediately went out to get them. Somebody told us that the mayor was the head of the *Werewolves*. This time we got the message back to the corps and the military authorities came up. They took control of them all.

We were up near the war's end now, near the Czech border. I guess I made my last patrol there. I got called back to battalion and was told to take a patrol in through a small town and bring back some German prisoners. I assumed I could do it my way like I always did, but the battalion commander had already picked the men he wanted me to take. Twelve men. I said, "Sir, I don't need a 12-man patrol to get one prisoner." He said, "Just do what you're told."

"Yes, sir." He gave me the names of the men. They were from various companies. They were some of the guys that had gone back to the States and all of them were pretty well decorated with DSCs and Silver Stars. These were the real combat veterans. I thought, "Well why in the hell are we doing this? Why risk these people? They've had enough."

I took the patrol. We got out about a mile and I stopped and cut off nine of them. "There's no need risking all of us. Courtney and Dreher here will go with me." Eventually they all agreed with the plan, but to their credit, each of them was willing to go.

We came up to a bridge going right across into the town. I was carrying a Tommy gun which put me out in front. Dreher had the BAR and Courtney had an M-1. I lost it there; I lost my nerve. I told Courtney, "Give me the BAR. You take the Tommy gun and go across the bridge. I'll cover you."

He looked at me like I had beat him with a club or something. He started out and I said, "The hell with that!" I got my nerve back again.

He took the BAR and both of us walked right across the bridge. We let it all hang out. We climbed up to the top of the a little hill where we could look down. There were probably twenty German soldiers down there. Some of them were shooting craps on a blanket. We pulled some grenades and killed a bunch. But there were three or four left. We took them prisoners.

Courtney had gone into a barn there and found a bunch of rifles. I told him, "You go ahead and take the prisoners and head on back.

I'll bust up these rifles." I'm not sure why I said that.

I took three or four of the rifles and one at a time I swung them by the barrel, up against a post. I splintered them so they couldn't be used again to shoot us. I started swinging one and thought, "If that thing had a round in the chamber it might go off and hit me in the stomach." So I switched it around and swung it by the butt. I hit it up against the pole and the damn thing went off. Man! I dropped to my knees and I was sick, vomiting. I heard a noise and turned and there were Courtney and Dreher, both had come back when they heard the gunshot. They thought I had gotten hurt. They helped me up. I got over it pretty quick, but I kept thinking, "That was one stupid thing to do!"

We got back with the prisoners and turned them over to the battalion.

Our Commander-in-Chief, Franklin D. Roosevelt died on April 12, 1945, before the war was officially over. In my opinion, Roosevelt was the greatest president that ever was. I thought he was great. I felt he had saved this country. Of course, a lot of people thought that. The rich people didn't think that way, though. We were in a depression when he came into presidency. Nothing wrong with Hoover as the Depression was going to happen regardless of who was president. Roosevelt just overrode the Congress. He developed the WPA and the CCC and put young people to work.

When Roosevelt died, I think I felt like Frank South did. When he heard about it, he told me he had just sat down under a tree and cried.

Dave Jacobus Private Collection

My platoon on VE day.

16

THE WAR ENDS

I'd been doing this for four years. All of a sudden my job was gone.
–Robert Edlin

STARS AND STRIPES in the European Theater of Operations 1Fr.
Wednesday, May 9, 1945
'Cease Fire' Order at 0001 Today

Peace came to Europe at one minute past midnight this morning when the cease-fire order to which Germany had agreed went into effect.

Formal announcement of Germany's unconditional surrender had come nine hours earlier–at 3 PM, Paris time–when President Truman and Prime Minister Churchill proclaimed it in radio broadcasts.

At that moment the last "all-clear" sirens sounded in London and Paris, and the streets in both cities were the scenes of frenzied celebrations. America took the announcement calmly and quietly, having staged its celebration Monday when the premature Associated Press dispatch brought the news of surrender.

We were moving down the road when a jeep came by with someone in it hollering, "The war is over! The war is over!" I remember that moment. It was May 9th and I had just turned 23 years old three days earlier. We pulled off to the side of the road and stopped. Nobody disarmed themselves. Nobody did anything silly. It was hard to realize that the war was over.

Dave Jacobus Private Collection

Dave Jacobus Private Collecti

Dave Jacobus Private Collection

Pictured top, Bucher and Jacobus; bottom, Wade
Prague, Czechoslovakia, June 1945

Dave Jacobus Private Collection

I think Pfc. Prince put it eloquently:

We had traversed a road which had had many traps and pitfalls .
. . Many who had started out on this road fell by the wayside before
they had taken a couple of steps. Others had managed to come part
way, before they were overcome by the obstacles in the road. Yet
some of us did make the complete journey . . . It is hard to realize the
starring role that our company and battalion played in this history-
making epoch. It is hard to visualize that we were the actors in the
greatest play of all civilization; that we performed our parts with per-
fection. It is not difficult to recall the trials and tribulations we had to
endure in order to bring about the final curtain in this saga. It is heart
rending to review the time when we had to leave behind the main
stars . . . it is with greatest sorrow that we repeat their names and
remember their features as they went forward so gallantly and so
bravely. It is because of them that today this play has its conclusion;
it is because of them that hopefully despotism, tyranny and Nazism
are to be forever banished from this world.

Then we started thinking about the future and what we were
going to do. Talk about losing a friend. For me it was like losing the
greatest friend I'd ever had in my life. I'd been doing this for four
years. All of a sudden my job was gone. Now my whole way of life
would change. Nothing would be the same. It would become a
whole different world.

I thought, "Now what do I do? Can I better myself? Should I
stay in the military or what?" We sat around and talked about stuff
like that.

The very next day we went into a Polish prisoner of war camp.
The Germans had impounded these people. There were also some
Czechoslovakians in there. It was like the rest of them, Dachau and
the other prisoner of war camps, only it hadn't been there that long.

We saw racks of dead bodies, just skeletons piled up. That's
when I met a little Polish girl about 14 or 15 years old. I saw her
standing by herself, alone and very lost. I went up to her and started to talk to her. I was told that I couldn't talk to her by one of the
military police. I replied back that I would do what I wanted. I outranked the soldier.

I discovered she spoke perfect English. I alerted some people in charge about her talents and that they should consider using her as an interpreter somewhere. I thought it might give her a chance at survival.

I was pleased when, several months later, I came upon her working in one of the government agencies there. Evidently someone had listened to me. I was glad that I had helped her. It was probably her only chance.

For the first week after the war ended, we did a lot of drill and platoon action. Then finally higher headquarters realized that this was foolish, so they let us be on our own. We could do whatever we wanted to do if we had the money. Which we didn't.

Everybody was clamoring to go home. The mammas and the grandmas caused that. They wanted to get their boys home. We sang the words: *Oh, Mr. Truman why can't we go home. We've conquered Berlin. We've conquered Rome. We've defeated a super race. Now why is there no shipping space? Mr. Truman, why can't we go home?*

Then we got active in sports—boxing, basketball, fast-pitch softball and played other teams. We formed a battalion softball team. Everybody in the battalion wanted to play. Somehow I wound up as manager. I was also a pitcher, but not as good as a lot of them, like Zalaski. There were some great guys on the team including Dreher and Ray Alm. We had a record of 18 wins in a row and beat everybody including the 5th Rangers three or four times. You can emphasize that. We also won the olympics that some of the Army staff had organized.

We heard the Rangers were not going to the Pacific. We were going to be shipped home instead. Major Arnold and I went to talk to Colonel Rudder. We asked Colonel Rudder, a full colonel now, to transfer us into the 28th. We understood they were going to the Pacific to attack Japan. My brother, Marion, was still fighting there on Bataan. Sam, my other brother, was just getting out of the submarine service. However, Rudder wouldn't take us. He told us we'd had enough and to go on back to the States with the rest of the Rangers.

We went back to Camp Miles-Standish, Virginia and they disbanded the Rangers there. It was a heartbreaking time.

Dave Jacobus Private Collection

Dave Jacobus Private Collection

Bob Edlin Private Collection

This was my house in Czechoslovakia, June 1945

Bob Edlin Private Collection

My future wife Dodie, May 1945

I went to Atterbury and was given a thirty-day leave to go home, and did so. I was then ordered to report to Camp Chaffee, Arkansas. I went down there and the weather was pretty bad. I was promoted to captain. I had a battalion commander there, a lieutenant colonel who had spent the war in the Pentagon. He didn't like Rangers; he didn't like DSC winners; and he didn't like officers that had been recruited as enlisted men. He let me know that right quick.

We were on maneuvers, the second of three nights, when it started to rain. It was raining terrible. These guys were new recruits and had only been in the service about six weeks. I asked the colonel what I should do with the men. I felt they weren't ready for these conditions. He said, "Well, you're a Ranger. Just do it the Ranger way."

So I did. I outposted the area like I should and pulled the men back into some barns. I got some warm blankets and some warm clothing, hot food and we spent the night. The next day, of course, he heard about it. He chewed me out. I told him, "Colonel, I don't have to put up with any more of this. How do I get out of this outfit?"

He told me I'd have to go back to headquarters and more or less insinuated that he'd be glad to get rid of me. So I went back to headquarters and asked them how to get out. They said I had to have 85 points. I told them that I thought I had those. They checked and I had 145. They told me I could be discharged twice. I went back to New Orleans and got discharged from active duty March of 1946.

I took a job with my dad at Boyd Cummings but that didn't work out. I just couldn't do anything right. So I went back to New Albany and drank and fought. I had no money. But every Sunday night Dodie and I would go out to a movie or something. She was my Sunday girl. Finally, about November, I wised up and we sat down and talked. I told her I thought I was ready to settle down. "This stuffs over with."

She replied, "I think it's about time, too."

"Well, what do you think about getting married?" I asked.

"Well, to who?"

"Well, to me of course."

She said, "I don't know. I'm not sure about that."

I thought, what the hell, the world's coming to an end. I looked at her and I saw the twinkle in her eyes. She was kidding me. She asked me when did I want to get married. I told her just as soon as possible. We decided on December 7, 1946. So that's when we got married. It wasn't a fancy wedding. We started out with only seven silver dollars that I had won in a craps game. After the wedding we spent our honeymoon at Sam's house in Bennettville. I went back to work at Cummings Veneer making 22 ½ cents an hour.

Things were starting to heat up in the Korean War. I decided to join the National Guard and became company commander of K Company of the 152nd Infantry. They had only 18 men or so in their unit. I recruited my brothers Marion and Sam and within three or four months time we had a 185-man well trained outfit.

Bob Edlin Private Collection

1st Sgt. Klaus, front; S/Sgt. O'Connor, behind; S/Sgt. Bodner, right
Bavaria, May 1945

Indiana National Guard unit 1948.
Bob seated in center, with brothers Marion and Sam seated directly in front

17

RECRUITING BLACKS

In my estimation when the President of the United States, the
Commander-in-Chief, says to do something, I believe you ought to do it.
–Robert Edlin

President Truman in 1949, ordered all military units to integrate immediately. In my estimation when the President of the United States, the Commander-in-Chief, says to do something, I believe you ought to do it. So I tried to enlist four black people but I ran into some difficulties. The fact that they were all 6'4" and 6'5" and we needed good basketball players certainly didn't have anything to do with it. Actually, I didn't care how tall they were. They just happened to all be big fellows. But my superior officers turned them down; they wouldn't let me recruit them. A lady reporter actually interviewed the Adjutant General of Indiana and Governor Henry Shricker at the time and they both told her that regardless of what the President said, they were not going to let integration happen. Indiana wasn't ready.

But I figured the President outranked them so I went ahead with plans to recruit them. However, I had to resign to keep from getting court martialed. It's a story that's substantiated in the papers. It really happened.

After that my brother, Marion, resigned. My brother, Sam, resigned and about thirty other guys did the same. Al Singleton, a 2nd Ranger with me in France, also resigned.

I was elected to the Black Hall of Fame that year. They had my picture, in uniform, in the paper with the story about the Guard captain who was threatened with court martial for enlisting black people.

At about the same time, in 1950, some people told me I should run for sheriff. So I ran for sheriff of Floyd County, Indiana. In spite of receiving support from the mayor, I got beat. Shortly after that, the mayor of New Ulm, Indiana, called. He wanted me to join their police department. I took the job.

Robert "Bob" Edlin
Democratic Candidate for Sheriff
Floyd County
Primary May 2, 1950

New Albany Officer Has Close Call Disarming Man on Shooting Spree

Hoosier Misses 2 Other Persons

A man police described as "drunk crazy" shot at three persons and fired two bullets into a taxicab before he was overpowered by four officers at a New Albany service station at 4:40 p.m. yesterday.

Lawrence E. Watson, about 50, who gave his address as 514 E. Main, New Albany, was charged with shooting with intent to kill, carrying a concealed and deadly weapon, disorderly conduct, and public intoxication.

Misses at Close Range

Patrolman Robert Edlin, dubbed "that fool lieutenant" when he singlehanded caused surrender of 800 Nazi soldiers in World War II, had a close call as he disarmed Watson. Watson fired at Edlin at close range. A 32-caliber bullet from an Italian pistol penetrated Edlin's heavy leather pistol holster. The bullet was deflected and passed along his leg, grazing a path in the side of his trousers.

ROBERT EDLIN
Bags one more prisoner

Police Capt. Claude Neafus sent two cars of policemen to the service station, operated by John O. Ludlow at 202 W. Main, where Watson was reported to have shot at two persons and into the taxicab.

Police said the man shot at James E. Wayman, 721 E. Eighth, driver of the taxicab. When Ludlow went out of the station to investigate, he saw Wayman fleeing. Ludlow said Watson then fired at him. Police arrived about that time.

Overpowered by Officers

Patrolmen Edlin, Edward Hubbuch, Raymond Nale, and Robert Thurman rushed at Watson, who leveled his revolver at them. Edlin lunged for the man's gun and as he did so, Watson fired. Edlin then forced the weapon from his hand and the four policemen overpowered Watson.

18

POLICEMAN BOB

. . . they gave me a gun and a badge and away I went.
–Robert Edlin

At that time there was no training for police officers. I went in and they gave me a gun and a badge and away I went. An old friend of mine for many years taught me the ropes.

I was promoted to captain. To be captain you're supposed to be on the police department two years. So they gave me a temporary promotion. I told the mayor I didn't really deserve it; I didn't want it. I told him that I thought some of the other guys were much more qualified. He said, "Well, it's yours." All the guys told me to go ahead and take it, so I did.

I enjoyed the job thoroughly as a captain. I had a couple of tough cases that I think I handled pretty well. In about 1955 the chief of police changed. The new chief and I didn't get along but he was a good friend of the mayors and it was strictly a political town.

There was a lot of gambling going on. I went to the chief and I told him I thought we should raid the gambling joints. He said he'd take care of it. I waited about a week. I went back in and he told me to keep my nose out of it. I told him if he didn't do it then I was going to do it on my own. I got the warrants and I went. Everyone in the department knew that I was going to make the raid at 11 o'clock that night. When I got there, there was no gambling going on, nothing at all.

The chief called me in and informed me he was going to suspend me for 39 days for disobeying orders. We had some words and I told him I was going to get a lawyer. My first attorney was good but he was a Republican, just like the chief of police and the mayor. So that didn't work. Another lawyer volunteered his services. He was a good one, a Democrat and later a judge in Jeffersonville, Indiana.

We went before the city council and they listened to my side and the whole story. I lost my temper a time or two and then they fired me. This is exactly what my attorney wanted; he wanted me to get fired. Then we could file suit for civil damages. The judge was a good friend of mine. Testimony went on from each side. The mayor testified, the chief, everybody! One of the high points was when Officer Thurman testified that I'd saved his life. Somewhere in the testimony, the Hurtgen Forest came up and the judge leaned over to the clerk lady and told her how to spell it. I knew then that he knew all about Hurtgen.

When the testimony was over in the trial, the judge said it would be about 90 days before he came back with a decision. We went on home. We were in pretty dire straits. We didn't have any money. I was selling insurance part time and I started working a little harder at it. I started getting a little better.

After three weeks had passed, the judge announced he'd made a decision. He held court and ordered everybody to show. Just before the proceedings started, Sergeant Joe Friberger, head of the police department, came over to me. He told me, "Bob I think you won it, because the judge told me to arrest anyone that created a disturbance or anybody that made any noise, even if it was the mayor. That ought to give you a clue."

The judge announced I had won. They called it fraud and everything else. They awarded me back pay and reinstated me to my job plus a substantial settlement. I told him I didn't want the cash settlement if it wasn't from the mayor or the chief. If it was money coming from the taxpayers, then I didn't want to take it. I don't remember how much it was but I remember he said, "Are you sure?" I said, "Yeah, I don't want to do that." He said he'd take care of it. So I didn't get the cash settlement. He ordered me back to work at 10 o'clock.

I went back at 10 the next night. The department refused to issue me a uniform, a badge, or a gun. The chief told me, "You can walk around downtown if you want to, but you're no police officer." I didn't argue with him. I walked across the street to the county jail and Marion, my brother and deputy sheriff at that time, was there. We talked a while and I called my lawyer. He said he expected that to happen. He would file the papers in the morning.

So the next morning about 11 o'clock I was over at the sheriff's office. My attorney came in with the court order, ordering the mayor and the chief of police to be arrested for contempt of court. Alec, the sheriff, said, "Marion, do you want the honors or do you want me to do it."

Marion replied, "I'll be happy to do it." He walked across the street to the mayor's office and arrested the mayor. Then he arrested the chief and brought them back to the jail.

Alec told him, "Get up against the wall. I'm gonna have to shake you down."

The mayor said, "Wait a minute. This thing has gone far enough. Let's straighten it out." He turned to the chief and said, "Put Captain Edlin back to work right now, tonight, and put him back to work with everything." I was standing there and he said, "Well, are you coming back tonight?"

I said, "I'll be there at 10 o'clock." I was there at 10 and they issued my uniform, badge, and gun back to me. I went back in charge, just like it had been.

This went on for four or five nights. Things were going along pretty smoothly. I was on the night shift from ten at night till six in the morning.

One Saturday night the chief came in and said he would take over the desk for a while. He told me to take the number one car and go out and patrol the area. So I did. I was waiting for him to call me back in. It got to be about 1:30 in the morning and I hadn't received a call yet. I continued to ride around. On the radio there were a lot of other radio transmissions coming in, assigning other cars to missions and so forth. It got quiet.

Then the radio came on and it was the chief giving the car number one an emergency run. A man with a shotgun was threatening to kill his wife and family. I started off. Like we always did, I radioed back to ask how long before my backup got there. He said there wouldn't be any backup; everybody was tied up. So I went to the address by myself. I wasn't there more than a minute and a half, I guess. I couldn't go in and try to take the man's gun without any back up.

About that time two more cars pulled in behind me. They hadn't been ordered there but they came. We disarmed the man quickly. There was no problem.

I got back to the department and told them we had a 10-15, a prisoner. We brought him back to the jail and locked him up. The chief said, "Well, I think I'll go home for the night." I thought, "That son-of-a-gun had been waiting for an opportunity to do me in. They continued to expose me to every danger in the world.

The next Saturday night I got another one of them lonesome coyote calls. I went by myself and when I got there Alec and Marion were both there to back me up. A chief marshall from Clarke County pulled up with some police cars from a town across the bridge. Against all orders he had come across the bridge to back me up. An FBI agent was also there.

For the next month, I kept getting those lonesome calls and all my friends continued to back me up. It got bigger and bigger. Finally they quit treating me that way, but I figured it wasn't the place for me anymore. I was developing stomach ulcers. I went to the hospital and had an operation.

During this time I got my GED from high school. When I wasn't on the police department I took courses with the FBI and various courses on handwriting to become an expert.

Then I decided to go to law school. I contacted the LaSalle Extension University in Chicago. They had a four-year correspondence course that would make me eligible to practice law in a few states, provided I passed the exam. I got through the course in two and a half years. But we decided it wouldn't be right for the kids to leave the state we were in, to go to one that I could practice. Rocky was getting a little older.

I decided I had better resign from the police department before they killed me. So I did. Then I went into the insurance business.

Eventually, my brothers and I established a bail bond business. Being good friends with the judge, the sheriffs, and the prosecuting attorney, we just about sewed up the bail bond business in the area. We did real good with it.

Then Sam and I opened a service station. But cold, miserable weather had us looking for a warmer climate to live. I phoned General Rudder and he suggested Corpus Christi, Texas. My whole family moved to Corpus Christi in 1963.

Ret .General James Earl Rudder
suggested my family move to
Corpus Christi

Courtesy of Erin Warfield

Courtesy of Erin Warfield

19

EDLIN'S AUCTION HOUSE

Well, then we're going to have to get the auction business out of the hobby
stage and into the profit stage . . .

–Robert Edlin

Our first business we owned in Corpus Christi was a billiard room. Rocky, our son, was out of school and could run the billiard room with a little help from my daughter, Emma Lee and my wife. The billiard room was doing pretty good.

My brother had an auction house over at Kingsville. I got into the business also, more or less as a hobby. When I first started my own auction place, we sold $200 worth of goods the opening night. The auction kept getting bigger and bigger, so we eventually had to move out of that first building.

In the meantime the billiard business went bad. The kids (customers) started bringing drugs around. My wife couldn't stand the alcohol and Rocky wouldn't put up with the drugs. They agreed we were going to have to close it down. I told the family, "Well, then we're going to have to get the auction business out of the hobby stage and into the profit stage so we can make a salary out of it." And we did just that.

I got an idea and placed an advertisement in the world-wide circular, the *Antique Trader.* It stated, "Shippers wanted from England, Scotland or France to ship open consignments to U. S." Terry and William Clark in Scotland, had just started a shipping business. They picked up the *Trader* and read my ad. Then they called me but I couldn't understand a word.

272   MOEN AND HEINEN

I said, "Are you sure you've got the right number? I can't understand you."

Terry Clark responded in a strong Scottish brogue, "I'm from Scotland. I saw your ad in the paper." Then we began to get on a bit. After some negotiating we agreed that he would put together a container of antiques and pay for shipping and duty and that I would get a commission to sell it at my auction house.

A few weeks later the container came in and he came with it. I met him down at the airport. When the plane came in I was looking for a business man. The airport emptied out. Nobody was left except a long-haired hippy-type man carrying a back pack. I thought, "That can't be Clark." He had a big old beard and looked like one of those hippies of the sixties. I went over to him and I said, "I don't suppose your name is Clark."

He said, "Yes it is. You can't possibly be Edlin."

"Yeah, I am."

A couple of years later when we had become close friends, he told me his thoughts that day. And I told him mine. "I thought you were a long-haired hippie. You looked like hell."

He said, "Well, you told me that you were a poor guy. There you were sitting, smoking a cigar. Cigars cost eight dollars in Scotland. I thought you were a rich man and couldn't possibly be Edlin."

That first encounter, many years ago, was the beginning of a great relationship for us! Because of our relationship with the Clarks, my auction house specializes in antique furniture from Scotland, England and France and remains prosperous to this day.

Courtesy of Erin Warfield

Courtesy of Erin Warfield

Courtesy of Erin Warfield

20

THE BURGLAR THAT DIDN'T GET AWAY

He was in the Rangers. That's how he could do that.
–Corpus Christi resident

Living in Indiana and Corpus Christi, we never kept our doors locked. But we do now! I've had two burglars here and one of them was something else, let me tell you.

I was sitting in my living room chair at 9:30 on a Monday morning, reading the paper with a drizzling rain outside. My nephew, Shorty, was asleep upstairs. I heard a tremendous crash. I walked out into the kitchen and there was a guy that had smashed the whole kitchen door in and was standing there with a crowbar in his hand.

I asked him, "What the hell are you doing in my house?"

He said, "I'm just getting ready to leave." Then he started out the door.

"Wait a minute," I said. He dropped the crowbar and started to run. I picked up the crowbar and ran only three or four steps after him. Then I threw the crowbar at the back of his head and hit him in his foot. He went over the fence and ran.

I hollered, "Shorty! Shorty!" Shorty came down the stairs. I told him, a bit excited, "A guy broke in here with a crowbar. He could have hit me in the head and killed me."

He said, "Let's go find the guy."

I said, "Let's go." So we drove over to the high school and around about six or eight blocks. We couldn't find anything.

We came back and pulled into the driveway. Shorty asked, "Did you say that he had kind of a red coat and coveralls on?"

"Yes he did."

"Well he's walking behind the house." The man had gone back in the house and broke in again while we were gone. So Shorty jumped out of the car. Shorty's a big guy. He told me to wait in the car. The guy reached inside his coat pocket. Shorty thought that he was grabbing a gun. Shorty ducked behind the car. I threw the car in gear and ran at the burglar. The guy ran down the street. Shorty started chasing him on foot and I was chasing him in the car. He went over a fence but Shorty couldn't get over the six-foot fence. I circled over two blocks and found him again. He was running down the street. He ran back through another yard. I didn't have a car phone. I thought, "I'm going to catch this guy."

I circled around about eight or ten blocks. I learned a long time ago, if you want to catch somebody, you've got to go beyond where they are going to be and then circle around in tighter circles until you catch them. He was walking up a street about 10 blocks from my house. I pulled up to him, almost hit him and stopped. I said, "You might as well quit running because I'm going to catch you."

"You caught me."

I said, "Get down on the street, lay down facing the street." So he did.

"Bob, don't turn me in."

He knew my name. "Who the hell are you?"

He said, "Sam was trying to help me." Sam was my brother.

I said, "Who are you?" He told me his name.

"Are you the man that broke into Sam's house two or three weeks ago?"

He said, "Yeah, but they didn't file charges. They let me go."

I told him, "I'm going to file charges before you kill somebody." Now, I couldn't handle this guy by myself. He was just a young kid, about 22 years old. I saw a guy in a pickup truck coming down the street, a typical Texan with a cowboy hat on. I flagged him. He pulled up. "What's the problem?"

I said, "This guy broke into my house and I ran him down and caught him."

He said, "How old are you?"

"I'm 78."

He said, "I don't know who's right and who's wrong. But neither one of you is leaving until the police get here." An old man came out from across the street, older than I was, carrying a sack of garbage. I said, "Could you make a call for me to 911 and call the police."

He said, "You only call 911 if it's an emergency."

I said, "This is an emergency." So, he called right then and within minutes I heard sirens coming. I don't know what he told them but the police car came roaring up and slid in sideways. A policeman jumped out with a gun in his hand and said, "Mr. Edlin, you just take it easy." He knew me from the Auction House. "I'm going to shake this guy down. We're going to find out what the problem is."

So this guy said, "Officer, be careful. Don't you reach into that pocket there."

The policeman said, "Why not?"

He told him, "There's a syringe in there. It's got drugs in it and I don't want you to hurt yourself." He wasn't completely bad. Then two or three other cars came. They put him in the back of the car and came over to me. I was shaking, just scared to death by then.

The policeman kept asking me, "How could you run this guy down? At your age, how could you lie him down?"

Another guy said, "He was in the Rangers. That's how he could do that."

Ceremony inducting Bob Edlin into Ranger Hall of Fame in 1995
Fort Benning, Georgia

21

RANGER HALL OF FAME

I didn't know him but it didn't matter. Certain things need to be recognized.
–Dr. Robert S. Rush, CSM (Retired) USA

On July, 17, 1995, Robert T. Edlin joined a select group of Rangers to become a member of the Ranger Hall of Fame. The Ranger Hall of Fame was instituted in 1992. Selection criteria are as unique as the Ranger history. To be eligible for selection for the Ranger Hall of Fame a person must be deceased or have been separated or retired from active military service for at least three years at the time of nomination. He must have served in a Ranger unit in combat or be a successful graduate of the US Army Ranger School. A Ranger unit is defined as those army units recognized in Ranger lineage or history. Achievement or service may be considered for individuals in a position in state or national government after the Ranger has departed the Armed Forces.

One day, early in 1995, Len Lomell called me and insisted that I call the Ranger Association to find out what I needed to do to get into the Hall of Fame. He thought I should be nominated. But after making a few phone calls, I found out that it was too late. They already had their two nominees from WWII.

In March of that same year, Bob Edlin received a letter from Lieutenant General John P. Otjen, Commander First U. S. Army, informing him that he had been nominated for the Ranger Hall of Fame. It read: "Your exploits in almost single-handedly eliminating the Graf Spee Battery at Lochrist, France, certainly deserves recognition and am confident the nominating board will agree. I am proud you were a member of America's First Army and am honored in forwarding your packet."

Cooper Addison, a Viet Nam War veteran and a Corpus Christi resident, played a major role in getting Bob inducted into the Ranger Hall of Fame. Here is his story of how he got the nomination process started:

I had seen Bob's name and story in the newspaper. I went down to Edlin's Auction House and asked Bob if he'd sign a copy of *Rudder's Rangers* for a friend of mine. It was really not a big deal. Sometime later, I met Sergeant Major Rush of the First Army on an on-line WWII history discussion group. I'm an amateur historian. He was in the process of writing a book about the 22^d Infantry Regiment in the Hurtgen Forest. I was with the 2^d Battalion in Viet Nam as an infantry platoon leader. We got to talking to one another and actually became virtual friends. We've exchanged e-mail and have talked to one another on the phone for years.

I had mentioned to Robert how I met Bob Edlin. When I told him about Bob Edlin's story, he said that he'd never heard of that. Robert Rush knows more history than any human I've ever known - he's like this incredible encyclopedia and he had never heard of it. Nobody has ever heard of it! About a year later he called and said the First Army had a quota to nominate somebody for the Ranger Hall of Fame and asked if I thought Bob Edlin would be interested. Well, all of that gets pretty political. Bob had told me previously that he would not accept the nomination because they had told him that he didn't have a shot at it - because it wasn't his battalion's turn. It's just ridiculous because if *he* didn't deserve to get in, no one does.

Anyway, Robert Rush's general was Lieutenant General Otjen and he was then Commander of the First Army. So Robert talked to him and General Otjen decided that it would be a neat thing to do. I went to Bob's house and collected the data and sent it to Robert. I was just in the fortunate position of being able to do it. I was in the right place at the right time. Robert's really the guy that did it. I think Edlin has gotten some recognition out of it and I think that it's stupendous! He's a good man!

Dr. Robert Rush, retired Command Sergeant Major and military historian, adds his vital part in getting Bob Edlin inducted:

Cooper had told me about Bob several times. I had gone back and had done some research on my own. I had served four years myself in the Ranger battalion back in the 70's so I knew that there was a Ranger Hall of Fame. I read more about the Ranger Hall of Fame and talked to Cooper about it. He had told me that members of the WWII Association had told Bob that there was no chance in the world that he would be able to get in because they only picked one or two people a year, or whatever.

I went back and did even more research and asked Cooper to send me the information that he had on this. I looked at his award packet for his Distinguished Service Cross that's at the National Archives and determined that his actions demanded recognition fifty years after the fact. Then I wrote the letter for General Otjen's signature. I didn't know Edlin but it didn't matter. Certain things need to be recognized. At the time, I was the Sergeant Major for First US Army.

I went in to Lieutenant General Otjen's office, the First Army commander, which at the time encompassed 23 states in the northeast and midwest. I said, "This would really be a nice thing to do. He not only deserves it but Edlin's Ranger battalion back in 1944 was a member of the First Army." So he signed the forwarding letter and sent it off to the nominating committee of the Ranger Hall of Fame. Normally a nominee does not come from a regular active unit. Usually they are nominated from the Ranger Associations or from within the regiment. I guess a Lieutenant General's signature helped a lot because Edlin was selected. I had no doubt that he would not be. And Cooper helped a lot too. Without his efforts in gathering the information, perhaps Edlin's remarkable exploits in capturing the Graf Spee Battery in Brest, France, would not have made it to the selection committee. It is not often, during this hectic period, that individuals go out of their way to help one another like he did.

Attending the ceremony were Bob's family and some of his dearest Ranger friends of many years.

Jim Tate, a 28th Infantry old friend, wrote an enthusiastic description of the proceedings to members of the Jackson Muster. Here's part of that letter:

Wouldn't you know it? Edlin stole the show! What show? The 1995 Induction Ceremony to the U. S. Army Ranger Hall of Fame held on July 17 at Fort Benning. Here's the story: After parking, it was a good walk to the ceremony area and I kept looking for Bob. Didn't see him but as I approached the area, I did spot one little ol' white-haired geezer trailing along behind a bunch of other white-haired geezers. Then I realized it was Bob and yelled at him. We howdied and walked on into the ceremony area where a goodly crowd was gathering…soon the ceremony got under way…the inductees were honored individually…As the inductee's name was called, a Ranger (modern day) would escort him to the center of the amphitheater where he stood while his citation was read. As that concluded, there was polite applause. He then was escorted to the microphone where he said a few words… Again…polite applause. The remarks made by these men (and two widows) were the highlight of the entire ceremony for me. They were truly inspirational - all entirely different, but meaningful from the heart.

After a few citations were read, I have to admit that I began to think that none of these guys had done nearly what Bob had done. But when they read his citation, it was so valorous and inspirational that the "polite" applause that had gone before was replaced by all the Rangers spinning to their feet, yelling the Ranger yell and giving him a standing ovation. After his remarks they gave him another standing "O" and the crowd all joined in. The next morning there was a good story of the affair (in the newspaper), featuring - who else? - but that "fool lieutenant."

From the Columbus, Georgia Ledger-Enquirer, Tuesday, July 18, 1995:

'Fool Lieutenant' Edlin joins
Ranger Hall of Fame ranks
By Clint Claybrook
Staff Writer

Lt. Robert T. Edlin, labeled "the fool lieutenant" after he captured 850 German soldiers on the Brest peninsula during World War II by threatening to blow himself up with a hand grenade, joined the ranks of those in the U. S. Army Ranger Hall of Fame at Fort Benning on Monday.

Edlin was among 18 men honored at an induction ceremony at the Ranger Memorial…Edlin said, however, that today would be a better day.

"That's the day I get to go home. I don't usually go to these things," he said...But his family made him come,...and the crowd gave him one of the heartiest "HooAahs" of the day when today's Rangers heard about Edlin's bravado at Brest. "It wasn't that easy, fellows," the slight, gray man told the crowd, drawing a laugh. "I just took a calculated risk."

Edlin, 73, said he thinks back on his World War II exploits "almost every day. I lost my wife of 50 years in September, and that makes it all the worse." When he looks back, he's still 20 years old, Edlin said, "Not in health, but in how I feel. I'm not old."

Bob Edlin Private Collection

**Bob Edlin standing beside Ranger Memorial
at Fort Benning, Georgia in 1995,
wearing Ranger Hall of Fame medal**

Bob Edlin in Weymouth, England, 1999

EPILOGUE

Some old soldiers just wither away and people don't appreciate them. But his family does.

—Terry Potts (Edlin's Niece)

*N*umber 218, a miniature oak wardrobe. We'll start the bidding at $50, go 50 – 50 –50, do I hear 35, 35, 35 now 40, 35 now 40, now 45, 45,45 now 50, $50 now 5, $50 now 5, Sold at $50!

Bob Edlin, 78 years old, still is the lead auctioneer at Edlin's Auction House, three blocks south of the City Hall in Corpus Christi, Texas. He's been doing this for almost thirty years now. People come from miles around. Deals? Absolutely, but the regulars come for Bob's quick sense of humor and his feisty character. The twinkle in his eyes and his great smile make you forget his age.

The auction patrons not only attend the auction for Bob's personality and to get a good bargain, but also to see the Edlin family work like clockwork together. Bob's family that are involved in the business include: his son, Rocky, who works as the second auctioneer and business partner; his daughter, Emma Lee, clerk; daughter-in-law, Jan, cashier; son-in-law, Warren, ring man and business partner; grandsons Casey, Chris, Curt, and Clay; Curt's wife, Stephanie; Casey's girlfriend, Jennifer; and friends Cal McWhirten, Hershel Sessions and David Billarel. These grandchildren help out when needed: Travis, Doug, and Melanie. Other helpers include: Travis's wife, Nicki and Melanie's husband, Shaun.   Everyone gets involved!

Slagle, O'Connor, Arnold, Edlin, Klaus, Tollefson and Jacobus
Ranger reunion in Orlando, 1997

Burmaster, Slagle, Klaus, Drake, Edlin, Tollefson and O'Connor
Ranger reunion in Orlando, 1997

Loyal auction goers, Mr. and Mrs. John Paul Jones, look forward to the auction on their weekends. Mrs. Jones speaks for the couple:

> Well, we've known Bob for about thirty years, ever since he's been in the auction business. We've been married for 66 years and we're both 87 years old. We come every Friday and Saturday night. They're such a fine family, a close-knit family. He's just the nicest fella, very kind and accommodating. He's just a doll.

Hershel Sessions, a volunteer worker at Edlin's Auction House and expert on antique glass, told us:

> I've been hanging around here for ten years more or less. There's just something about being at an auction; there's an adrenaline flow here. I've spent a lot of time around Bob. Bob is one of the greatest individuals you will ever meet . . .unassuming, funny, witty. He's a gem. He's the cement that the family is built around.
>
> It's an oxymoron to say "honest auctioneer" but he's as close as you will ever get to it. Forget about what he did during the war, he's just a nice individual.

Though the business is a big part of his life now, the most defining time in Robert Edlin's life will always be his years as a Ranger in WWII. Some of his strongest relationships have come from those "life and death" moments. He and his Ranger brothers remain as close as any family bond can be.

The World War II Rangers first started having reunions in 1949. It gives them an opportunity to talk about old times and to be a group dedicated to bettering future soldiers and Rangers. They have reunions every two years that are well attended. Bob has not made it to every reunion but he still keeps in touch by letter and phone with his special buds. Of the fabulous four patrol, Bob and "Halftrack" (Burmaster) are the only two still alive.

When we separated at the marshalling area, Stateside, Fort Patrick, Virginia, that was the last time I saw Whitie, Bill Courtney and Bill Dreher. I never saw the three of them again.

I got in touch with Dreher just before he died. He had Alzheimer's. He called me and then I called him. We talked for ten

Bob Edlin shaking hands and signing autographs in Weymouth,
England, 1999. Betty Hockey at right in lower photo

Bob Edlin standing by American War Memorial in Weymouth, England, 1999

minutes. That's the last I heard from him.

Ray Tollefson, Company A, 2nd Platoon, in 1994 attended the 50th D-Day Anniversary ceremonies in Weymouth, England. He could see the special feelings Weymouth had for Bob. Bob's picture boarding the landing craft on June 1, 1994, hung everywhere. To the Weymouth residents it represented the liberty and freedom they enjoy today. In 1999, Ray and his wife, Peggy, personally financed Bob's trip back to England and France for the 55th Anniversary of the Normandy invasion. It was the trip of a lifetime for Bob. He thoroughly enjoyed himself and remains in gratitude to the Tollefsons for their generosity.

Bob's memories of that trip and how it all came to be are very special:

Betty Hockey, a D-Day Committee member for Weymouth and a famous British singer and dancer, found me in 1994 on the 50th Anniversary. They had that picture of me boarding the assault craft. They knew the soldier in the picture was the first American soldier to board a landing craft at Weymouth Harbor for the invasion of Fortress Europe. Betty wanted to find out who was in that picture; nobody knew who it was. They had thought it was someone from the 1st Infantry Division. They sent copies of it around and tried to locate me. I think that Eichner got a copy of it in Boston. He was the secretary of the Ranger Battalion Organization at that time. He sent it to me. "I believe that this is you, but I can't be sure."

I called him back and told him that was definitely me, no doubt about it. In the meantime Betty Hockey had just taken hold of this project and she was going to find me. Early in 1994 they hired a private detective and found me.

After finding me, the people of Weymouth got a fund together to fly my wife and I over to England— to pay for all our expenses and make the tour. At the time, my wife was very sick and I was worried to death about her. So I told them I just couldn't come. That was in June and she died in September. Thank goodness that I didn't go. The last few months were good months that we had together.

The mayor of Weymouth sent me a letter expressing her regrets that we weren't able to attend:

```
12-06-94
Dear Bob:
    We regret that we were unable to welcome you dur-
ing our D-Day Commemorations and we all hope that
your wife is well on the way to recovery.
    Your photograph taken as you entered the land-
ing craft on your grim voyage to the terrible events
that followed, is one many Weymouth people know
well, and it is a constant reminder to us all of
the cheerful young men who gave so much for the
freedom we know today.
    We will never forget, nor must we, and I hope
that the younger members of our society will learn
from the horrific events of 50 years ago.
    It is therefore, with great pride that the peo-
ple of Weymouth. . . send you our warmest greet-
ings, and hope that you may still be able to visit
us in the not so distant future, and be assured of
the warmest welcome.
    Our sincere thanks and best wishes to you both.

    Brenda Dench, Mayor of Weymouth and Portland.
```

When I finally was able to return to Weymouth in 1999, thanks to Ray and Peggy Tollefson, I was approached by hundreds of people that knew me. They have a picture of me on the side of a hotel, the one where I am getting into the assault craft. Longshore men on the ships in the harbor would holler, "Hi Bob." When they took a survey of the townspeople there, they found that my picture was in 80% of the homes: in closets, on fireplace mantles and tops of pianos. I had no idea.

They had a big reception for us. Betty Hockey was there and signed her book for me. Then we went with a BBC national commentator. He did an interview with Tollefson, O'Connor, and myself. Also Lomell and Salomon and the rest of them.

To summarize my life, go back to the first grade when Chief

Ritter and I had those fights. It was then that I learned that if you keep fighting you win some. I guess I look back on my life and I think I kept fighting most of the time and I won some. Lord knows, I lost a bunch of them too.

I have no regrets about the way my life has gone. None whatsoever. When I was a little kid, seven or eight years old, I thought, boy, I'd sure like to be a soldier. I want to be a soldier! Every time I'd see a policeman, I'd think, boy, I'd like to be a policeman. Then, I went to a couple of cattle auctions with my dad. Boy, I'd like to be an auctioneer. As it turned out, I was a soldier with the best soldiers in the world, the Rangers. I saw my share of combat as a police officer. Then I became an auctioneer. Everything I wanted to be I became. And not by skill, but just by luck.

We, however, the writers, wish to disagree. Bob Edlin chose to travel the roads that led him to fulfillment. He achieved the high ground by sheer determination. He fought for what was right at every turn. Though he is modest in his own special way, he is to be admired. Robert T. Edlin, "the fool lieutenant," we hope your story wins the hearts and admiration of many. You deserve it!

Just as we were going to print, a wonderful thing happened to Bob Edlin. He was recognized by the city of Corpus Christi for his life accomplishments and they proclaimed the month of October in the year 2000 to be "Robert Edlin Day." This came about through the hard work of Richard Hinojosa, a well-known Corpus Christi resident owning a trucking company and a big heart.

PROCLAMATION

WHEREAS, Bob Edlin at the age of twenty-two was one of America's World War II soldiers to go down in history; and because First Lieutenant Robert Edlin was the first GI to board a landing craft at Weymouth for the D-Day battles at Pointe du Hoc and Omaha Beach; and because he was wounded while leading his platoon in an assault across Omaha Beach; and

WHEREAS, Bob Edlin along with brothers, a sister and some very close friends, sold property and some possessions and migrated from New Albany, Indiana to find a warmer climate and as a result Corpus Christi's population increased by approximately 50 persons; and because they became viable assets to the community, starting businesses and raising families; and

WHEREAS, Bob Edlin has been a member of the Eagles Lodge, the Veterans of Foreign War and the Persons With Disabilities to name a few; and because at the age of 78 continues to operate Edlin Auction House, a successful auction business, along with his son and son-in-law.

NOW, therefore, pursuant to the powers vested in me as Mayor of the City of Corpus Christi, I do hereby proclaim October, 2000 as

"ROBERT EDLIN DAY"

Samuel L. Neal, Jr., Mayor

THE END

ROSTER

COMPANY "A" SECOND RANGER BATTALION
(Roster Prior to D-Day)

COMPANY HEADQUARTERS

Comd. Officer	1st Lt. Joseph Rafferty
1st Sergeant	1st Sgt. Edward Sowa
Clerk	Sgt. Charles Berg
Messenger	T/5 Harry Brewster

FIRST PLATOON

Plat Ldr 1st Lt Robert Edlin   Msrgr   Pfc William Dreher
Plat Sgt T/Sgt Bill White   Sniper   T/5 Kenneth Bladorn

First Section	Second Section
Section Ldr S/Sgt Elmer Cawr	Section Ldr S/Sgt Harry McCue

Assault Squad		Assault Squad	
Sqd Ldr	Sgt John Donovan	Sqd Ldr	T/5 William Courtney
Rifleman	Pfc Clyde Pattison	Rifleman	Pfc Peter Swedo
Rifleman	Pfc Garland Hart	Rifleman	Pfc Carl Cerwin
Rifleman	Pfc Harrz Ware	Rifleman	Pfc Roy Culp
Rifleman	Pfc John Shannahan		

Light Machine Gun Squad		Light Machine Gun Squad	
Sqd Ldr	S/Sgt Ralph Hoyt	Squad Ldr	S/Sgt William Klaus
Gunner	T/5 Garfield Ray	Gunner	T/5 Percy Bower
Asst Gnr	Pfc George Salepec	Asst Gnr	T/5 George Lawrence
A. Bearer	Pvt Rea Carroll	A. Bearer	Pvt Earl Shireman
A. Bearer	Pvt Martin Painkin	A. Bearer	Pfc Roy Latham

Special Weapons	
Sec Ldr	S/Sgt Robert Davis
Asst Sec Ldr	Sgt Charles Rich
Gunner	T/5 Charles Bollia
Asst Gnr	T/5 Orville Wright
A. Bearer	Pfc Coy Stanley
A. Bearer	Pvt Louis Broncek

SECOND PLATOON

Platoon Ldr   1st Lt Stanley White
Platoon Sgt   T/Sgt Ronald Swanson

Msgr   Sgt Robert Gary
Sniper   T/5 William Kuasnicki

First Section
Sec Ldr   S/Sgt John Biddle

Second Section
Sec Ldr   S/Sgt Frederich Smith

Assault Squad
Sqd Ldr   Sgt Theodore James
Rifleman Pfc Elmer Davison
Rifleman Pfc Edward O'Connor
Rifleman Pfc Charlie McCann
Rifleman Gerald Schroader

Assault Squad
Sqd Ldr   Sgt Donald Fendley
Rifleman Pfc Dailey
Rifleman Pfc Durbert Ferguson
Rifleman Pfc Donald Ashline
Rifleman Pfc Ervin Bealinoki

Light Machine Gun Section
Sqd Ldr   S/Sgt Leonard Lavandoski
Gunner   T/5 Julius Remmers
Asst Gnr T/5 James Slagle
A. Bearer Pfc Joseph Daniels
A. Bearer Pfc John Balalar
A. Bearer Pfc Ray Tollefson

Light Machine Gun Section
Sqd Ldr   S/Sgt Gerald Belmont
Gunner   T/5 Mike Drobick
Asst Gnr T/5 Innes Robertson
A. Bearer Pvt George Cutoweld
A. Bearer Pfc Morris Prince

Special Weapons Section
Sec Ldr   S/Sgt Fred Culbreatt
Asst Sqd Ldr T/5 George Hellers
Gunner   T/5 John Bodnar
Asst Gnr   Pfc Richard Rankin
A. Bearer   Pfc Joe Trainer

Czechoslovakia 1945

A COMPANY

1st PLATOON

Top rows standing, left to right

Virgin	"Gabby" Hart*
Lansome	"Potts" Cerwin*
Ware*	Taylor
Murphey	McCaleb
Korb*	Jackson
Anton	Carroll
Schobee	Sargent
"Kitty" Carr*	Simon
Tolson	Cooper
Sinbine*	Dassaro
"Doc" Guerra	Carman
Drake	Devito
	Wilson*
	Lt. White

Seated top and bottom rows

"Dusty" Donovan*	"Pete" Ruta*
Courtney*	Noland
Klieve	Toft
Steele	Dreher*
Silagy	Hurley
"Duck" Lupin	Serrette
"Slim" Hart	May
Lt. Edlin*	Cory
Lt. Porubski	Knight
Capt. Arman*	Lavandoski*
Lt. Roquemore	Klaus*
Lt. Wilson	

A COMPANY

2nd PLATOON

Top rows standing,, left to right:

		Seated top and bottom rows:	
Schroeder*	O'Connor*	Celles	Bodnar*
Jacobus	Rachabinsky	Bruce	Ferguson*
Andrews	Nassett	Gary*	Gutowski*
Janistek	Kohl	Prince*	Douglas
Ewaska	Sorger*	Pulaski	Fagan
Mabbitt	Mickewiecz	Pies	Schouw
Freeman		Barnard	Days
Kwasnicki*		Stater	Conner
Drobick*		Freisen	
		Robertson*	

Names followed by asterisk (*) indicate D-Day veteran

Dave Jacobus Private Collection

GLOSSARY

.45	A common term for the standard issue automatic pistol of the US armed forces, the Colt 1911A1, chambered in .45 ACP (Automatic Colt Pistol).
88's	German 'Flak' Fliege Abwehr Kannon M36/37. Heavy antiaircraft gun chambered in 8.8 cm (3.46 inches) caliber, hence the name "88." Designed for use against air, ground, and sea targets, proven to be accurate and powerful against Allied forces. Weighed 5.5 tons and 15 feet in length, firing at a range of 16,200 yards.
Doughboy	Nickname for US troops originating in the Mexican War. Soldiers marching along dusty roads looked as though they were covered in flour, hence the term "doughboy." Later used more popularly for US infantryman during WWI.
AWOL	Absent Without Leave. A serious offense for a soldier to be missing from duty without permission. Also associated with desertion.
BAR	Browning Automatic Rifle model 1918/A1 developed by John Browning in 1917 for service in WWI. A select fire (semi-or fully automatic), magazine fed, gas operated, shoulder fired rifle, firing a .30 caliber cartridge from a 20 round magazine. Issued at the squad level for infantry support.
Barrage	A prolonged concentration of artillery fire on ground or air targets.
Billeted	To be quartered in housing or sleeping quarters. Many times civilian homes, hotels, etc. were used.
Bivouac area	A temporary encampment of soldiers in the field.
Boot Pac	The M1944 Boot Pac was issued in the winter of 1944 and consisted of a rubber boot over a felt lining. Designed to be worn over the combat boot, it was usually worn alone, causing foot problems on the march. The commercial "Sorel" winter boot was based on this design.
Burp guns	Generally used as a slang term for the German MP40

	machine pistol, a fully automatic submachine gun, derived from the unique report of the weapon when fired in short bursts. Can also mean any submachine gun.
CCC	Civilian Conservation Corps. Created by President Roosevelt in 1933, the CCC assisted in employing youths without work during the Depression. Run by the US Army and directed by the Departments of Interior and Agriculture, the CCC ran camps in every state of the union. The CCC mainly improved state parks and forests with restoration, fire protection, and building recreational facilities.
Carbine	Any rifle which has been shortened in length and/or lightened in weight for ease of handling. Here meant to describe the M1 carbine, based on the M1 rifle, but with its own .30 caliber carbine cartridge. Designed to give rear echelon troops more firepower than their issued pistols and issued to officers for its lighter weight.
C.O.	Military abbreviation for commanding officer.
Commando	A term for special forces dating back to the Boer War of 1899-1902 with the Dutch Boer settlers of South Africa. A "kommando" meaning a command of troops of no particular size. Because of the hit and run style of tactics used by the Boers, this term came describe that type of action, as well as the units and finally the members tasked with this type of mission. The British formed their first commando units in 1940, the name suggested by Lieutenant Colonel Dudley Clark of the Imperial General Staff.
CP	Command Post. Any particular area indoors or out, designated as a headquarters for commanding officers.
C-rations	Field ration containing similar contents to the K-ration but with larger crackers, tins of meat, etc. Packaged in a large soup size can.
D-Day	Term used by military to denote day of invasion.
D-Day+	Term used to signify how many days had transpired since the first day of an invasion or assault.
D-rations	Emergency ration consisting of a large brick-like

	chocolate bar weighing four ounces and containing 600 calories.
Dog Face	Slang term for infantryman, possibly derived from the dirty, unshaven look of soldiers on the front lines.
ETO	European Theater of Operations including all actions on the European continent - i.e. Italy, France, Germany, etc.
Father Lacy	Rev. Joseph Lacy. Captain, Chaplain, staff officer of Headquarters Company, 5th Ranger Battalion.
FFI	Forces Francaises de l'Interieur. French forces of the Interior. The organized free French resistance forces which actively aided Allied forces with sabotage, intelligence, and armed resistance.
Flank	Military term for the right or left side of a formation, in military action, or to attack or pass around the side of an enemy formation.
Foot Slogger	Slang term for an infantryman derived from their main mode of transportation, marching.
Fox hole	A field fortification consisting of a rectangular or round hole dug into the earth for protection against shrapnel and small arms fire. Dug to varying depths depending on time spent in the area, although seven feet deep by regulation, and usually large enough for one or two soldiers.
Furlough	A leave of absence for military personnel.
Glider plane	Motor-less aircraft capable of carrying troops, and/or small vehicles, or artillery. Towed by a larger powered aircraft in flight and released over the target area for a silent approach and landing.
GI	Government Issue, a slang term for American soldiers as well as all of their equipment and belongings.
Goldbrick	A slang term for a lazy soldier who avoided work or duties, a shirker.
Hedgerow	A dense row of shrubs atop an earth embankment with overgrowth of plants. Found especially in Northern France and throughout Normandy, used to divide agricultural fields and roadways.
Heinies	Slang term for German soldiers.

Jerry	Slang term for German soldiers.
K-rations	Field ration consisting of canned meat, crackers, cheese, powdered coffee, cigarettes, etc. Packed in paraffin-coated boxes, these featured different contents for breakfast, dinner, and supper.
LCA	Landing Craft, Assault. The British made version of the US LCVP (Landing Craft, Vehicle, Personnel). Could carry troops only, and included armor plating for protection from small arms fire.
LST	Landing Ship, Tank. A large US Navy ocean going ship designed to land several tanks or other vehicles, also used at Normandy to transport the wounded.
M-1 Rifle	The standard issue infantry rifle of the US in WWII. Also known as the Garand after its designer, John C. Garand. Adopted in 1936, this shoulder fired, gas operated, semi-automatic rifle, weighs eight pounds, and fires a 30.06 cartridge from an 8 Round end block clip, with an effective range of up to 600 yards. Its' rugged dependability, accuracy, and rate of fire made it a popular weapon.
Mauser	Term used to describe the standard German rifle, the model Kar98k Mauser. Designed by the firm of Peter and Paul Mauser, the bolt action Kar98k fires a 7.92mm cartridge from a five round magazine.
Married	One unit attached to another unit.
Mae West	Slang term used for the Navy M5 lifebelt issued to soldiers for the Normandy invasion.
Mess hall	Military dining area.
Messerschmidt	A term commonly used to describe any German fighter plane regardless of its make and model. Willie Messerschmidt was Germany's top aircraft designer; many German planes used the heading "ME" (as in ME 109, ME 262), to signify this.
Mortar	A short range, small bore artillery piece, designed for small unit support. Consisting of a steel tube with sights mounted to a heavy base, the mortar is loaded from the muzzle with self-projecting shells, which fire in a high

	arching trajectory.
N. C. O.	Military abbreviation for non-commissioned officer. The enlisted ranks above that of Private First Class and up to Master Sergeant.
Non-coms	Slang term for non-commissioned officers, or "NCOs."
OCS	Officer's Candidate School. At various military bases around the country, these schools were established to test and train military officers.
Old Man	Any soldier slightly older than the average. This was a common term for men in their early 30s and late 20s.
Potato Masher	Slang term for the standard German hand grenade. The "stielhangranate" utilized a short stick handle attached to the explosive head, which gave the thrower more leverage and thus increased range. This nickname comes from the grenades' resemblance to kitchen potato mashers.
Pup Tent	Slang term for the two piece, two man shelter tent issued to US ground forces, resembling a dog house. May have come from the Civil War term of "dog tent."
PW	Abbreviation for Prisoner of War, also/or POW.
Quonset Hut	A pre-fabricated, semi-permanent shelter used for the housing of troops, offices, etc. Generally made of corrugated iron sheets in a semi-circular shape with doors at either end.
Ranger	Originally used to describe a forester or frontiersman-hunter, later used to describe scouts and raiders during the French and Indian Wars of the 1700's and the American Revolution. Influenced by the successes of the British commandos, President Roosevelt directed General George Marshall to form "American commando" units. Due to a strong British association with the name "commando," the name "ranger" was used in order to form an American identity.
The "Rear"	Slang term used by front line soldiers for any distance behind the front lines where small arms fire could not reach. This area could still be subject to artillery fire and bombing from aircraft. Can also mean a rest area many

	miles behind the front lines.
S.P.	Abbreviation for self-propelled applied to mechanized artillery, howitzers, cannon, etc. meaning that the artillery is contained in/on a motorized vehicle.
Tommy Gun	Thompson submachine gun M1928 A1. Air cooled, recoil operated, chambered in .45 ACP, and firing from a 20 round magazine or 50/100 round drum magazine. Derived from the name of its inventor/designer, Brig. Gen. John Thompson.
U-boat	Abbreviation for the German term "Unterseeboot" meaning "under sea boat," or submarine. Also commonly used in English.
USO	United Service Organization. An organization to provide US troops with entertainment and relaxation through performances, concerts, dances, etc. Made popular by the appearance of Bob Hope.
V-E Day	Victory in Europe day. The day that war was ended in the ETO, May 8, 1945.
WP's	White phosphorous explosive usually used in hand grenades. Causes casualties upon explosion by showering burning phosphorous particles. Can also be used for concealment as the explosion emits thick clouds of white smoke.
WPA	Works Progress Administration. Created by President Roosevelt in 1935, the WPA was designed to relieve unemployment in the US during the Depression through preserving and developing the arts. Various artists produced work in the theatre, writing and publishing, and fine arts.
Wehrmacht	German for defense forces. The overall term for the German Armed Forces, including all branches.
M1	Steel helmet with insignia painted on the back for the 2nd Ranger Battalion to help with identification of following troops.

RANGER ATTIRE

M5	Amphibious assault gasmask bag/assault gasmask. A rubberized, waterproof bag designed to carry the M5 assault gasmask for short-term use in amphibious landings.
M1941field jacket	Worn over the issue wool shirt with diamond shaped Ranger insignia worn only by the 2nd and 5th Rangers on the left shoulder.
Assault vest	Modeled after the British "battle jerkin" the assault vest was designed to aid troops in carrying the vast amount of equipment required. Various pockets, pouches, and loops were provided to carry all manner of ammunition and field gear. Issued to Rangers and some first wave troops at Normandy.
Gas brassard	A chemically treated brassard which changed to a bright color in the event of gas attacks to warn troops of its presence.
M1940 canteen	With cup, inside an insulated cover.
M1942 field dressing pouch	Contained a Carlisle first aid dressing consisting of a large pad of gauze attached to a strip of gauze for wrapping. To be used if the soldier is wounded to control bleeding.
US Navy M1926 lifebelt	Inflatable by CO_2 cartridges or manually by mouth, the lifebelt was also attached to equipment to aid buoyancy.
Trousers	Made of herring bone twill. Issue utility trousers worn over wool trousers, made of lightweight cotton twill. Sometimes these were coated with a gas resistant impregnate.
M1938 dismounted leggings	To protect the feet from mud, water, etc. when in the field or on the march. Made of canvas material.
Service shoes	Made of russet leather with the toecaps and a rubber composition sole. Also called ankle boots.

INDEX

INDEX

INDEX

INDEX

INDEX

Margo Heinen, Bob Edlin, and Marcia Moen
Edlin's Auction House, July 2000

ABOUT THE AUTHORS

Marcia Moen and Margo Heinen, twin sisters, are both natives of Minnesota. Their first book, *Reflections of Courage on D-Day and the Days that Followed*, was written about their uncle, Charles "Ace" Parker, 5th Ranger Battalion, Company A Commander. Their next book, *Heroes Cry Too—A WWII Ranger Tells His Story of Love and War*, will be be released in August 2002. In this book, Ranger "Bing" Evans tells about his experiences in North Africa, Sicily and Italy with the 1st Battalion Rangers.

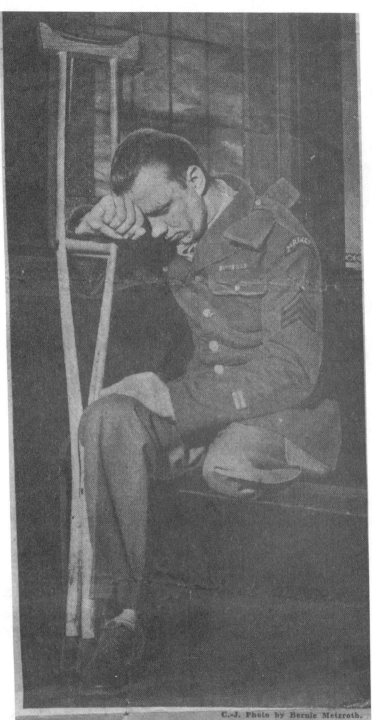

C.-J. Photo by Bernie Meizroth.

A PRAYER ON V-E DAY for his two brothers in the service is offered at his mother's church by Sgt. Raymond Middleton, Jeffersonville, who lost a leg in Germany.

MEADOWLARK PUBLISHING, INC.

Order Form

Reflections of Courage on D-Day
and the Days that Followed by Moen and Heinen
A personal account of Ranger Ace Parker, Company Commander of A Company, 5th Ranger Battalion. Credited with moving further inland on D-Day than any other group.

_____ ISBN 0-9649922-6-4 $15.95

The Fool Lieutenant
a personal account of D-Day and World War II by Moen and Heinen
A personal account of Ranger Robert Edlin, Platoon Commander of A Company, 2nd Ranger Battalion. Credited with capturing a fort of 800 Germans along with his 4-man patrol.

_____ ISBN 0-9705257-3-7 $15.95

The Road to Victory
The story of the elite WWII 2nd Battalion Rangers by Pfc. Morris Prince
Written in Czechoslovakia in 1945, this is the history of A Company, 2nd Battalion Rangers from the day the outfit left the States until V-E day in Europe.

_____ ISBN 0-9705257-1-0 $14.95

Heroes Cry Too
A WWII Ranger Tells His Story of Love and War by Moen and Heinen
Ranger Warren 'Bing' Evans tells an emotional story of falling in love and then being shipped overseas to fight in Africa, Sicily and Italy with the legendary Darby's Rangers.

_____ ISBN 0-9705257-2-9 $15.95

Please send me the books I have checked above.
I am Enclosing $_____ (Add $2.50 to cover postage and handling.)
Send check or money order, no cash or C.O.D.'s please.
Add $1.00 postage for each additional item.

Name_____

Address_____

City/State/Zip_____

Send order to: Meadowlark Publishing, Inc.
P.O. Box 741
Elk River, Minnesota 55330

Please allow three to four weeks for delivery.

MEADOWLARK PUBLISHING, INC.

Order Form

Reflections of Courage on D-Day
and the Days that Followed by Moen and Heinen
A personal account of Ranger Ace Parker, Company Commander of A Company, 5th Ranger Battalion. Credited with moving further inland on D-Day than any other group.

_____ ISBN 0-9649922-6-4 $15.95

The Fool Lieutenant
a personal account of D-Day and World War II by Moen and Heinen
A personal account of Ranger Robert Edlin, Platoon Commander of A Company, 2nd Ranger Battalion. Credited with capturing a fort of 800 Germans along with his 4-man patrol.

_____ ISBN 0-9705257-3-7 $15.95

The Road to Victory
The story of the elite WWII 2nd Battalion Rangers by Pfc. Morris Prince
Written in Czechoslovakia in 1945, this is the history of A Company, 2nd Battalion Rangers from the day the outfit left the States until V-E day in Europe.

_____ ISBN 0-9705257-1-0 $14.95

Heroes Cry Too
A WWII Ranger Tells His Story of Love and War by Moen and Heinen
Ranger Warren 'Bing' Evans tells an emotional story of falling in love and then being shipped overseas to fight in Africa, Sicily and Italy with the legendary Darby's Rangers.

_____ ISBN 0-9705257-2-9 $15.95

Please send me the books I have checked above.
I am Enclosing $_____ (Add $2.50 to cover postage and handling.)
Send check or money order, no cash or C.O.D.'s please.
Add $1.00 postage for each additional item.

Name_____

Address_____

City/State/Zip_____

Send order to: Meadowlark Publishing, Inc.
P.O. Box 741
Elk River, Minnesota 55330

Please allow three to four weeks for delivery.

MEADOWLARK PUBLISHING, INC.

Order Form

Reflections of Courage on D-Day
and the Days that Followed by Moen and Heinen
A personal account of Ranger Ace Parker, Company Commander of A Company, 5th Ranger Battalion. Credited with moving further inland on D-Day than any other group.

_____ ISBN 0-9649922-6-4 $15.95

The Fool Lieutenant
a personal account of D-Day and World War II by Moen and Heinen
A personal account of Ranger Robert Edlin, Platoon Commander of A Company, 2nd Ranger Battalion. Credited with capturing a fort of 800 Germans along with his 4-man patrol.

_____ ISBN 0-9705257-3-7 $15.95

The Road to Victory
The story of the elite WWII 2nd Battalion Rangers by Pfc. Morris Prince
Written in Czechoslovakia in 1945, this is the history of A Company, 2nd Battalion Rangers from the day the outfit left the States until V-E day in Europe.

_____ ISBN 0-9705257-1-0 $14.95

Heroes Cry Too
A WWII Ranger Tells His Story of Love and War by Moen and Heinen
Ranger Warren 'Bing' Evans tells an emotional story of falling in love and then being shipped overseas to fight in Africa, Sicily and Italy with the legendary Darby's Rangers.

_____ ISBN 0-9705257-2-9 $15.95

Please send me the books I have checked above.
I am Enclosing $_____ (Add $2.50 to cover postage and handling.)
Send check or money order, no cash or C.O.D.'s please.
Add $1.00 postage for each additional item.

Name_____

Address_____

City/State/Zip_____

Send order to: Meadowlark Publishing, Inc.
P.O. Box 741
Elk River, Minnesota 55330

Please allow three to four weeks for delivery.

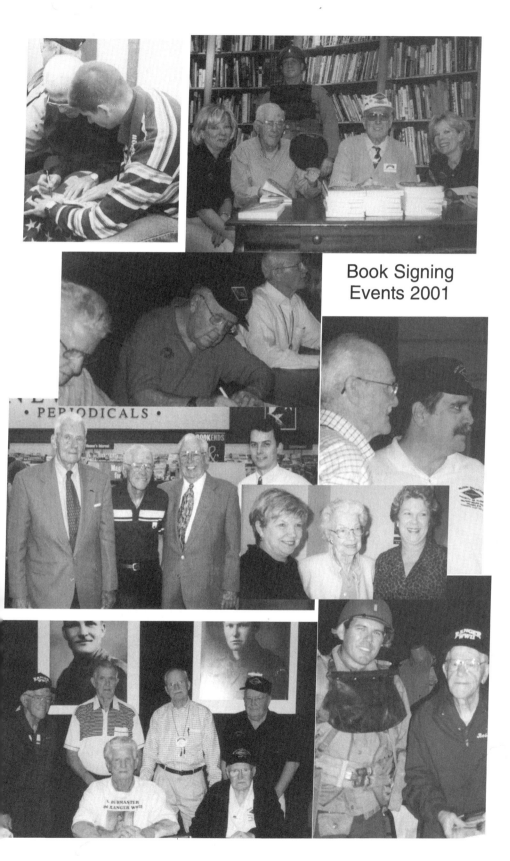

Book Signing
Events 2001